P9-EGK-355

Assisting Workers Displaced by Structural Change

An International Perspective

Duane E. Leigh
Washington State University

1995

W. E. UPJOHN INSTITUTE for Employment Research
Kalamazoo, Michigan

Library of Congress Cataloging-in-Publication Data

Leigh, Duane E.
Assisting workers displaced by structural change / Duane Leigh.
p. cm.
Includes bibliographical references and index.
ISBN 0–88099–154–2 (cloth : alk. paper)— ISBN
0–88099–153–4 (paper : alk. paper)
1. Unemployed—Services for—Case studies. 2. Displaced workers—Services for—Case studies. 3. Insurance, Unemployment—Case studies. 4. Structural unemployment—Case studies. 5. Hard-core unemployed—Employment—Case studies. 6. Occupational retraining—Case studies. 7. Public service employment—Case studies. 8. Job creation—Government policy—Case studies. I. Title.
HD5707.5.L45 1995
331.13'77—dc20 95–21004
CIP

300 S. Westnedge Avenue
Kalamazoo, Michigan 49007–4686

Cover design by J. R. Underhill.
Index prepared by Shirley Kessel.
Printed in the United States of America.

The Author

Duane E. Leigh is a professor economics and economics department chair at Washington State University, Pullman, Washington. He earned his Ph.D. in economics from Michigan State University in 1969, and he has held teaching and research appointments at the University of Wisconsin—Madison and the University of Virginia. In recent years, his research has centered on the operation and labor market effects of training programs directed toward displaced workers and welfare recipients. Dr. Leigh is also the author of two earlier monographs published by the Upjohn Institute—*Assisting Displaced Workers: Do the States Have a Better Idea?* (1989) and *Does Training Work for Displaced Workers? A Survey of Existing Evidence* (1990).

Acknowledgments

The seed for this project was planted about half a dozen years ago when I began gathering materials on displaced worker programs in Canada and Australia. These materials became the basis for two relatively brief chapters in my 1990 Upjohn Institute monograph titled, *Does Training Work for Displaced Workers? A Survey of Existing Evidence.* In 1991, a contract received from the World Bank allowed me to initiate a broader study of displaced worker programs in several additional countries including Sweden, Japan, and Britain. Arvil Van Adams supervised the larger World Bank project of which my contribution was a small part and provided useful comments on my chapter in the final report. In 1993, I received a grant from the Upjohn Institute to expand my study to include Germany among the countries considered and to begin to develop a monograph-length manuscript. The generous financial support provided by the Institute, with additional support from the International Labour Office, permitted me to take professional leave from my usual teaching responsibilities during the 1992–93 academic year to work on this monograph.

The final version of the manuscript benefited enormously from the detailed and very helpful comments of my project monitor, Christopher O'Leary, and two outside reviewers, Lisa Lynch of Tufts University and Louis Jacobson of Westat Incorporated. Judy Gentry expeditiously handled the final steps of preparing the manuscript for publication.

CONTENTS

1
Introduction

Competing in the global marketplace implies that a national economy will be in a constant state of change, with new commodities and technologies supplanting old commodities and technologies. At the same time, the mobility of capital increasingly obliges workers in highly industrialized nations to compete with willing and cheap labor in developing countries around the world. While contributing greatly to economic well-being, this process of change generates each year large numbers of enterprise closures and business restructurings, each associated with the permanent layoffs of experienced workers. The term "displaced" is applied to these unemployed workers because they face a low probability of being recalled to their old jobs or perhaps even to jobs in their old industries. Unfortunately, many displaced workers who received high wages to perform the repetitive tasks required by mass production technologies find, after a period of job search, that their reemployment options are restricted to less-well-paying jobs. Displaced workers typically differ from other unemployed workers by the continuity of their prelayoff work experience, the duration of their postlayoff joblessness, and their lower wages upon reemployment.

The availability of the first biannual Displaced Worker Survey (DWS) in 1984 gave researchers and policy makers a much better handle on the number and characteristics of displaced American workers.[1] In these data, displaced workers are distinguished from other unemployed workers by affirmative answers to a question asking whether within the last five years the respondent was separated from his or her job because of a plant closing, an employer going out of business, or a layoff from which the respondent was not recalled. Using three years of prelayoff job tenure as the cutoff point to further distinguish displaced workers, the benchmark analysis by Flaim and Sehgal (1985) calculates a population of 5.1 million displaced workers during the January 1979 to January 1984 period.

More recent estimates of the size of the displaced worker population are provided by Ross and Smith (1993). Merging the five DWS data sets available for the 1984-92 period and using a slightly different definition of the displaced, they estimate that on average two million full-time workers were displaced from their jobs each year during the 1980s.[2] Not surprisingly, the annual number of displaced workers is found to vary with the overall state of the economy. In the recession year of 1982, 2.7 million workers—about 1 of every 25 full-time wage and salary workers—lost their jobs and were not recalled. But even during the relatively strong labor market existing in 1988, 1.5 million workers—about 1 in every 50 full-time workers—are estimated to have permanently lost their jobs.

The governments of most industrialized nations, including that of the United States, have committed themselves to help shoulder the adjustment costs borne by displaced workers by providing an arsenal of both active and passive labor market programs. Active labor market programs are basically intended to shorten the duration of postdisplacement unemployment spells and to restore long-run earnings potential. These programs typically include job search assistance to sharpen job search techniques that may have grown dull from disuse, and retraining in job skills to enable workers to qualify for jobs opening up in growing industries. In contrast, passive labor market measures provide income support to prevent unemployed workers and their families from slipping into poverty. Thus passive labor market programs are often collectively referred to as the "social safety net." Included among passive programs are unemployment compensation, pensions and early retirement benefits, continuation of health insurance, and welfare benefits.

During the 1980s, concern over an increasing incidence of long-term unemployment as a fraction of total unemployment led many industrialized nations to shift their mixes of public expenditures toward active and away from passive labor market programs. The Organization for Economic Cooperation and Development (OECD) has been instrumental in leading policy makers in member countries to redirect their focus toward active labor market policies. In the United States, events occurring during the first few years of the 1990s dramatically heightened the attention paid by policy makers to the needs of displaced workers. These events include:

- job losses in the defense sector—both federal civilian and military personnel and private sector defense industry workers—associated with large-scale cutbacks in the defense budget;

- concern that the implementation of the North American Free Trade Agreement (NAFTA) would cause U.S. producers to shift operations to other countries, thereby eliminating domestic jobs; and
- the perception that the corporate restructuring ongoing during the 1990-91 recession and the years immediately following is, for the first time, substantially increasing joblessness among white-collar workers in services as well as blue-collar workers in manufacturing (see, for example, Karr 1991).[3]

This heightened attention to the needs of the displaced was apparent in policy deliberations leading to the very sizable expansion in the 1994 fiscal year budget of the U.S. Department of Labor and to the drafting of the proposed Reemployment Act of 1994 (see, for example, U.S. Department of Labor 1993). Prominent issues considered in these deliberations include early identification of unemployed workers unlikely to be recalled to their old jobs, enhancement of the long-term retraining options available to displaced workers, establishment of national skills standards, imposition of a national payroll training tax, improvement of the school-to-work transition of youth, development of one-stop career centers supplying workers and employers better labor market information and career development services, and provision to states of the flexibility to offer unemployed workers reemployment bonuses and self-employment programs.

Other highly industrialized nations possess a wealth of experience gained from the design and actual implementation of these kinds of active labor market policies in permanent, nationwide programs. The perspective taken in this monograph is that increased awareness of how active labor market programs operate in other nations can substantially improve the way in which we deal with worker displacement in the United States. Nations examined in detail are Sweden, Germany, Japan, Britain, Canada, and Australia. These countries fall naturally into two groups. The first group, consisting of Sweden, Germany, and Japan, provides their workers with stable, nationwide employment and training systems. On the other hand, the countries in the second group—Britain, Canada, and Australia—have all anticipated U.S. policy with recent major restructurings of their employment and training programs involving the shift of resources from passive to active labor market policies.

Increased insight into the adjustment assistance needs of displaced workers, no matter in what nation they reside, requires a discussion of the costs of displacement. We turn to this issue next.

Costs of Worker Displacement

Some amount of job change plays a positive allocative role in assuring that workers are appropriately matched with employers and that inappropriate matches are terminated. While it is widely perceived that society as a whole benefits from maintaining a dynamic, generally open domestic economy, it is also recognized that displaced workers bear the brunt of the inevitable adjustment costs. It is this recognition that has prompted the governments of many nations to provide special assistance to the displaced.

A large body of literature exists dealing with the identification of the private and social losses incurred by displaced workers (see, in particular, Hamermesh 1987, 1989). A worker is said to experience an economic loss when an income stream expected to continue into the future is unexpectedly and permanently lost. Income streams considered in this literature are generated by either of two factors: (1) investment in human capital specific to the firm (or perhaps to the industry or geographic location), and (2) economic rents accruing to the beneficiaries of union-induced job queues. Upon a permanent separation from the firm, the private cost of displacement includes lost income streams generated by either or both of these factors, whereas a social cost of displacement arises only in the case of forgone returns to specific training. Both cost measures must also include the value of resources lost during the adjustment process. Special assistance to displaced workers is commonly rationalized on the basis of the first factor. The argument is that unless compensation is available, risk-averse workers and their employers will be discouraged from investing in specific human capital. The second factor also plays a role to the extent that compensation to displaced workers is needed to buy off unions and other politically powerful interests that would otherwise block socially desirable policies such as free trade and the introduction of labor-saving technology.

The empirical literature measures economic losses incurred by displaced workers in terms of length of postlayoff spells of unemployment and reduction in wages upon reemployment. Hamermesh (1989) summarizes the evidence found in thirteen studies of the effects of displacement on wage and employment losses. Six of these studies utilize DWS data. A key finding in all of the studies is that workers with the longest tenure on the job from which they were displaced suffered the greatest losses in subsequent wages and time employed. Kletzer (1989) finds, using 1984 DWS data, that the direct relationship between predisplacement tenure and wage loss is particularly strong for blue-collar workers since the returns to tenure for these workers are more job-specific, reflecting both job-match heterogeneity and specific human capital.

A second conclusion reached by Hamermesh (1989) is that poorly educated workers spend more time unemployed and suffer disproportionate wage losses. He reports no consensus, however, that particular demographic groups, such as women, minorities, or older workers, suffer especially large losses from being displaced (though minorities are more likely to be displaced).

Several more recent studies generally reinforce these findings and add new insights. Jacobson, LaLonde, and Sullivan (1993a, 1993b) examine a large sample of both displaced and nondisplaced Pennsylvania workers for whom administrative data are available on quarterly earnings covering the 1974-86 period. Focusing on prime-age, high-tenure (six or more years of tenure) workers, their evidence suggests that studies based on data such as the DWS, which lack a long earnings history or an appropriate comparison group, are likely to understate earnings losses associated with worker displacement from distressed firms. The reason is their finding that earnings of displaced workers tend to be abnormally low in the year prior to separation. Without a longer earnings history or a suitable comparison group with which to measure normal predisplacement earnings, earnings losses would be substantially underestimated. These earnings losses are also long term, with little evidence of substantial recovery even after the third year following displacement. Similarly, Ruhm (1991) finds, using data for both displaced and nondisplaced workers, that while the initial rise in joblessness associated with displacement dissipates after several years, there is a significant long-term loss of earnings potential. Ruhm's analysis is based on the University of Michigan's Panel Study of Income Dynamics (PSID) data set.

Three other findings supplied by Jacobson, LaLonde, and Sullivan are of interest. First, they find that while earnings losses were substantial for displaced workers who found new jobs in the same industries, losses were even greater for those who changed industrial sectors. Using 1984 DWS data, Addison and Portugal (1989) also report that wage losses associated with a change in industry or occupation, but not location, are greater than wage losses for displaced workers not obliged to make such shifts.[4] Similarly, Carrington (1993) finds, using 1984, 1986, and 1988 DWS data, that much of the wage loss suffered by displaced workers is the result of downturns in entire industries rather than of firm-specific declines in demand. That is, displaced workers tend to be victims of "industrial restructuring."

A second additional finding by Jacobson, LaLonde, and Sullivan is that sizable earnings losses occur even in relatively strong labor markets. Finally, the authors find that earnings losses are substantial across a broad range of industries and firm sizes. Nevertheless, losses are especially large for workers separating from highly unionized industries and large firms. This finding suggests that loss of rents, including union wage premiums, may contribute to earnings losses of displaced workers.

Farber (1993) adds to these findings evidence on employment losses as distinct from earnings losses resulting from worker displacement. To provide a comparison group of nondisplaced workers, he appends to the 1984-92 Displaced Worker Surveys data from outgoing Current Population Survey rotation groups from 1982-91. Several of Farber's main findings should be highlighted. First, male displaced workers face a dramatically lower probability of reemployment compared with nondisplaced males. Displaced females also face a lower reemployment probability, although the displaced/nondisplaced difference is not as great. Second, displaced workers are less likely to obtain full-time jobs upon reemployment; and this cost of displacement is especially great during recessions. Since part-time wage rates are substantially lower than full-time wages, the increased incidence of part-time employment during recessions is an important component of the cost of job loss to the displaced. Third, even conditioning on reemployment in a full-time job, displaced workers earn substantially less than either otherwise comparable nondisplaced workers or what they themselves earned prior to displacement. Moreover, length of previous job tenure and a less-than-high-school level of education are strongly and negatively related to wage change. In the case of job tenure, an additional year of predisplacement tenure is estimated to result in about 1 percent lower wage growth.

Finally, Farber finds that while the effects of displacement on the probability of reemployment and on full-time reemployment appear to be temporary, there is no evidence that the earnings gap between full-time reemployed displaced and nondisplaced workers narrows over time. This finding reinforces evidence on the persistence of earnings losses reported by Jacobson, LaLonde, and Sullivan (1993a, 1993b) and Ruhm (1991). Farber's interpretation of the permanence of the full-time wage effect is that wage losses are directly related to tenure, and lost tenure is never recovered. It might also be noted that the wage loss is considerably larger for workers displaced in 1990-91 than it was for workers displaced earlier.

One last study, by Crossley, Jones, and Kuhn (1994), is noteworthy because it uses recently available Canadian data to examine the costs of displacement for women relative to men. Data analyzed by the authors are derived from a survey of 1,736 workers (612 women and 1,124 men) laid off from their jobs in twenty-one establishments located in Ontario. For both male and female Canadians, postdisplacement wages are found to decline as predisplacement tenure increases. As noted, this is a common result in the literature utilizing U.S. data. More novel is the authors' finding that women lose more from displacement than men, and that the magnitude of women's losses increases faster with tenure. For example, predicted hourly wage losses for workers with three to five years of service are 4 percent of predisplacement wages for men and 13 percent for women. For workers with fifteen to twenty-five years of service these estimates rise to 15 and 26 percent, respectively, for men and women.

An Evaluation Framework

With this background on the costs of worker displacement, a next issue to consider is how government programs designed to reduce these costs are evaluated. Haveman and Saks (1985) point out an interesting contrast between program evaluation in the United States and in other industrialized countries, particularly those in Western Europe. In Western European nations, stable, well-funded, and highly professional employment and training systems receive constant feedback from employers and workers on the quality of their activities. In these countries, there is little formal evaluation of marginal program impacts. In the United States, by contrast, government-sponsored programs are less stable, funding often fluctuates dramatically, and the professional quality of program managers is uneven. Program evaluation in the United States is therefore largely based on statistical analyses of program effects in limited-duration demonstration projects, and the United States clearly leads the world in the quantity and sophistication of its program evaluations. Even so, available evaluation evidence is subject to enough qualifications, particularly with respect to skill training, that it is not easy to draw strong policy recommendations.

In summarizing this situation, Wilensky (1985, p. 9) proposes as "Wilensky's law" the following proposition: the more evaluation, the less program development; the greater the number of demonstration projects, the less follow-through. Underlying his proposition are three problems Wilensky identifies with existing program evaluations: (1) evaluation research is typically quite narrow, politically naive, and often seriously flawed in design and execution; (2) research focused on a single program, which is usually the case, obscures the interaction and interdependence of many programs; and (3) evaluated success has little to do with program funding.

The United States is clearly at one extreme in terms of the application of this proposition. At the other, Wilensky (1985, p. 3) points to Sweden as the country that combines the least program evaluation with the most action and greatest achievement in utilizing its human resources. Given its stable institutional structure, heavy national investment, and staff of well-trained professionals, it is quite likely that there are important lessons to be learned from the experience of Sweden as well as from other European nations about the design and implementation of active labor market policies. We can also gain insight from other non-European nations, including Britain, Canada, and Australia, that have preceded us in restructuring their employment and training systems.

In the absence of quantitative evaluations allowing program benefits and costs to be measured and compared, how might a discussion of the experience of other nations be made meaningful to U.S. policy makers? The approach taken in this monograph is to specify an evaluation framework against which alternative active labor market programs may be consistently assessed. The six criteria listed below, which make up the evaluation framework, are drawn from the current labor economics and labor market policy literatures. They are not necessarily mutually exclusive.

1. *Program services should facilitate the transition of displaced workers to jobs in expanding industries and growing sectors within existing industries.* By definition, adjustment assistance services are intended to make it easier for displaced workers to respond to market signals by moving from markets in which there is an excess supply of labor to those in which there is an excess demand. Growing markets may be in entirely different industries from declining markets or, as appears to be the case in manufacturing, growth may be centered in small, nimble single-plant firms at the expense of large, centralized corporate giants. Clearly, the more complete the coverage of job vacancy information and the faster vacancy information is conveyed to unemployed workers, the more rapidly the reemployment process can be completed. Sweden's system of employment exchange offices represents a model to be studied for insight into how to improve the matching process between available workers and vacant jobs.

The flip side of this criterion is that labor market services that distort or retard the response to market signals should be substantially modified or eliminated entirely. As mentioned earlier, recent concern over rising long-term unemployment has led most industrialized nations to increase their emphasis on active labor market measures and to deemphasize passive programs. Among active programs, moreover, funding for direct job creation programs has been reduced. Motivating this decision is the desire to decrease reliance on "make-work" schemes that over the longer run cannot ensure sustainable jobs, and instead to switch resources to measures that improve the skills of the workforce. Even the highly regarded Swedish adult training system has been criticized for doing little more for some workers than keep them off the unemployment rolls.

2. *Program activities must meet the needs of displaced workers.* Two important factors emerge from discussions of the characteristics of displaced workers and the costs of worker displacement. The first is that lengthy job tenure with the predisplacement employer often means that the job search skills of displaced workers will typically be rusty from disuse. Employment services, including job matching, assessment and testing, counseling, training in job search skills, and job development, are therefore an essential part of a comprehensive labor market system. As has been widely noted (see, for example, Marshall and Tucker 1992, p. 223; and Baily, Burtless, and Litan 1993, pp. 136-37), the U.S. Employment Service is basically limited to the referral of unskilled workers to low-paying and often temporary jobs. In its current form, the Employment Service does not come close to offering the employment services provided in other nations.

The second factor is that displaced workers are interested in jobs, not training. An immediate implication of this point is that on-the-job training may be preferred to classroom training as a vehicle for providing job skills. However, targeted employment subsidy programs have not always proven successful in attracting a sufficient number of employers willing to provide on-the-job training opportunities. Voluntary employer participation in the firm-based German and Japanese training systems is especially important to study for insight into how to increase the interest of American employers in supplying on-the-job training opportunities. An interesting policy initiative to be considered in the context of stimulating firm-based training is the payroll training tax recently imposed in Australia.

Regarding skill training provided in a classroom setting, workers' interest in jobs rather than training suggests that classroom training programs be designed with three goals in mind. First, training courses must be timely and flexible. Circumstances such as layoffs that generate a demand for retraining can occur at any time, and training programs should be designed to be available on a timely basis and flexible enough to fit into workers' schedules. Second, training programs must demonstrate to enrollees a clear connection between skills learned and employment opportunities. This goal is especially important, albeit difficult to accomplish, in the context of basic education programs. Finally, since most adult workers support families, the tuition charged for training courses must be low or paid for by government subsidies. Strong consideration should also be given to providing trainees with a form of income maintenance while they are engaged in training.

3. *Programs must serve the entire spectrum of displaced workers, not just those easiest to place.* Evidence for the United States suggests that only a small fraction of the eligible displaced worker population is served by Job Training Partnership Act (JTPA) programs.[5] Of those served, in addition, relatively few displaced workers are provided with skills training and even fewer eligible workers receive basic education (see Levitan and Gallo 1988, pp. 57-62). This is a not unexpected result since basic education is expensive relative to other adjustment assistance services and program administrators have a natural propensity to "cream" (i.e., to select those individuals who are the most job-ready) in the applicant selection process.

Yet on equity grounds the case can be made that it is adults at the low end of the skill distribution who should be first in line for access to training services. With the possible exception of Japan, the displaced worker populations of the countries considered include a substantial fraction of workers in need of basic education. Swedish experience offers some insight into the operation of basic education programs, and the limited formal education and vocational skills of British workers make the ongoing restructuring of the employment and training system in the United Kingdom especially interesting to study. Guidance on the design and operation of basic education programs can also be gained from evidence generated from state welfare employment demonstration projects in the United States.

4. *Training programs must supply marketable skills to program graduates.* As suggested in the discussion of criterion 2, it is reasonable to suppose that firm-based training is more likely to enhance labor market opportunities than classroom training, since it is directly demand-related. Clearly, one of the most difficult problems in design-

ing classroom training programs is to guarantee that the training will supply program completers with job skills currently in demand in local labor markets. All of the countries examined recognize that some degree of employer involvement is necessary to solve this problem. Most countries, including the United States in the JTPA program, involve employers in helping to set policy and provide feedback. In Britain, for example, this type of employer involvement is a major emphasis of the national network of Training and Enterprise Councils (TECs) recently established to deliver training services and promote small business development at the local level. Sweden has gone one step further in seeking to decentralize decision making and increase responsiveness to changes in market demand. Created in 1986, the Swedish National Employment Training Board is responsible for being financially self-sufficient through the sale of training services to any customer willing to buy.

5. *Programs should effectively utilize existing educational and training institutions.* The existence of an extensive postsecondary schooling system makes it most unlikely that the United States will follow the Swedish model in establishing a government-funded adult training system independent of the regular educational infrastructure. Rather, the presumption for our country, as well as for Britain, Canada, and Australia, is that existing institutional training providers will be heavily utilized in supplying adult training services. This presumption raises the issue of how to encourage third-party providers to adapt to the special needs of adults while supplying training that leads to job placement.

The contractual mechanism often used to deal with this issue is performance-based contracting. This form of contracting is used in the JTPA program in the United States and in contracts entered into by TECs and the training providers with which they subcontract in Britain. The operation of performance-based contracting in JTPA programs, in the British network of TECs, and in an important state program, California's Employment Training Panel, will be examined for direction in establishing policies that preserve the incentive to provide training leading to job placement while restraining the incentive to cream in the participant selection process. Also to be considered is the role of nationally recognized credentials in Sweden, Germany, and

Britain in certifying the quality of program graduates to employers and in helping potential trainees make informed choices between training curricula and institutional providers.

6. *A broadening of the concept of job skills should be encouraged.* Reports of recent national commissions and discussions in the popular press and professional journals stress the need for a radical change in skills that workers should possess in order for American firms to be competitive in the international marketplace.[6] As recently described by Lynch (1994, p. 63), concern during the 1970s over how to absorb "overeducated Americans" into the labor market shifted during the 1980s to how to stimulate the skill development of "undertrained Americans." Rather than simply achieving competency at a particular narrowly defined job, it is frequently argued that American workers need to be able to think creatively and solve problems, work effectively in teams, adapt flexibly to rapid shifts in product demand, and engage in lifetime learning. Frontline workers in this model, termed "high-performance work organizations" by former Secretary of Labor Ray Marshall and Marc Tucker (1992), often operate in teams and are expected to substantially supervise themselves while assuming responsibility for quality control, equipment maintenance, ordering supplies, and many other functions traditionally reserved for management and technical staff. Countries that are often presented as being far ahead of the United States in developing most or all of these productive characteristics in their workers are Japan and Germany.

Empirical evidence is just beginning to appear on the extent of upskilling within the American labor market. For goods-producing industries in particular, this evidence indicates that the breadth of skills required of American workers is in fact increasing. Using data collected by Hay Associates, Cappelli (1993a) examines changes in skill requirements for production jobs in ninety-three manufacturing establishments between 1978 and 1986 and for clerical jobs in 211 firms between 1978 and 1988. His results for manufacturing indicate a highly significant upskilling within all but one of the ten production job families considered. (The lone exception is "housekeeping.") For eight clerical job families, on the other hand, there is an even split between job families experiencing significant upskilling and those experiencing deskilling. New office technologies appear to explain the deskilling of specific clerical jobs.

In a second recent study, Osterman (1994) finds that about 35 percent of the 694 manufacturing establishments he surveyed in 1992 made substantial use of "flexible work practices," which he defines as the use of teams, job rotation, quality circles, and Total Quality Management. Moreover, Osterman is able to isolate several important factors that are highly correlated with the adoption of flexible work practices. These include an international product market, a complex production technology, a "high-road" competitive strategy (one that emphasizes service, quality, and variety of products rather than low costs), and a commitment to increasing the well-being of employees' families.

Organization of the Study

Chapter 2 provides an overview of labor market policies in place in the seven countries examined (including the U.S.). The purpose of this overview is to supply the necessary background for understanding basic differences between countries in their labor market institutions and in the levels and mixes of their active and passive labor market program expenditures. The chapter also investigates a possible linkage between these countries' labor market policies and differences in their unemployment rates and especially in the incidence of long-term unemployment.

With this background, chapter 3 reviews the evaluation evidence available for demonstration projects and experiments implementing various kinds of active labor market programs in the United States. This evidence includes evaluation reports on five major displaced worker demonstrations and on a number of additional experiments implementing three proposed reforms of the unemployment insurance (UI) system. The proposed UI reforms involve (1) enhanced employment services and stricter enforcement of job search requirements, (2) reemployment bonuses paid to UI recipients who find jobs quickly, and (3) self-employment as an alternative reemployment strategy. Also discussed in this chapter are selected evaluation reports examining the effectiveness of training and basic education programs in demonstration projects targeted to economically disadvantaged workers (i.e., welfare recipients).

Chapters 4 and 5 examine the design and operation of particular active labor market programs in other countries. Adult retraining programs are considered in chapter 4. Beginning with classroom training, this chapter investigates in detail the operation of the highly regarded government training model in Sweden and Britain's employer-led/school-based model with its requirement of performance-based contracting. Concerning on-the-job training, the firm-based training systems in place in Germany and Japan are discussed, with emphasis on the questions of how best to give employers an incentive to provide on-the-job training opportunities and whether important features of these firm-based systems might be transferable to the U.S. labor market. Also considered in this chapter are the payroll training tax implemented in Australia and the national skill certification system in Britain.

Chapter 5 focuses on employment services, including the traditional labor exchange function matching unemployed workers to job vacancies, as well as more proactive job search assistance services. Carefully examined are the job matching system provided by the Swedish public employment service and job development services supplied by the Canadian Industrial Adjustment Service. This chapter concludes with a consideration of recent policies implemented in Britain, Canada, and Australia to link eligibility for income support payments to participation in active labor market programs in order to maintain the work incentive of the unemployed.

A final chapter pulls together the findings presented in chapters 2 through 5 and outlines an agenda for assisting displaced Americans.

NOTES

1. DWS data sets are supplements to the January Current Population Surveys (CPS) produced by the Bureau of Labor Statistics.

2. In defining the displaced, Ross and Smith count only workers who lost full-time jobs and ignore length of prelayoff job tenure.

3. Farber (1993) presents empirical evidence supporting the impression that recent events have changed the demographic and industrial composition of the displaced worker population. Using DWS data from the 1984 through 1992 surveys, he compares the nature of job losses during the 1990-91 recession to job losses during the earlier 1982-83 recession and the more prosperous

1984-89 period. While job loss is still disproportionately concentrated in the goods-producing sector, Farber's evidence indicates that displacement was more common during 1990-91 than during the 1982-83 recession in important and growing nongoods-producing industries. In addition, the rate of job loss among older workers during the 1990-91 recession is found to be higher than during the earlier recession, especially for college-educated men.

4. Addison and Portugal also attempt to model the simultaneity noted by Hamermesh (1989) between unemployment duration and postdisplacement wages resulting from worker search behavior and to relax the strong restriction imposed by identifying the tenure coefficient with the return to firm-specific training investments.

5. The major federal program providing reemployment services to displaced workers is Title III of JTPA.

6. Examples of national commission reports are the Secretary's Commission on Achieving Necessary Skills (1991) and the Commission on Workforce Quality and Labor Market Efficiency (1989). In the academic literature, Bound and Johnson (1992) conclude from their study of the dramatic changes in the U.S. wage structure during the 1980s that the rise in the relative wage position of women and the highly educated stems largely from an increase in the relative demand for skilled labor stimulated by changes in computer-based technology.

2
Fundamental Differences Between Nations in Labor Market Policies

A useful way to begin analyzing international differences in labor market policies is to look at the level and mix of government expenditures on active and passive labor market programs. As discussed in chapter 1, passive programs provide a social safety net to prevent unemployed workers and their families from slipping into poverty. In contrast, active programs are intended to speed up reemployment and to improve long-run earnings potential. Active programs are commonly broken down into three categories: employment services, including job search assistance and job placement; adult training programs; and job creation and employment subsidies.

Table 2.1 displays, for the nations mentioned in chapter 1, OECD estimates of public expenditures on active and passive labor market programs expressed as a percentage of Gross Domestic Product.[1] Annual averages calculated over the 1985-88 period are presented. Table 2.2 links these expenditure estimates to national unemployment rates and measures of the incidence of long-term unemployment for the same years. The 1985-88 period is chosen to represent a period of relative economic and political stability just prior to the disruptions created in the early 1990s by the worldwide recession and the breakup of the Soviet Union. Unemployment rates generally fell during the latter half of the 1980s, bottoming out in 1989 or 1990. Except for Japan and western Germany, unemployment rates then rose in 1991 and 1992.[2] This rise was moderate for the United States and more pronounced for Sweden, the United Kingdom, Canada, and Australia. Particularly striking is the rapid increase in the Swedish standardized unemployment rate from 1.5 percent in 1990 to 4.8 percent in 1992 and 9.0 percent in the first quarter of 1994 (Economist Intelligence Unit 1994b). Forslund and Krueger (1994) offer an analysis of the dramatic rise in Swedish unemployment during the 1990s in which they predict that the unemployment rate will remain at historically high levels for at least the next few years, and probably longer.

Table 2.1 Public Expenditures on Active and Passive Labor Market Programs as a Percentage of GDP, Seven Countries, Annual Averages for 1985–88

Country	Active	Passive[a]	Total	Active/ passive
Sweden	1.96	0.80	2.76	2.45
Germany	0.95	1.36	2.31	0.70
Japan[b]	0.19	0.40	0.59	0.48
U.K.	0.80	1.89	2.69	0.43
Canada	0.58	1.74	2.32	0.33
Australia	0.36	1.20	1.56	0.30
U.S.[c]	0.26	0.51	0.77	0.51

SOURCE: OECD (1989, table A.1).

a. Includes unemployment compensation and early retirement for labor market reasons.

b. For 1987 and 1988.

c. For 1986-88.

Table 2.2 Unemployment Rates and Incidence of Long-Term Unemployment, Seven Countries (in percent)

Country	Standardized unemployment rate, 1985–88[a]	Long-term unemployment, 1987[b]	
		6+ months	12+ months
Sweden	2.3	23.4	8.2
Germany	6.5	64.2	48.1
Japan	2.7	40.4	20.2
U.K.	10.2	62.8	45.2
Canada	9.1	24.1	9.4
Australia	7.9	48.7	28.7
U.S.	6.4	14.0	8.1

SOURCE: OECD (1989, tables 1.5 and M).

a. As a percentage of total labor force.

b. As a percentage of total unemployment.

Among the seven nations, Sweden and the United Kingdom are reported in table 2.1 to have the highest total expenditure ratios on active and passive programs combined. The expenditure mix is dramatically different between the two countries, however, with Sweden's active program expenditure ratio more than double the ratio for passive programs while just the opposite is true for Britain. At the same time, Sweden enjoyed the lowest unemployment rate shown in table 2.2 and the United Kingdom suffered the highest. Long-term unemployment is a particularly severe problem in Britain, as it is in Germany. At the other end of the spectrum, Japan ranks lowest among the seven nations in terms of public expenditures on both active and passive labor market programs. The Japanese unemployment rate, nevertheless, is also very low at 2.7 percent, a rate that is only slightly higher than Sweden's rate (2.3 percent). Labor market program expenditure ratios for the United States are seen to be only slightly higher than those for Japan, while the U.S. unemployment rate is roughly in the middle of the pack at 6.4 percent. Long-term unemployment is a relatively minor problem for American workers.

This chapter provides background information intended to help in understanding the differences across nations in labor market program expenditures and unemployment rates shown in tables 2.1 and 2.2. The discussion is divided into four main sections, which contrast the historical development of labor market programs in Western Europe, Japan, the United Kingdom, and North America and Australia. The Western European model is illustrated by programs in Sweden and Germany. A final section summarizes the discussion.

The Western European Model

The centerpiece of the Western European model is a comprehensive and stable institutional structure for addressing employment and training issues. Haveman and Saks (1985) characterize this structure as follows:

1. A single primary agency established by the national government but often independent of it.

2. An extensive network of local offices emphasizing outreach to employers and workers.

3. Participation in policy formulation and implementation by employer groups and trade unions.

4. Substantial expenditures on developing a large professional staff of placement, counseling, and training personnel.

Along with a stable institutional structure for implementing labor market programs, most Western European countries maintain an industrial relations system that imposes advance notice and severance pay requirements on employers who dismiss workers and that encourages adjustment of work hours in lieu of layoffs.

The structure of the Western European model can be understood more clearly by examining labor market programs in place in Sweden and Germany. As indicated in table 2.1, Sweden and Germany ranked one and two, respectively, in the level of public expenditures devoted to active labor market programs during the second half of the 1980s.

Sweden

The Swedish labor market has long been identified with centralized collective bargaining. Milner (1990, p. 85) remarks that by the 1930s the labor movement in Sweden had transformed itself from "a network of organizations designed to defend workers from capitalist exploitation to a confident alternative source of national leadership." Vandewalle (1991) estimates that currently about 95 percent of Sweden's blue-collar workers and some 80 percent of salaried workers are part of the Trade Union Confederation.

In the immediate postwar period, Swedish union leaders faced a perplexing dilemma (see Rehn 1985). On one hand, they could pursue a militant wage policy that would contribute to inflation and ultimately erode away the real wage gains of their members. On the other, they could present moderate wage demands and be judged as ineffective by a rank and file interested in a union movement that delivered the goods in terms of rising money wages.

The solution hammered out by the Trade Union Confederation in 1951 to solve this dilemma is known as the "Rehn-Meidner model." There are three main elements to the model.

1. Maintenance of a level of aggregate demand necessary to avoid inflation.

2. Implementation of a "wage solidarity" policy requiring wage equalization across industries and regions.

3. Protection of workers from the unemployment that would otherwise result from limited aggregate demand management (element 1) and rigid wages (element 2) by active labor market programs intended to facilitate worker mobility across industries and regions.

The second of these elements reflects the Trade Union Confederation's position that allowing wage differentials across labor markets amounts to subsidizing firms and industries with low productivity and profits while restraining the growth of highly productive firms and industries. At the same time, a policy of wage equalization has the unfortunate side effect of eliminating market signals that encourage the efficient movement of labor from contracting to expanding industries.[3] As a substitute for wage differentials responsive to market forces, the active labor market policy called for by the third element seeks to equip laid-off workers to locate and qualify for new jobs in growing industries. An active labor market policy reflects the central place of work in the Swedish value system. Work is perceived as part of living a normal life; income transfers cannot replace employment for the able-bodied and even for those who are handicapped (Milner 1990, p. 101). Thus, Swedish labor market policies have historically been strongly oriented toward satisfying the first of the six evaluation criteria outlined in chapter 1.

By the mid-1950s, the Swedish government was persuaded to implement the Rehn-Meidner model. The active labor market policy called for by the model is administered by the National Labor Market Board, which consists of a national board and twenty-four regional boards. Each board is composed of labor, employer, and government members, with representatives of labor and employer organizations dominating the decision-making processes of the boards. The national board administers the local boards and the national Employment Service, while regional boards administer local employment exchange offices. Also administered under the National Labor Market Board is a nationwide system of employability institutes, which is responsible for serving the occupationally handicapped.

Created in 1986, a parallel institution—the National Employment Training Board (AMU)—was given responsibility for operating Sweden's nationwide system of 100 skill training centers.[4] Like the National Labor Market Board, the AMU is composed of a national board and twenty-five regional boards, each board consisting of employer, union, and government members. The AMU does not receive direct government funding. Instead, it sells training services to any customer willing to buy, although the Employment Service is its

Figure 2.1 Structure of Sweden's Labor Market System

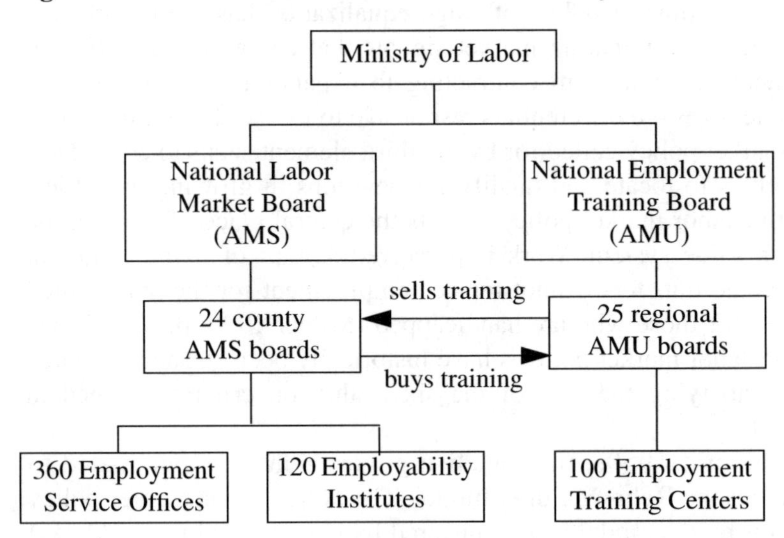

primary customer. Figure 2.1 summarizes the organizational structure of the Swedish labor market system.

The broad range of Swedish labor market programs can perhaps be best visualized in the list presented below.[5]

1. Counseling and Job Placement

2. Supply-Side Programs
   a. Employment training
      - Vocational training and basic education courses taught at AMU employment training centers
      - Vocational rehabilitation at employability institutes
      - In-house employment training—grants paid to companies to subsidize the cost of sending employees to training courses
   b. Relocation grants paid to workers

3. Demand-Side Programs
   a. Relief work—public sector jobs lasting no more than six months
   b. Recruitment subsidies—a subsidy of up to 60 percent of wage costs for six months targeted to job seekers aged 18-24, the hardcore unemployed, and unemployed workers whose unemployment benefits are about to expire
   c. Youth traineeships—a 100 percent wage subsidy for six months targeted to workers under age 25
   d. Start-up grants—grants to assist unemployed workers to start up their own small businesses
   e. Wage subsidies—subsidies of up to 100 percent to assist the placement of disabled persons in public- or private-sector jobs
   f. Sheltered employment—subsidies of 75 percent of labor costs to municipal employers who hire the occupationally handicapped

4. Income Support to the Unemployed
   a. Benefits from an unemployment insurance society
   b. Unemployment assistance

An unemployed Swedish worker typically encounters a sequence of active labor market programs. Initially, job seekers pass through a series of counseling and placement services provided at a local employment exchange office of the Employment Service. The system of employment exchange offices is the focal point of Swedish labor market policy. The system is completely computerized, and by law all job vacancies (with certain exceptions) in both the public and private sectors must be registered with the Employment Service. If a job for which an unemployed job seeker is qualified is not available in the local area but is available elsewhere in the country, the employment office will pay the cost of travel to interview with the potential employer and will subsidize moving expenses if a job is located.

Those who remain jobless are placed in a training program in a nearby skill center where they are retrained to qualify for jobs in growing industries. Training is free to participating workers, and trainees are eligible to receive an income-maintenance allowance, the size of which depends on number of dependents. For handicapped workers, the system of employability institutes offers vocational rehabilitation and intensive counseling. As emphasized in table 2.3, adult training is the active labor market program that, by international standards, is funded at an especially high level. Since training through the AMU is widely used by Swedish workers—those employed as well as the jobless—to enhance their labor market skills, government training is a key element in the Swedish concept of lifetime learning.

Retrained workers who have still not been placed in a job are eligible for temporary employment in relief work projects (typically public construction projects) and wage-subsidy (or "recruitment") programs intended to create jobs in both the public and private sectors. These demand-side programs are designed especially to increase the employment opportunities of youth, the disabled, and the hardcore unemployed. In terms of table 2.3, these measures show up in the large expenditure ratios for youth and disabled worker programs, as well as in the substantial expenditure ratio for direct job creation/employment subsidy programs. It should be noted that the OECD includes subsidies for in-house workplace training in the adult training category of the table rather than in the job creation/employment subsidy category.

The Swedish Institute (1990) estimates that 3 to 4 percent of the labor force is involved in a government-sponsored active labor market program at any point in time. The impact of this level of labor market program participation on Sweden's unemployment rate is vividly

Table 2.3 Breakdown of Public Expenditures on Active Labor Market Programs as a Percentage of GDP, Seven Countries, Annual Averages for 1985–88

Country	Employment services	Adult training	Job creation/ employment subsidies	Special youth measures	Measures for the disabled	Total[a]
Sweden	0.24	0.52	0.30	0.16	0.76	1.96
Germany	0.22	0.27	0.20	0.05	0.21	0.95
Japan[b]	0.03	0.03	0.12	--	0.01	0.19
U.K.	0.15	0.11	0.26	0.25	0.04	0.80
Canada	0.23	0.22	0.02	0.12	--	0.58
Australia	0.11	0.04	0.13	0.06	0.03	0.36
U.S.[c]	0.07	0.11	0.01	0.03	0.03	0.26

SOURCE: OECD (1989, table A.1).

a. Categories may not sum to total because of rounding error.

b. For 1987 and 1988.

c. For 1986–88.

brought out in a recent analysis by Sorrentino (1993), in which she calculates alternative measures of unemployment for nine countries in 1989. As seen in table 2.4, Sweden's unemployment rate in 1989 rises sharply from 1.4 percent (the official or U-5 measure) to 3.4 percent (the U-6 measure) when involuntary part-time work is treated as at least partial unemployment.[6] But an even bigger change from the U-5 rate occurs when account is taken of the absorption by active labor market programs of persons who otherwise would be either unemployed or discouraged workers. Sorrentino (1993, p. 17) estimates that Sweden's official unemployment rate in 1989 would have more than tripled to 4.5 percent if all labor market program participants had otherwise been unemployed. Similarly, the U-7 rate would have increased from the 3.8 percent shown to 7.3 percent if all program participants would otherwise have been either unemployed or discouraged workers. While a U-7 rate of 7.3 percent would have ranked Sweden in a virtual tie with Japan as the lowest among the countries analyzed, it is much closer to the U.S. U-7 rate of 7.9 percent than are the two countries' U-5 rates.

Table 2.4 Alternative Unemployment Indicators, Six Countries, 1989 (in percent)

Country	U–1	U–2	U–5	U–6	U–7
Sweden	0.5	0.7	1.4	3.4	3.8
Germany	4.6	1.7	5.8	6.0	n.a.
Japan	1.1	0.4	2.2	2.8	7.2
U.K.	5.2	1.5	7.4	8.7	9.3
Canada	3.1	3.9	7.5	9.5	9.9
U.S.	1.2	2.4	5.3	7.2	7.9

SOURCE: Sorrentino (1993, table 1).
NOTE: alternative unemployment indicators are defined as:
U–1: long-term (13+ weeks) unemployment rate,
U–2: job loser rate,
U–5: conventional unemployment rate,
U–6: unemployment rate including per sons working part-time for economic reasons, and
U–7: U–6 plus discouraged workers.
n.a. indicates not available.

Workers who remain jobless even after their exposure to government employment services, training programs, and demand-side programs are eligible to receive unemployment insurance benefits. Most unemployment insurance coverage in Sweden is administered by unemployment insurance societies associated with labor unions. In addition, the government offers unemployment assistance (known as KAS) to workers who are not members of insurance societies, to new labor market entrants, and to unemployed workers older than age 60 who have exhausted insurance benefits (see Burtless 1987, pp. 131-33).

At this point, it may be useful to pause a moment to emphasize the distinction between the unemployment insurance (UI) and unemployment assistance (UA) programs found in Sweden and many other industrialized countries, especially in Western Europe (see table 2.5). As described by Atkinson and Micklewright (1991, pp. 1688-97), UI plans are broadly characterized by the following provisions:

1. Benefits are not paid to persons who enter unemployment voluntarily.

2. Benefits may not be paid for an initial period.

3. Benefits are conditional on the person making a genuine effort to search for new employment.

4. Refusal of suitable job offers, beyond some specified number, leads to disqualification for benefits.

5. Benefits are contributory, meaning that eligibility depends on the past record of insured employment.

6. The amount of benefits received may depend on past earnings.

7. Benefits are paid for a limited period of time.

8. Eligibility for benefits is not affected by the level of income of other household members.

Failure to satisfy provisions 1, 3–5, and 7 typically means that a sizable fraction of the unemployed is not covered by UI.

Unemployment assistance plans share provisions 1–4 with UI. The key difference between the two is that the amount of UA benefits received depends on other income and on assets via a means test. As a consequence, eligibility for UA benefits is not related to past employment, and benefits may be received for an indefinite period. In addition, UA benefits do not depend on previous wages but are affected by the earnings of other household members. Atkinson and Micklewright (1991, pp. 1693-94) comment that a particular country's unemployment compensation system is frequently difficult to classify as either a UI or UA plan or as a dual UI/UA plan. A case in point is the Swedish KAS scheme, which is intended for those who do not satisfy UI eligibility requirements and is thus classified in table 2.5 as a UA plan. Nonetheless, KAS is of limited duration, is not means-tested, and depends on employment history—all characteristics of UI.

Germany

Germany's "dual system" of apprenticeship training is well known for producing highly skilled frontline workers. At the same time, table 2.1 shows that Germany ranks second only to Sweden in terms of active labor market program expenditures and third behind Britain and Canada on passive labor market expenditures. One other consideration is that both table 2.2 and the U-1 measure in table 2.4 indicate that Germany faces a relatively high incidence of long-term unemployment.

Marshall and Tucker (1992, p. 206) argue that key to understanding the paradox of a highly skilled workforce coexisting with relatively large labor market program expenditures and high long-term unemployment is the strong identification of German workers with a trade or occupation that develops over time as they progress from apprentice to journeyman to master craftsman. This system clearly produces exceptionally well-qualified workers. Moreover, the high skill level of the workforce when coupled with restrictions on layoffs imposed in industrial relations and by law provides employers a strong incentive to make further investments in firm-specific training.[7] The consequence is a workplace that is highly flexible in terms of both the tasks that can be taken on by workers and the freedom enjoyed by employers to introduce new technology. The downside of this system is that increased job security with the firm ("internal flexibility") is accomplished at the

Table 2.5 Income Support Programs in Place in Seven OECD Countries

Country	Type of program	Duration of benefits	Description
Sweden	UI and UA	14 months	UI for 60 weeks if age under 55; 90 weeks if age 55 or older. UA (KAS benefits) dependent on employment history for 150 days (longer if age 55 or older).
Germany	UI and UA	Indefinite	UI for between 6 and 32 months depending on employment history and age. UA instead of UI or following UI.
Japan	UI only		UI subsidy paid to employers to keep temporarily laid-off workers on the payroll. UI paid directly to permanently laid-off workers.
U.K.	UI and UA	Indefinite	UI for up to 12 months depending on employment history. UA instead of, during, or after UI.
Canada	UI only	50 weeks	Up to 50 weeks depending on regional unemployment rate and employment history.
Australia	UA only	Indefinite	
U.S.	UI only	6 months	UI for up to 6 months depending on the state, employment history, and unemployment rate.

SOURCE: Atkinson and Micklewright (1991, tables 2 and 3) and discussion in text.

expense of employment security provided through the market ("external flexibility"). That is, workers who are laid off or seek a voluntary job change face a difficult transition in moving to jobs comparable in wages and responsibilities in other occupations or industries.

Apprenticeship training

Formal vocational training in Germany dates back to the middle ages.[8] Medieval craft guilds established the concept of Master Craftsman or *Meister,* whose responsibilities include the task of training apprentices. By the end of the nineteenth century, Crafts Chambers and Chambers of Industry and Commerce assumed the role of coordinating apprenticeship training programs; and in 1938 a law was passed requiring all apprentices to receive formal schooling in conjunction with their on-the-job training. The Vocational Training Act of 1969 established the legal framework for the German apprenticeship approach to training. Under this act, most high school graduates not going on to college become apprentices at the age of 15 or 16 in one of 378 classified occupations. Wilfried Prewo, chief executive of the Hanover Chamber of Industry and Commerce, reports that some 70 percent of young Germans sign up for apprenticeship training, and that 6.5 percent of the labor force in 1992 was enrolled in apprenticeships (see Prewo 1993). It is not unusual for the chief executive officers of large German companies to have begun their careers as apprentices with their firms.

The dual system for training apprentices is based on a partnership between schools, labor unions, employers, and the government. A secondary school graduate who wishes to receive training applies for an apprenticeship position with an employer. Obtaining an apprenticeship with a desirable employer depends on the applicant having a strong academic record and good recommendations from his or her teachers. If the application is successful, the employer enters into a contract to provide the apprentice with training in accordance with the provisions of the Vocational Training Act. Length of training varies from two years to three and one-half years, depending on the occupation. Under the terms of the contract, the employer must provide accredited training that combines on-the-job training supervised by a *Meister* at the employer's workplace with one or two days per week of off-the-job training at a state vocational school (a *Berufsschule*). Program accreditation is the responsibility of self-governing Chambers of Industry and Commerce. Because of the obligation to ensure that the apprentice is properly trained, employers have a strong motivation to maintain close contact with vocational schools and the curricula they offer. All direct costs associated with workplace training are borne by the firm supplying the training, and the apprentice receives a monthly allowance. Monthly allowances for the first year of an apprenticeship vary between 20 and 27 percent of the earnings of a fully trained worker and increase yearly to between 27 and 53 percent by the fourth year (Her Majesty's Inspectorate 1991, p. 20). The government supplies a means-tested supplement to employer-provided allowances, which shows up as the major component of the "special youth measures" expenditure category in table 2.3.

At the end of the contract period, the apprentice faces a written examination and a careful review of selected samples of his or her work. Apprentices who successfully pass their final examination are awarded a certificate, honored by employers throughout Germany, which certifies that they possess the skills required to assume journeyman status in their trade or occupation. Responsibility for the development, administration, and grading of exams rests with the Chambers. The apprenticeship system substantially eases the school-to-work transition of young Germans, making the ratio of youth unemployment to adult unemployment in Germany by far the lowest of the nine counties examined by Sorrentino (1993). Lerman and Pouncy (1990) argue persuasively that a German-style apprenticeship program could substantially benefit non-college-bound American youth by strengthening the link between schooling and work and establishing ties with adult mentors.

Once they have completed an apprenticeship, adult workers have the opportunity to continue their training in a Meister or a Technician program. To become a Meister, a skilled worker may attend a full-time course at a Meister training center for one or two years or a part-time course for up to three years. It is interesting to note that all businesses providing services that fall within the 378 classified occupations covered by apprenticeship training must employ at least one Meister (Her Majesty's Inspectorate 1991, p. 15). Technician courses are usually full time for two years. Lynch (1993a, p. 27) observes that there is a current debate in Germany on whether further training should be subject to the same degree of regulation as apprenticeships.

Other labor market programs

As suggested by table 2.3, the German dual system of apprenticeship training provides initial training in a much larger system of labor market programs. Germany offers workers an unemployment compensation system that is fully integrated with its job matching and training programs. The system is operated by the Federal Employment Service (*Bundesanstalt fur Arbeit*), established in 1952 as a quasi-governmental agency governed by representatives of unions, employer associations, and public organizations.

The German government's employment and training policy, implemented through the Federal Employment Service, is aimed at assisting the movement of labor from declining to growing industries. As is the case in Sweden, a system of national wage determination keeps the wages of German workers high and wage differentials small, thus limiting the market's ability to signal labor shortages and surpluses. To facilitate labor mobility, the Federal Employment Service operates one-stop jobs centers called *Arbeitsamt,* located in cities and larger towns throughout the country, which serve as the universal intake point for the unemployed and for employed workers seeking to upgrade their skills. These jobs centers offer counseling and assessment services along with job matching with local employers. In addition, relocation grants are available to enable unemployed workers to expand the geographic scope of their job search.

Lynch (1994) points out that while the incidence of firm-based training for German workers 20 to 24 years of age is the highest in the world, it is much less common for workers older than age 24. Job seekers who require services beyond job matching and relocation allowances are eligible for financial assistance to enroll in a retraining program supplied by an institutional training provider. There is no central adult training agency like the Swedish AMU. Unemployed workers undergoing retraining are eligible for unemployment insurance benefits (*Arbeitslosengeld*), and the unemployed may be disqualified from receiving benefits for refusal to relocate or to participate in a retraining program. In addition, unemployed workers undergoing training are eligible for a subsistence allowance to cover part or all of their costs of tuition, educational supplies, travel, and lodging if trainees are away from home. Those who cannot be matched to vacant jobs even after completing a retraining program may be referred to a temporary public service employment program or to a private-sector wage-subsidy program.

Abraham and Houseman (1993, pp. 26-27) comment that beginning in the mid-1980s, the German government implicitly began to subsidize retirement at earlier and earlier ages by changing the rules about UI coverage for older workers. As of 1987, the maximum period of benefit eligibility was set at 18 months for workers aged 42 or 43, 22 months for those aged 44 through 48, 26 months for those aged 49 through 53, and 32 months for those aged 54 and over. A popular early retirement program allows workers aged 60 who have contributed to the retirement system for at least 15 years and who have been unemployed for at least 52 weeks out of the last year and a half to start receiving government retirement benefits. Thus, a worker aged 57 years and four months can be dismissed and receive UI, possibly supplemented by a company pension, for 32 months, and then begin collecting government retirement benefits at age 60.

As noted in table 2.5, unemployed Germans are eligible for two separate systems of jobless pay. Unemployment assistance (*Arbeitslosenhilfe*) furnishes income support for an indefinite period to the unemployed who have exhausted their unemployment insurance benefits. Currently, unemployed workers with children receive 67 percent of their previous after-tax earnings in UI benefits, while childless couples and single individuals receive 60 percent (Wessel and Benjamin 1994). UA benefits provide as much as 57 percent of previous earnings for those with children and 52 percent for those without. In contrast to these percentages, unemployed American workers are eligible for up to six months of UI benefits that rarely exceed half of what they previously earned.

UI and UA rank one and two among the expenditure categories the OECD reports for Germany under the heading of unemployment compensation (see OECD 1988, p. 101). Short-time work compensation is the third major unemployment compensation program component. To avoid layoffs by encouraging work sharing, German employers, with the approval of works councils and the Federal Employment Service, may reduce employees' hours of work, and employees working reduced hours are eligible to collect prorated UI benefits. Work sharing and the strong legal protection against layoffs cause employers to treat layoffs as a strategy of last resort. It is typical in German "employment plans" for redundant workers to remain with their employers at wages subsidized by public funds while they are being retrained. In a highly publicized recent example, Volkswagen announced in November of 1993 that it had reached an agreement with local government officials and its works council to introduce a four-day workweek for 100,000 VW employers. This plan would prevent—or at least delay—the laying off of 30,000 redundant employers who would receive retraining services while remaining on the company's payroll.

Burtless (1987, p. 146) concludes that the much higher incidence of long-term unemployment in Germany than in the United States arises because the generous German unemployment compensation system allows the unemployed to be more selective about the jobs they find acceptable. At the same time, as argued by Marshall and Tucker (1992), the internal flexibility of German firms decreases the number of job vacancies available to experienced workers from the outside. The consequence is that the unemployment rates appearing in tables 2.2 and 2.3 for Germany and the United States are very similar because, although German workers are less likely to lose their jobs through layoffs than Americans, their rate of reemployment is also lower, thereby increasing the incidence of long-term unemployment.

The Japanese Model

Japan's employment laws and practices, like those of Sweden, are aimed at preventing unemployment; and table 2.2 indicates that at 2.7 percent, the unemployment rate in Japan during the 1985-88 period exceeds only that of Sweden. Unlike Sweden, which relies primarily on government labor market policy, the Japanese model is based on a commitment of private sector employers to bear the major responsibility for maintaining a low level of unemployment. Tables 2.1 and 2.3 reflect this commitment, indicating that the Japanese government spends relatively little in public funds on both active and passive labor market measures and virtually nothing on adult training.

The Japanese firm-based model builds on a foundation of well-developed training provided by the educational system in the native language, science, and mathematics. Japanese high schools successfully retain a very high percentage of the population until age 18 and produce graduates who are homogeneous in basic knowledge, willingness to learn new skills, and ability to work with others. Hashimoto (1994) notes that employers stress academic achievement in their hiring decisions and often establish ongoing arrangements with individual high schools to help in recruiting their graduates year after year.

Young workers are hired on the expectation that job-specific skills will be learned in the workplace. It is important to emphasize, however, that learning does not end once a worker has achieved competency in a particular task. Rather, managers in large firms are responsible for designing work experience and training opportunities that continue throughout a worker's career. The Japanese practice of continuous improvement in skills is known as *kaizen.* Critical in the Japanese tradition of hierarchical training is the attitude instilled in senior workers that it is their duty to train younger, less-experienced workers. Instead of being considered a threat to the job security of incumbent workers, a successful trainee is regarded as a credit to the senior employee who, in turn, is judged to be all the more valuable to the employer. In this connection, Brown et al. (1993, p. 434) suggest that Japanese

> [P]erformance appraisal procedures reflect a delicate balancing of individual and group incentives. While it is individuals who are evaluated and rewarded, an important part of what is evaluated is contribution to the group. . . . The appraisal system explicitly encourages teaching of subordinates.

Firm-sponsored training in Japan can be broken down into three main components. First and most important are general but still firm-specific skills acquired primarily by rotation through various jobs within the firm. The rotation may be across different departments (e.g., new engineers spend time in sales and in rotations between research and manufacturing) as well as between related jobs in the same department that are grouped together in quality circles. Self-study of training manuals is an important aspect of on-the-job learning. A second component is training off the job, usually in special centers organized by the company. Few workers ever return to external educational institutions for further training. Third, workers develop skills by enrolling in correspondence courses, with the employer often underwriting the cost of the courses.

The underlying presumption of the Japanese model is that workers are expected to learn throughout their careers with an employer. The result is a broadly trained workforce capable of adjusting rapidly to changes in product demand, unforeseen problems on the shop floor, and the introduction of new technology. Dertouzos, Lester, and Solow (1989, p. 91) furnish an interesting example involving workers employed by Nippon Steel. In a major corporate restructuring, the prior computer experience acquired by production line workers allowed them to be placed in jobs in new businesses established by the company as it diversified out of steel. The authors report that in Nippon's new electronics and communications companies, 2,000 out of 2,500 new employees were former Nippon Steel workers. That is, blue-collar workers formerly engaged in producing steel were sufficiently well trained in computer skills to be hired in the new enterprises as programmers.

The discussion thus far of the broad-based training possessed by Japanese workers applies most directly to so-called regular employees of large firms (those covered by lifetime employment guarantees) in export-oriented industries. In the case of a demand shock, these workers are not typically laid off from their jobs. Rather, a slot is found for them in another department within the firm, in a subsidiary, or even in a different firm. Ono (1993) explains that redundant employees kept on the payroll but given no tasks to perform under Japan's lifetime employment system are said to be shown the "window seat," and he reports estimates that there are currently one million Japanese workers being supported in this way until they retire at age 60.

Nonregular workers and workers employed by small and medium-sized firms are more subject to layoffs during an economic downturn. Major categories of workers whose employment is governed by fixed-term contracts include part-time and so-called temporary workers—so-called because they may have been employed by the same firm for years. Although it is difficult to pin down with precision, there is little doubt that the proportion of Japanese workers covered by lifetime employment guarantees is declining. Williams (1994) reports that the lifetime employment system, which covered about half of all Japanese employees in the mid-1970s, now extends to roughly one-quarter of workers. Focusing on just part-time employment, Schlesinger and Kanabayashi (1992) write that nearly 20 percent of the Japanese workforce is believed to be part time—a proportion that has nearly tripled over the past twenty years. In the manufacturing sector, Houseman and Abraham (1993, p. 46) add that the percentage of part-time workers (most of whom are women) has increased rapidly from 4 percent of manufacturing workers in 1978 to 9 percent in 1988.

Once laid off, part-time workers—especially women and older workers—tend to drop out of the labor force.[9] In table 2.4, Sorrentino calculates a more than threefold jump from the U-5 or official Japanese unemployment rate to the U-7 rate which treats discouraged workers as unemployed rather than labor force drop-outs. This dramatic increase is driven by the U-5 and U-7 rates for females (not shown), which are 2.8 percent and 12.3 percent, respectively.

Because Japanese employment practices make it difficult for displaced workers to be reemployed, government adjustment assistance programs are designed to prevent workers from ever being unemployed. There are three major programs (see Dore, Bounine-Cabalé, and Tapiola 1989, annex; and OECD 1992, p. 139).

In the first of these programs, an Employment Adjustment Subsidy is paid to employers as an incentive to keep redundant workers on the payroll on a short-term basis. Hashimoto (1993) reports that following the 1973 oil shock, the Employment Insurance Law of 1975 shifted the usual concept of unemployment insurance benefits paid directly to unemployed workers to a system in which subsidies are given to employers who, in turn, provide compensation to workers on furlough. A novel feature of this law is that it enables furloughed workers to remain "employed" by the firm. The law also provides an employment subsidy to employers who wish to implement short-time work schedules involving reduced days per week or per month. Hashimoto (1993, p. 145) estimates that if all Japanese workers who were employed but not currently working were counted as being in fact on temporary layoff, the Japanese unemployment rate of 2.5 percent in 1988 would rise to 3.8 percent. That is, as much as 43 percent of the gap between the U.S. unemployment rate of 5.5 percent in 1988 and the Japanese unemployment rate is due to the difference in the statistical treatment of temporarily laid-off persons.

Longer-term adjustment assistance in Japan is provided through a second program—the Subsidy for Industrial Employment Stabilization—which is restricted to employers in designated depressed industries (i.e., industries that have undergone a 10 percent decrease in output or employment). Forms of assistance provided are (1) a subsidy to existing employers to keep redundant workers on the payroll while they are enrolled in a training program sponsored by a public training center (the training center may subcontract training to a private employer or an employer association), and (2) a wage subsidy of up to two-thirds of the first year's salary paid to receiving employers who hire eligible displaced workers. To qualify for longer-term assistance, an employer must satisfy the Employment Service that it has a realistic plan that will lead to permanent employment for affected workers. Both subsidy programs are funded by a 0.35 percent payroll tax assessed on employers.

The third major program is intended to accelerate the reemployment of especially disadvantaged workers. Known as the Subsidy for Employment Development for Specified Job Applicants, this program provides a subsidy to employers who hire handicapped workers, single mothers, and workers older than age 45 who have been displaced from designated depressed industries.

The government also provides unemployment insurance benefits in the event of a job loss although, as table 2.1 indicates, resources committed to unemployment benefits are meager. Early in their unemployment spell, job seekers receive a short placement/counseling interview primarily intended to speed up the job matching process. In 1985, Japan introduced a reemployment bonus program to stimulate active job search by the unemployed (see OECD 1992, annex 3.A). The reemployment bonus works as follows. An unemployment insurance recipient who finds a job during the first half of his or her benefit entitlement period is eligible to receive a lump-sum bonus equivalent to between one-third and two-thirds of the total value of the remaining benefit entitlement. For example, if the original entitlement to benefits is 90 days, an unemployed worker who found a job within the first 45 days would be eligible to receive a lump-sum bonus equivalent to 30 days of benefits. Evidence from several reemployment bonus demonstration projects carried out in the United States is reported in the next chapter.

The United Kingdom

As indicated by table 2.2 and the U-1 unemployment indicator in table 2.4, the United Kingdom has the dubious distinction of having the highest unemployment rate and, along with Germany, the greatest incidence of long-term unemployment of the nations considered. At the same time, Britain's combined expenditures on active and passive labor market measures displayed in table 2.1 are almost as high as those in Sweden. But while Swedish active program expenditures exceed passive expenditures by more than 2 to 1, the same ratio is less than 0.5 for the United Kingdom.

As in Germany, the British unemployment compensation system consists of two programs. First, unemployed workers are eligible for regular unemployment insurance benefits for up to 12 months. The size of these benefits hinges on previous commitment to the labor force. In addition, workers who are still unemployed after one year are eligible for the Income Support program, which provides benefits related to family size for an indefinite period and a housing allowance. The OECD (1992, annex 3.B) notes that for family heads, Income Support benefits exceed after-tax earnings from low-wage jobs. Given the generosity of the unemployment compensation system, it is not surprising that discussions of the economic malaise existing in many of Britain's industrial cities emphasize the long-term dependency of workers on safety net programs (see, for example, Horwitz 1991).[10]

Turning to active labor market policies, table 2.3 shows that Britain's expenditure ratio on job creation/employment subsidy programs is a close second to that of Sweden. For much of the postwar period, Britain has lagged behind other industrialized nations in economic growth and labor productivity. Trebilcock (1986, ch. 4) comments that despite the government's sensitivity to the challenges posed by industrial decline, Britain's industrial and labor market policies have been notable for their ad hoc attempts to preserve the status quo. In particular, a consequence of the joining together of the interests of politically powerful labor unions and employer organizations is government labor market policies that emphasized employment maintenance rather than reducing the adjustment costs of redundant workers. Such policies are clearly inconsistent with the criterion of encouraging worker mobility out of distressed industries.

An example of an active labor market policy that reduced rather than encouraged labor market mobility was the Temporary Employment Subsidy introduced in Britain in 1975. That program made a wage subsidy of £20 per worker per week available to firms that agreed to forestall laying off ten or more workers. At the time, £20 was equivalent to one-half the level of standard benefits available under the unemployment compensation program. Although the wage subsidy was limited to one year, further assistance for an additional six months was available under a supplementary program. Trebilcock (1986, p. 199) suggests that the government's inability to insulate itself from political pressure was particularly heightened when declining firms were concentrated in depressed regions or when the firms were nationalized.

Retraining in the United Kingdom has taken a similar industry-specific approach. The 1964 Industrial Training Act made the retraining of redundant workers in a particular British industry the responsibility of employers in that industry through the formation of tripartite Industrial Training Boards (ITBs). Each ITB was empowered to impose a payroll tax on employers in its industry to fund an industry-specific training program, with additional funding from the national government. In 1969, twenty-seven ITBs covered 15 million workers and levied hundreds of millions of pounds in taxes, which were then returned to employers in the form of grants for approved training programs (see Department of Employment 1988, p. 34). The ITB approach was apparently successful in attaining the objective of encouraging employers who had been poaching skilled employees from other firms in their industry to provide more training themselves. However, concerns were raised about whether the quality of training matched the quality provided by major competitors in other nations.

In 1979 the Thatcher government came to power and implemented a number of reforms broadly intended to restrict institutional intervention in product and labor markets and to stimulate market competition and entrepreneurship. In the labor market, the new government criticized ITB training on the grounds that it reinforced a narrow, craft-based approach to work organization in a world calling for more flexible arrangements (see Cappelli 1993b, p. 10).[11] By 1981 government subsidies to Industrial Training Boards were ended, and member companies were asked whether they wanted their ITBs to continue as totally industry-funded entities. Most firms declined, and by 1988 just seven ITBs remained.

For adult workers, two new programs implemented by the Thatcher government during the second half of the 1980s are especially noteworthy. The first establishes a national network of Training and Enterprise Councils (TECs) intended to decentralize the provision of training services to the local level and to increase the impact of the business community on training program decision making. TECs are business-led community partnerships responsible for the operation of programs providing training opportunities and training allowances to youth and unemployed adults, temporary public service employment, and self-employment assistance to unemployed adults. The second new program seeks to integrate job placement at the local level with the unemployment compensation system. These innovations are discussed in chapters 4 and 5, respectively.

Looking specifically at young workers, a final point to note in connection with table 2.3 is Britain's very high expenditure ratio for special youth measures. This largely represents spending on the Youth Training Scheme (YTS) introduced in 1983 to remedy a high rate of youth unemployment and a low rate, relative to other advanced OECD nations, of British youth enrolled in education and training programs. As described by Cappelli (1993b), YTS provided out-of-school youth with general work skills through programs that integrated employer-based job training with off-the-job classroom education. Operated by locally based Area Manpower Boards, the objective of the YTS program was to assist participants in working toward earning nationally recognized occupational credentials. In 1986, the National Council for Vocational Qualifications (NCVQ) was created to rationalize the diverse set of existing occupational qualifications. NCVQ accreditation is based on competencies determined by employers in the industry subject to the requirement that training be of sufficient breadth to provide a basis for further personal development (Department of Employment 1988, pp. 32-33).

Cappelli (1993b, pp. 16-17) notes that in 1988 the government concluded that the Youth Training Scheme was a "resounding success." Yet YTS was basically dismantled in 1989 and replaced by the Youth Training (YT) program. Reflecting a shift in political priorities due to a temporary decline in youth unemployment and a general lack of employer support, Youth Training reduced the length of training programs available to youth and cut back on the on-the-job training component. YT is currently one of a number of government-funded employment and training programs operated under the employer-led TEC framework.

North America and Australia

Compared to Western European and Japanese employers, custom and national labor market policy make it much more likely that employers in Canada, Australia, and the United States will respond to demand shocks by laying off workers rather than by adjusting compensation or hours of work. At the same time, workers in these nations are typically expected to prepare for and to locate vacant jobs with relatively little government assistance. For Canada and the United States, a high incidence of layoffs and an emphasis on worker self-reliance in locating new jobs is reflected in table 2.4 in the relatively high U-2 unemployment indicator measuring the unemployment rate only for job losers and the relatively low (especially for the United States) U-1 or long-term unemployment rate. Table 2.2 also captures the relatively low incidence of long-term unemployment in Canada and the United States. Australia, on the other hand, does face a relatively high level of long-term unemployment.

Canada

Referring to table 2.1, probably the most dramatic difference between Canada and the United States is that Canadian expenditures on passive labor market programs are more than triple those of the United States. This difference reflects the much more comprehensive and generous unemployment insurance system in place in Canada.[12] One consideration is that unemployed Canadians are eligible for UI benefits for up to 50 weeks, whereas UI is available to American job seekers in most states for no more than 26 weeks. Another is that workers who quit their jobs are eligible for UI in Canada but not in the

United States. Still another consideration is that in many parts of Canada individuals are eligible for unemployment benefits after working a minimum of just 10 or 12 weeks a year. American workers, by contrast, are typically eligible for UI only after having worked a minimum of 20 weeks per year.

Green and Riddell (1993, p. S114) point out that an unemployed Canadian worker is more than three times as likely to receive UI benefits than an unemployed American, and that this difference has been growing since 1982-83. In addition, Card and Freeman (1994) provide evidence that, also in the early 1980s, Canada's unemployment rate jumped above that of the United States and continued above the U.S. rate for the remainder of the decade. The authors' analysis of this "unemployment gap" of 2 to 3 percentage points is that in Canada, but not in the United States, there was an increase in the fraction of jobless individuals reporting themselves as seeking employment, thereby increasing the count of the unemployed.

Turning to active labor market programs, the Canadian government has for over sixty years provided unemployed workers with employment information and job placement services delivered through a joint federal-provincial network of Canada Employment Centers (CECs). Table 2.3 indicates that Canada, along with Sweden and Germany, has the highest expenditure ratio for employment services of the seven nations considered. Beginning in 1966, the federal government initiated, in addition, a series of training programs intended to improve the reemployment prospects of adult workers through the purchase of classroom training from community colleges and other training institutions and of on-the-job training from private-sector employers. Classroom training and on-the-job training programs were augmented in 1982 by a third national program intended to expand the capacity of the economy to train workers for jobs in shortage occupations.

A change in administrations at the federal level resulted in 1984 in a comprehensive review of all federal labor market policies. The outcome of this review was the creation in 1985 of an umbrella program called the Canadian Jobs Strategy (CJS). The CJS was designed to provide labor market assistance to those clients (individuals, employers, and communities) perceived to have the greatest need for federal labor market intervention. As a consequence, the CJS includes in a single comprehensive initiative five major component programs designed to assist the following client groups: (1) the long-term unemployed, (2) women and youth who face difficulty in making the transition to full participation in the labor market, (3) employed workers whose job security is threatened by technological or market changes, (4) employers who need workers possessing skills in short supply, and (5) communities with chronic high unemployment or faced with major layoffs. It is worth noting that in assisting these client groups, CJS programs serve employed workers in need of skill enhancement in addition to jobless individuals. The Skill Investment program assists experienced workers (client group 3) to retain their jobs by enabling them to update their skills. The Skill Shortages program subsidizes employers (client group 4) to train workers in high-demand occupations in order to head off likely shortages of skilled workers.

In 1991, the Canadian government introduced a restructuring of the CJS intended to make the program more responsive to the needs of workers at the level of the local labor market. A second initiative announced two years earlier in 1989 was designed to reform the Canadian UI system. Specifically, the UI initiative proposed to tighten the work requirements for UI eligibility and to shift resources from income maintenance to active training and job search assistance programs. More detail on both of these initiatives is presented in chapter 5.

The United States

Beginning with passive labor market programs, an issue of concern to U.S. policy makers is the downward trend over the postwar period in the fraction of the unemployed who receive UI benefits. Particularly notable declines in this fraction occurred in the early 1960s and again in the early 1980s. At present, although over 90 percent of employed workers hold jobs that are covered by the UI system, less than 30 percent of the unemployed receive UI benefits.

A careful analysis by Blank and Card (1991) makes use of annual Current Population Survey data to decompose changes in the fraction of insured unemployment into three components, due to (1) changes in state UI laws, (2) changes in the eligibility-determining characteristics of unemployed workers, and (3) changes in the take-up rate for UI benefits. Their analysis suggests that, over the 1977-87 period, there was no significant change in the fraction of unemployed workers eligible for benefits. Rather, the decline in the fraction of workers who received regular UI benefits in 1980-82 is mainly due to an abrupt decrease in the take-up rate. In turn, this take-up rate decrease is primarily the result of changes in the regional distribution of unemployment. States in the Northeast have significantly higher take-up rates for UI benefits than states in the South, so as the distribution of unemployment shifted away from northeastern to southern states, the national take-up rate declined. Still to be explained is the wide historical variation in UI participation across states.

Like Canada, the United States has had lengthy experience with the design and implementation of active labor market programs. Haveman and Saks (1985, p. 36) characterize this experience as lurching from one direction to another, developing some high-quality but many low-quality programs. With few low-quality programs ever terminated, the consequence is a proliferation of active labor market programs directed to assist jobless workers. Recent congressional testimony by Crawford (1993) reports that the U.S. General Accounting Office has identified 125 federal programs administered by 14 departments or independent agencies that spend over $16 billion annually to provide employment and training services.

By most accounts, one of the low-quality programs is the federal-state Employment Service (ES), created in 1933 to provide job matching services. Job seekers must register with the ES to obtain unemployment insurance benefits. Employers are under no obligation to list job vacancies, however, and the ES caters mostly to the hard-core unemployed. Comparing the U.S. Employment Service to the Swedish employment exchange system, Burtless (1987, p. 149) comments that the ES is relatively ineffective in aiding and monitoring the search for jobs. Since the Swedish government requires employers to register all job vacancies with its Employment Service, it is quite simple to refer insured job seekers to suitable jobs and penalize workers who refuse to engage in search or accept available job offers. In contrast, the U.S. Employment Service is unaware of most available vacancies and is therefore in a weak position to enforce UI job search requirements. Marshall and Tucker (1992, p. 223) also criticize the ES for failing to computerize many of its offices and note that inadequate funding prevents the agency from doing a serious job of counseling the unemployed.

The federal government's first attempt to design an adult training program dates back to 1962 with the passage of the Manpower Development and Training Act (MDTA). MDTA represented the response to a rising national unemployment rate coupled with a growing concern over the effects of automation and new technology on the employment options of mid-career adult workers. By the mid-1960s, however, an improved labor market and reduced concern over automation led to a shift in interest and funding away from the employment problems of displaced workers and toward the employability of economically disadvantaged youth and adults.[13] In 1973 MDTA was consolidated into the newly created Comprehensive Employment and Training Act (CETA). Two distinct types of programs were funded under CETA. Title I provided disadvantaged workers a program mix including classroom training, on-the-job training, and public-sector work experience. In contrast, Titles II and VI offered public service employment (PSE) to workers who had recently lost jobs in high-unemployment geographic areas. As unemployment rose during the 1970s, CETA expenditures shifted away from Title I training programs toward the provision of PSE jobs offering little or no formal training.

In addition to MDTA, the year 1962 saw the creation of a second major federal program specifically intended to assist displaced workers —the Trade Adjustment Assistance (TAA) program. TAA provided income support and, to a lesser extent, retraining to workers who lost their jobs as a consequence of trade agreement concessions. Legislation passed in 1974 removed the linkage between tariff reductions and job loss by making workers eligible for adjustment assistance if expanding trade alone was an important contributor to layoffs.[14]

The CETA program expired in 1982, with the economy mired in the trough of its deepest recession since the 1930s. Once again, the displacement of experienced adult workers became an important national issue. Rather than renewing CETA with its widely criticized emphasis on PSE programs, Congress enacted a broad new program—the Job Training Partnership Act (JTPA)—intended to train and place workers in private-sector jobs. Overall responsibility for administering the program was given to state governors, who then delegated authority for designing and administering local programs to business and labor representatives on what are called Private Industry Councils (PICs). The important role assigned PICs gives local JTPA programs something of the tripartite flavor of the Western European model. The federal government monitors the performance of local site operators by means of enrollment requirements and performance standards. Available empirical evidence on the effectiveness of performance standards imposed under JTPA is reviewed in chapter 4.

Title III of JTPA relates specifically to the adjustment assistance needs of displaced workers.[15] Services provided include skills training, job placement, worker relocation assistance, and support services such as child care and transportation while in training. However, because of limited funding, at most 7 percent of eligible workers received any JTPA Title III program services through June 30, 1986, according to the U.S. General Accounting Office (1987). Moreover, most Title III participants received relatively inexpensive job placement assistance, rather than more intensive and expensive classroom skills training and on-the-job training.

In 1986 a task force appointed by the U.S. Secretary of Labor issued a report recommending development at the state level of the capacity to respond quickly to plant closings and mass layoffs with the coordinated delivery of adjustment assistance services offered on-site (see U.S. Department of Labor 1986).[16] Acting on the recommendations of the task force, Congress passed the Economic Dislocation and Worker Adjustment Assistance (EDWAA) act of 1988, which amended the existing Title III of JTPA. EDWAA's main impact is to require states to develop displaced worker units with the ability to react to major layoffs and plant closures with on-site offers of job search assistance and retraining. Funding for displaced worker programs increased sharply from just $200 million in 1987 to about $517 million annually in 1991-93 (see Ross and Smith 1993, p. 31). A second piece of legislation passed in 1988—the Omnibus Trade and Competitiveness Act—made appropriate training an entitlement for all TAA-certified workers and required that recipients of income-maintenance benefits participate in retraining unless they received a waiver from this requirement.[17] The TAA program now essentially extends the duration of UI benefits to up to one and one-half years for eligible workers undergoing retraining. Nevertheless, Bednarzik (1993) estimates for the 1982-87 period that among manufacturing industries deemed import-sensitive, only about 9 percent of the long-term unemployed were certified for TAA benefits.

Expenditures on TAA benefits were $116 million in 1991, which is down substantially from about $1.5 billion annually in 1980 and 1981.

During the 1980s, the small fraction of displaced workers actually assisted by JTPA Title III and TAA programs suggested an important gap between perceived need and available federally funded services. Virtually all of the states developed programs attempting to fill this market niche. As discussed by Leigh (1989), however, state programs differ from comparable JTPA programs in two key respects. First, state programs are not exclusively targeted to specific jobless groups such as displaced or disadvantaged workers. Rather, training is also made available to currently employed workers in order to avoid layoffs and plant closures. Second, training programs are usually tailored to meet the needs of individual employers. That is, retraining is viewed as an economic development tool in addition to its traditional supply-side role of raising the level of workers' skills to enable them to compete for existing jobs.

Osterman and Batt (1993) group innovative state employment and training programs into what they term agency-based programs and public education-based systems.[18] As described in Leigh (1990, ch. 4), the largest and best-known state agency-based program is the California Employment Training Panel (ETP). In operation since 1983, ETP is noteworthy for being almost entirely employer-driven. Employers initiate the process by proposing individual projects to the Panel. If a project is approved and a contract negotiated, the employer selects trainees according to its own specifications, sets standards for successful program completion, and approves the training curriculum if an outside training provider (e.g., a state postsecondary educational institution) is selected. In return for the training subsidy and the discretion given them in all aspects of the retraining process, participating employers must make a good-faith commitment to hire or retain program graduates. Stringent performance standards mean that training providers receive full payment for their services only if program graduates find and remain in jobs that meet minimum wage standards.

Public education-based systems build on what in many states is a large, well-developed community college system. Osterman and Batt (1993, pp. 460-61) note that American community colleges are currently undergoing a transformation from feeder institutions to four-year colleges and universities to the major institutional source of retraining for adult workers. In addition to regular associate degree programs, many community colleges provide nondegree short courses for adults and create "customized" or "contract" courses in which they develop special training programs tailored to meet the needs of particular employers.

Australia

Australian labor market policies in many ways represent a hybrid of the policies described for Britain, Canada, and the United States. Table 2.1 shows that Australian expenditures on passive labor market programs are distinctly higher than in the United States but lower than in Canada and the United Kingdom. As in Britain, table 2.2 indicates that Australia faces a significant long-term unemployment problem. Active labor market program expenditures in Australia are only slightly above those for the United States and substantially lower than those in Canada and Britain. But like Britain, the largest component of Australia's active program expenditures is seen in table 2.3 to be job creation/employment subsidies.

Trebilcock (1986, ch. 5) suggests that Australia's labor market policies since the 1960s can best be understood in the context of the high level of import protection provided to important domestic industries, notably manufacturing. The government's policy of high barriers to imports reflects, at least in part, the inherent limitations of a small domestic market and the high costs of penetrating distant export markets. Beginning in the early 1970s, a policy of trade liberalization carried out to encourage greater efficiency and productivity in protected industries was made politically palatable in highly unionized Australia by labor market programs designed to assist workers made redundant by policy changes. Like the TAA program in the United States, the first of these programs—the Structural Adjustment Assistance program—was designed to provide income-maintenance assistance to workers directly and adversely affected by the relaxation of tariffs on imported goods. But in a program review carried out in 1975, it was severely criticized for its effect of reducing efficient labor mobility and its favoritism of unemployed workers in particular industries over others who were equally needy. The program was terminated in the early 1980s.

Despite these criticisms, the Structural Adjustment Assistance program was followed in 1982 and 1986 by two other targeted programs. The Labour Adjustment Training Arrangements program created in 1982 provided retraining and income-maintenance allowances to workers displaced from their jobs in the steel industry. That program was later extended to cover coal mining and auto and auto parts manufacturing. The basic rationale for targeting special assistance to workers displaced from their jobs in these industries is that displacement is especially likely to be the outcome of mass layoffs and plant closings, and these events present communities with the difficult problem of absorbing large numbers of workers with similar skills who are all dumped on the local labor market at once. In 1986, the Heavy Engineering Labor Adjustment Assistance program was introduced as part of an industrial assistance package intended to revitalize the "heavy engineering" industry (i.e., the capital goods industry). This program assists displaced workers by subsidizing the costs of classroom and on-the-job training programs and providing relocation assistance. Workers undergoing retraining are also eligible for income-maintenance allowances.

During the early 1990s, the Australian government legislated two initiatives designed to place greater emphasis on firm-based training and to realign the unemployment insurance system by making retraining or participation in some other adjustment assistance program a condition of income support. The first initiative, adopted in 1990, imposed on all employers with annual payrolls greater than $200,000 a payroll training tax called the Training Guarantee. The Training Guarantee required employers to spend 1.0 percent of their 1991 payrolls on training, with the tax rate rising to 1.5 percent beginning in 1992. An employer who fails to spend the required percentage on training is obliged to remit to the government the difference between the required tax and what was actually spent. This tax revenue, in turn, finances additional government-sponsored training. The payroll training tax initiative is discussed at greater length in chapter 4.

While income support has for some time been paid to displaced Australians enrolled in a retraining activity, the government implemented in July 1991 a second initiative designed to fundamentally reform its unemployment benefit program by making income maintenance more directly related to self-help. Termed Newstart, this program is a response to a growing number of long-term unemployed Australian workers. Instead of providing unemployed workers with a fixed number of weeks of income support and leaving it up to them to conduct their own job search, Newstart is intended to diagnose the difficulty the unemployed are having in locating new jobs and then to deal actively with their needs through retraining and other forms of assistance. Australia's Newstart program will receive more attention in chapter 5.

Summary

This chapter provided an overview of the evolution of labor market policies in seven industrialized nations including the United States. Focusing on the latter half of the 1980s, much of the discussion was organized around differences between counties in the level and mix of their public expenditures on active and passive labor market programs. Measuring public expenditures as a fraction of Gross Domestic Product, total expenditure ratios vary at the low end from 0.6 percent and 0.8 percent, respectively, for Japan and the United States to, at the high end, 2.7 percent and 2.8 percent, respectively, for the United Kingdom and Sweden. Except for Sweden, the countries examined spent from one and one-half to over three times more on passive than active labor market policies. Public expenditure ratios for passive programs are particularly large for Britain, Canada, and Germany. Sweden, in contrast, spent more than twice as much on active than passive policies. Since the mid-1950s, the Swedish government has committed itself to active labor market policies intended to encourage the efficient movement of labor from contracting to expanding industries.

By far the most important component of passive labor market programs is unemployment insurance, and several of the nations examined also provide unemployment assistance payments to workers who have exhausted their eligibility for UI benefits. There is some indication looking across countries that more generous unemployment compensation systems prolong the duration of unemployment spells, even though the relationship may not be a simple one. Concern over a rising incidence of long-term unemployment is leading many countries, including Britain, Canada, and Australia, to more closely link receipt of unemployment compensation benefits to participation in active labor market programs. This linkage, in turn, necessitates a careful look at the kinds of active labor market programs—namely, employment services and adult training—that are designed to reduce adjustment costs and increase the mobility of unemployed workers between declining and expanding industries.

Of the seven nations considered, Sweden, Germany, and Canada report the largest expenditure ratios on employment services. In Sweden and Germany, local employment service offices serve as the universal intake point for unemployed workers to initiate their job search process. Sweden is also noteworthy for spending a much larger share of its Gross Domestic Product on public adult training programs than any other nation considered, with Germany a distant second. There is a strong contrast between the permanent, integrated, and well-funded employment and training system in Sweden and the unstable, fragmentary, and underfunded employment and training programs available to jobless Americans. But even the Swedish adult training system was reorganized in 1986 to decentralize decision making and increase the system's responsiveness to labor demand conditions. In 1988 a similar reorganization occurred in Britain, decentralizing the provision of training services to the community level and elevating the role of employers in formulating and implementing training policies.

At the other extreme from Sweden, an almost negligible public expenditure ratio for adult training is reported for Japan. But this statistic certainly does not imply that adult training is neglected by the Japanese. While Sweden operates a government training system, Japanese employers accept the responsibility for designing work experience and training opportunities that continue throughout a worker's career. Despite this fundamental difference in their approaches to adult training, both Sweden and Japan enjoyed very low national unemployment rates during the latter half of the 1980s.

The other example of firm-based training discussed in detail in this chapter is the German dual system of apprenticeship training. The dual system combines on-the-job training supervised by a master craftsman (or *Meister*) at the employer's workplace with one or two days per week of off-the-job training at a state-sponsored vocational school. Germany and Japan offer an interesting contrast in that apprenticeship training opportunities are available primarily to German youth, while on-the-job training continues over the working lifetime in Japan. Nevertheless, as noted in chapter 1, both Germany and Japan are frequently pointed to as being far ahead of the United States in producing workers who can adapt readily to new production techniques and more flexible production systems.

NOTES

1. The OECD (1988, pp. 84-85) reports that its objective in collecting these data is to include all public outlays for relevant labor market programs, regardless of which branch or level of government is involved.

2. The Economist Intelligence Unit (1994a) reports a substantial rise in western Germany's unemployment rate from 6.6 percent in 1992 to 8.2 percent in 1993.

3. Ramaswamy (1994) argues that the current "crisis" of the Swedish economy is due in large part to the rigidities imposed by the system of centralized bargaining and solidaristic wages which preclude employers from tailoring their own internal wage structures to enhance worker productivity.

4. More detail on the decentralization and increased market responsiveness of the Swedish training system is presented in chapter 4.

5. The programs listed are described in more detail in the Swedish Institute (1992) and Trehörning (1993, ch. 5).

6. Other unemployment indicators reported by Sorrentino but omitted from table 2.4 are U-3—the adult unemployment rate, and U-4—the full-time unemployment rate. Sorrentino does not calculate unemployment indicators for Australia.

7. Abraham and Houseman (1993, pp. 17-23) note that laws regulating permanent layoffs have deep historical roots in Germany, as in many other European nations. (There is no such thing as a temporary layoff in Germany.) Dismissals for economic reasons (i.e., permanent layoffs) are justified only if the affected individuals cannot be reasonably transferred elsewhere in the company and the company has exhausted all other means of avoiding layoffs, such as reducing overtime or introducing short-time work. Worker-elected works councils must be consulted before every dismissal, and a "social plan" specifying compensation for laid-off workers must be negotiated with the works council before a collective dismissal can be carried out.

Some feel for the reluctance of employers to lay off workers may be gained from the following passage describing the situation facing the executive responsible for dismissing more than 5,700 of the 15,000 workers at a western German plant (see Benjamin 1993, p. A8):

> He did it the traditional German way: with fat payoffs. He persuaded 90% of those targeted to take voluntary severance packages, which averaged about $16,500, or early retirement, which was accompanied by unspecified payments. The rest were laid off and, by law, got packages running slightly under $16,5000.
>
> Mr. Dittert [the executive] was vilified, he says. "My family was threatened. We got anonymous phone calls at home," a dramatic event in a culture where co-workers are so formal that, even after decades, they may not know each other's first names. . . . "In school," he says, "my kids were hassled by others who said, 'Your father is the one firing people.' This was by far the most unpleasant thing I've ever gone through in my professional life."

8. The discussion of the German dual system is largely based on a report of Her Majesty's Inspectorate (1991). This document is the result of a visit in 1990 to the former West Germany of a group of British government officials. Also useful is a recent study of youth training in Germany by Steedman (1993).

9. Houseman and Abraham (1993) report evidence for the manufacturing sector, showing that Japanese women bear a disproportionate amount of employment adjustment compared to Japanese men. Even so, the authors (1993, p. 50) suggest that Japanese women enjoy greater employment security than either American men or American women.

10. An additional program—The Family Credit Benefit—is designed to increase the incentive of family heads eligible for Income Support to work even at low wages. Restricted to persons working more than 16 hours per week, the benefit paid is subject to a marginal implicit tax rate of 70 percent assessed against net earnings. Thus, Family Credit payments are received only when earnings are low or when one wage earner is supporting a large family (OECD 1992, p. 144).

11. Evidence related to the labor market effects of British apprenticeship programs and associated nationally recognized qualifications is presented in chapter 4.

12. In perhaps a bit of an overstatement, *The Wall Street Journal* (1993) writes that in Canada

> [U]nemployment insurance is so generous that in some parts of the country it has become a way of life: three months of work and nine months on the dole. In the little province of Prince Edward Island, the New Democratic party lays off its leader for three months each year so he can collect federal unemployment benefits and save the party about $3,100.

13. Economically disadvantaged refers to individuals who receive (or are members of families who receive) cash welfare payments or to members of a family whose total family income falls below the poverty line.

14. In addition to easing TAA eligibility criteria, the Trade Act of 1974 allowed qualifying workers to receive combined UI and Trade Readjustment Allowance (TRA) benefits that replaced 70 percent of previous earnings, with a maximum benefit of 100 percent of previous earnings for workers in the manufacturing sector. Combined UI/TRA benefits could be received for up to 52 weeks, and workers in an approved training program were eligible for benefits for an additional 26 weeks. Legislation passed in 1981 restricted the level of cash payments to the level of UI benefits, and stipulated that TRA payments could begin only after UI benefits were exhausted.

15. The other major titles of JTPA are Title II-A, which funds employment and training services to economically disadvantaged adults and youth, and the Title II-B summer youth program.

16. This recommendation is based on the task force's favorable assessment of the Canadian Industrial Adjustment Service program. Established in 1963, this is a federally funded agency which serves as a catalyst in bringing together local labor and management officials to help locate job opportunities for workers about to be laid off (advance notice of plant closings and layoffs is required by law). The Industrial Adjustment Service is discussed in chapter 5.

17. A third major piece of legislation passed in 1988 is the Worker Adjustment and Retraining Notification Act, requiring firms employing 100 or more workers to give 60 days' notice of a plant closing. In the case of a layoff, the bill requires the 60 days' notice if the layoff involves 50 or more workers representing at least one-third of the workforce at a place of employment.

18. The authors also distinguish a third category of state programs they call income-targeted initiatives, an example of which is the California GAIN program discussed in chapter 3. Income-targeted initiatives represent the approach that characterizes most current federal programs.

3
An Overview of Existing Evaluation Evidence for the United States

Chapter 1 noted that the evaluation of social programs in the United States is largely based on statistical analyses of program effects on economic outcomes such as employment and earnings, as opposed to internally generated feedback from employers and workers on the quality of program services. This is clearly the perception of foreign observers. Schellhaass (1991, p. 104) comments that program evaluation in Germany has never grown into a research industry as it has in the United States. Björklund (1991, p. 74) concludes his survey by noting that, by American standards, Swedish evaluation research is not impressive. Riddell (1991, pp. 52-53) observes that in contrast to the United States, in which an important private-sector evaluation industry has developed, evaluation research in Canada is largely internal to government agencies with little involvement of the social science community. In addition, he notes that experimental studies in which there is random assignment of eligible individuals to treatment and control groups is virtually unknown in Canada.

Fortunately, the range of programs that have been evaluated by American social scientists is sufficiently broad to cover most of the categories of active labor market programs summarized in table 2.3. The purpose of this chapter is to synthesize what can be learned about the labor market effects of active labor market programs from U.S. evaluation studies. The chapter is divided into four sections. The first reviews the evaluation evidence available for displaced worker programs that offer a reasonably comprehensive menu of services to clients. These displaced worker programs include four federally funded demonstration projects carried out in particular states or communities during the 1980s. Also described is a recent evaluation of the Trade Adjustment Assistance (TAA) program.

The second section of the chapter focuses on evaluation evidence available for three proposed reforms of the unemployment insurance (UI) system. The first UI reform emphasizes enhanced job search assistance and tighter monitoring of job search, while the second reform involves implementation of the reemployment bonus concept. Assistance to help unemployed workers to start up their own small businesses is the third reform considered.

In the third section of the chapter, additional evaluation results are presented for on-the-job and classroom training and basic education programs targeted to economically disadvantaged workers. In contrast to displaced workers, the economically disadvantaged are typically defined as individuals with limited work experience who are eligible for cash welfare benefits.

The final section summarizes what we can learn from these three sets of evaluation studies and points out some gaps in the evidence.

Displaced Worker Studies

During the early 1980s, rising unemployment and an increasing number of plant closures led the U.S. Department of Labor (USDOL) to fund a series of demonstration projects intended to test the effectiveness of alternative reemployment services in placing displaced workers in private-sector jobs. In chronological order, these projects are (1) the Downriver, Michigan program; (2) the Buffalo program of the Dislocated Workers Demonstration Projects;[1] (3) the Texas Worker Adjustment Demonstration (WAD) projects; and (4) the New Jersey Unemployment Insurance Reemployment Demonstration Project.

Later in the decade, the USDOL responded to legislative changes made in the TAA program in 1981 and 1988 by initiating a major study to assess the labor market impact of TAA extended benefits (called Trade Readjustment Allowances or TRAs) and retraining services. During the 1970s, as described in chapter 2, TAA provided generous income-maintenance payments, and relatively few displaced workers received retraining. This situation changed substantially in 1981. In addition to increased funding for retraining, income-maintenance benefits were reduced to the level of workers' regular UI benefits and made available only after a worker exhausted his or her UI entitlement. Legislation passed in 1988 continued the emphasis on adjustment services by requiring that TRA recipients participate in an approved retraining program unless they qualified for a waiver from this requirement.

Study Characteristics

Table 3.1 furnishes an overview of some of the main features of the five displaced worker evaluation studies. One common element is the type of reemployment services provided. As the table indicates, the demonstrations supplied a mix of services including job search assistance (JSA), classroom training (CT), and on-the-job training (OJT). JSA services typically included initial orientation and assessment sessions, a job search workshop, and job development and referral services. The New Jersey UI Demonstration added to this mix a cash bonus for early reemployment. Only in the case of the TAA program were extended income-maintenance benefits provided along with retraining.

An important difference among the studies is the approach program designers followed in distinguishing displaced workers from other unemployed workers. In the Downriver and Buffalo projects, workers displaced from their jobs by large layoffs in local auto and steel plants are targeted for program services. Displaced workers served in these two demonstration projects are male blue-collar workers with lengthy job tenure who enjoyed high wages prior to being laid off. Program services were provided promptly after plant closings to Downriver participants, while in Buffalo there was a long period of postlayoff unemployment prior to program participation.

Rather than targeting services to workers displaced from their jobs by particular mass layoffs, the Texas WAD, New Jersey UI, and TAA studies identified displaced workers by their eligibility for an ongoing adjustment assistance program. The Texas WAD project served workers eligible for JTPA Title III programs, while the New Jersey project was targeted to UI claimants older than age 25 who had at least three years of tenure with their prelayoff employer and who could not provide a date at which they expected to be recalled.[2] Targeted in the TAA study are TRA recipients. These are laid-off workers typically receiving UI who, as a group, have been certified by the USDOL as having suffered trade-related injuries.

Table 3.1 Characteristics of Major U.S. Displaced Worker Demonstration Projects

Project	Enrollment period	Method for distinguishing the displaced	Worker characteristics	Reemployment services delivered
Downriver	July 1980–Sept. 1981 and Nov. 1981–Sept. 1983	Workers laid off from particular auto and auto parts plants	Experienced male production workers earning high prelayoff wages	JSA followed, where necessary, by CT
Buffalo	Oct. 1982–Sept. 1983	Workers laid off from selected steel and auto plants	Experienced male production workers earning high prelayoff wages	JSA followed, where necessary, by CT or OJT
Texas WAD:				
Houston	1983–85	Workers eligible for JTPA Title III	Adult male professional workers earning high wages laid off from petrochemical plants	JSA-only (Tier I) or JSA followed by CT (Tier I/II)
El Paso			Adult Hispanic males and females earning low wages laid off from light mfg. plants	JSA followed by CT (Tier I/II)
New Jersey UI	July 1986–fall 1987	UI claimants with 3+ years of prelayoff job tenure	Adult males and females laid off from jobs in mfg., trade, and services	(1) JSA-only, (2) JSA followed by CT or OJT, or (3) JSA followed by reemployment bonus
TAA Study	1988–89	TAA recipients	Mostly mfg. workers with relatively high prelayoff wages and lengthy job tenure	(1) TRA benefits and (2) TAA retraining (largely CT)

Of the six WAD projects operated between 1983 and 1985, two projects in El Paso and one in Houston are available for evaluation. As noted in table 3.1, WAD program services were provided to groups of displaced workers other than the mostly white male steel and auto workers targeted for assistance in the Downriver and Buffalo projects. The Houston WAD project also served white males, but sizable groups of blacks, Hispanics, and Asians are represented among sample members. Over 90 percent of the workers sampled in El Paso are Hispanics, with about equal numbers of men and women. In the New Jersey UI project, workers laid off from jobs in the trade and services industries, as well as in manufacturing, are included among UI claimants who met the eligibility conditions. Men and women are about equally represented in the eligible population, which also includes sizable proportions of blacks and Hispanics and workers age 55 and older. TRA recipients in the TAA study are predominantly white men and women between the ages of 25 and 54 who were displaced from jobs in manufacturing. Corson et al. (1993) point out that relative to UI exhaustees in manufacturing and to respondents in the Displaced Worker Surveys of 1988 and 1990, TRA recipients received high weekly earnings and had lengthy tenure in their prelayoff jobs. TRA recipients were also much more likely to be unionized.

Results

Table 3.2 presents net impact and cost estimates for the Downriver, Buffalo, Texas WAD, and New Jersey UI studies. (Results for the TAA study do not fit conveniently into this table's format and are reported later in table 3.4.) As indicated in the table, the evaluation design differs sharply between the Downriver and Buffalo projects and the Texas WAD and New Jersey studies. The two earlier projects used a treatment group/comparison group design where the two groups of laid-off workers were drawn from different plants. In contrast, the two later programs implemented a true experimental design in which program participants were randomly assigned to treatment and control groups.

Before getting into the details of the empirical results, a brief discussion of some methodological issues involved in program evaluation might be useful. To measure the effect of a particular program on a labor market outcome variable such as earnings, the key problem is

Table 3.2 Estimated Program Net Impacts and Costs for the Major U.S. Displaced Worker Demonstration Projects of the 1980s

Demonstration project	Net impact: Earnings[a]	Net impact: UI benefits[b]	Cost[c]	Evaluation method
Downriver	–$19 to 122**		Levels not available. Cost of training more than twice that of JSA	Treatment and comparison groups randomly drawn from different plants
Buffalo[d]	JSA: $134** or 15 JSA/CT: $122 or 141 JSA/OJT: $64 or 136**		JSA: $851 JSA/CT: $3,282 JSA/OJT: $3,170	Treatment and comparison groups randomly drawn from different plants
Texas WAD:				
Houston	$547	–$204	Tier I: $1,460–2,072 Tier I/II: $2,981–3,381	Random assignment of eligible workers to treatment and control groups
El Paso	Men: $770 Women: $1,148**	–$194 –$227**	Tier I: $406–702 Tier I/II: $725–1,099	
New Jersey UI	JSA: $263** JSA/training: $103 JSA/bonus: $278***	–$87* –$81* –$170***	CT: $2,723 OJT: $1,960	Random assignment of eligible workers to treatment and control groups

SOURCES: Downriver: Kulik, Smith, and Stromsdorfer (1984, tables 3.4 and 3.6); Buffalo: Corson, Long, and Maynard (1985, table IV.4); Texas WAD: Bloom (1990, table 8.2); and New Jersey: Corson et al. (1989, tables 2, 3, and VII.1).

a. Measured weekly for Downriver and Buffalo, annually for Texas WAD, and quarterly for New Jersey UI. New Jersey estimates are measured for the second quarter after initial UI claim.

b. Measured over 30 weeks for Texas WAD and over the benefit year for New Jersey.

c. Cost estimates are per worker who received services.

d. Target plant and non-target plant net impact estimates, respectively.

***, **, and * indicate significant at the 1 percent, 5 percent, and 10 percent levels, respectively.

that of obtaining a "counterfactual," that is, the level of earnings program participants would have received had they not gone through the program. (A program's net impact is its effect on an outcome variable net of the change in that variable that would have occurred in the program's absence.) Since a counterfactual can never be observed, it must be estimated using information for program nonparticipants. There are two main approaches to obtaining counterfactual estimates.[3] The nonexperimental approach makes use of data for an externally selected comparison group of workers and attempts to adjust statistically for inherent differences between the two groups. An important difficulty with this approach is the selection bias that arises if those who choose to enter or are selected into the program possess unobserved characteristics that make them likely to enjoy higher earnings even in the program's absence. In the alternative experimental approach, random assignment of eligible workers to treatment and control groups means that there are no inherent differences between the two groups that might lead to a correlation between the participation decision and post-program earnings.

An influential paper by LaLonde (1986) provides evidence that nonexperimental strategies involving the selection of comparison groups from alternative data sources and the application of available econometric techniques fail to replicate experimentally generated results obtained by comparing the earnings of randomly assigned treatment and control group members. His conclusion that randomized experiments are necessary to reliably determine program effects has been adopted by perhaps most labor economists, as well as by influential policy makers responsible for funding program evaluation studies. On the other hand, Heckman and associates have waged a persistent counterattack, arguing that while in principle randomized experiments represent the most desirable approach to program evaluation, actual implementation of experiments typically creates new forms of sample selection that require the application of nonexperimental econometric procedures for making statistical adjustments (see, for example, Heckman, Hotz, and Dabos 1987).

The Downriver project

Eligible displaced workers who opted to participate in the Downriver program initially received JSA services followed, for those judged likely to benefit, by some form of retraining (typically classroom training). Net earnings estimates for program participants are seen in table 3.2 to range up to $122 per week after controlling for worker characteristics and plant-specific variables. But the most striking aspect of the estimates presented by Abt Associates is their variability depending on the phase of the program and on the plants from which treatment and comparison group members were selected. The incremental effect of CT above that of JSA is not reported, but Kulik, Smith, and Stromsdorfer (1984, pp. 90-92) conclude that classroom training did not significantly improve participants' postprogram reemployment rates.

An interesting aspect of the Downriver program is the systematic approach taken by program designers in selecting classroom training curricula. Downriver staff first attempted to identify occupations for which demand was expected to grow in the local labor market. This task was accomplished by reviewing economic forecasts and studies conducted by local universities, studying trade journals, and analyzing labor market data collected by the Michigan Employment Security Commission. Next, the actual demand for labor in the occupations that survived this scrutiny was verified through interviews with local employers and representatives of trade associations. It is important to emphasize that Downriver officials sought to retrain workers for occupations for which there was projected to be sufficient demand on the part of a number of employers so that participants' reemployment opportunities were not tied to the fortunes of a single firm. For the most part, the training curricula selected provided classroom instruction in blue-collar trades. In contrast, as mentioned in chapter 2, state-funded programs generally follow the opposite approach of supplying customized training tailored to meet the specific needs of individual employers.

The Buffalo program

After receiving JSA services, participants in the Buffalo project were channeled into either CT or OJT positions. A noteworthy feature of the Buffalo project is the relatively large percentage of OJT slots provided. Stratifying the data by type of reemployment service, table 3.2 displays estimated program effects measured in terms of weekly earnings for the project's target-plant and non-target-plant samples. Looking at JSA services, for instance, estimated earnings effects are

$134 and $15 per week for the target-plant and non-target-plant samples, respectively. For the six area steel and auto plants included in the target-plant sample, available program slots were rationed among laid-off workers through a formal lottery mechanism. The non-target-plant sample includes workers displaced from three other area steel and auto plants and from over 300 area establishments in a variety of industries. Members of the non-target-plant sample differ from those in the target-plant sample because they applied for the program and were offered program services on a first-come, first-served basis as slots became available.

The Buffalo evaluation raises the important distinction between net impact estimates obtained for all program-eligible workers (who may or may not have received program services) and for eligible workers who actually participated in program activities. Corson, Long, and Maynard (1985, pp. 98-100) point out that if an unbiased estimate of the program's impact on program eligibles can be obtained, a similarly unbiased estimate of the impact on actual participants may be calculated by dividing this estimate by the take-up rate of program services. This calculation follows on the assumptions that (1) comparison group members would, if offered program services, choose to participate at the same rate as program eligibles, and (2) the program has no impact on program-eligible nonparticipants.

Corson, Long, and Maynard acknowledge, however, that impact estimates calculated as simple differences in mean earnings between treatment and comparison group members are not likely to be unbiased because of the low take-up rates of program services (only 16 percent and 28 percent, respectively, for the target-plant and non-target-plant samples). Such low take-up rates suggest that displaced workers who chose to participate in program activities differed in significant ways from those who chose not to participate. The net impact estimates reported in table 3.2 for program participants thus control not only for differences in observable characteristics between program eligibles and comparison group members but also, using the Heckman two-stage procedure to correct for selection bias, for unobservable differences affecting the program participation decision.[4]

Estimated program effects are seen in table 3.2 to differ considerably for the three program services, depending on the sample utilized. In particular, JSA is the only statistically significant treatment for the target-plant sample, whereas only JSA/OJT is statistically significant for the non-target-plant sample. The authors of the Mathematica Policy Research report place more confidence in the former results, however, because of the random selection of workers offered program services in the target-plant sample. There is no evidence from this sample of an incremental effect on average weekly earnings above that of JSA for either classroom or on-the-job training. Note also that the cost per participant for the JSA/CT and JSA/OJT treatments is nearly four times that of JSA-only. It is clear, at least for the target-plant sample, that JSA is the only potentially cost effective treatment of those evaluated.

The Texas WAD projects

The experimental design of the Texas WAD projects randomly assigned eligible workers to either of two treatment groups or to a control group. The first treatment group was offered JSA services only (referred to as Tier I). Members of the second treatment group were offered JSA followed, if necessary, by more expensive classroom or on-the-job training (the Tier I/II sequence). Unlike the Buffalo program, the take-up of program services was not a severe problem in evaluating WAD services, as 71 percent of those assigned to the treatment groups chose to participate. While a simple comparison of treatment and control group mean outcomes yields unbiased net impact estimates, Bloom (1990, p. 37) suggests that statistical precision can be improved using multiple regression to control for differences in observed individual characteristics. The impact estimates presented in table 3.2 are obtained controlling for differences in observed individual characteristics and adjusting for program take-up rates, so that the estimates measure program effects for participants only rather than eligible workers. Judging from these estimates, only for women in El Paso is there evidence that the Tier I/II WAD program had a permanent effect in increasing annual earnings. For these women, the program's effect on earnings at the end of the first year slightly exceeds program costs. WAD also reduced UI benefits by an average of $227 per participant measured over a 30-week period.

For a combined sample of men from both El Paso and Houston, quarter-by-quarter earnings estimates reported by Bloom (1990, p. 163) indicate that WAD participants were reemployed sooner than would have otherwise been the case. But ultimately, as seen in table

3.2, the employment opportunities of male participants located at both sites were no better than for members of the control group. The Houston program also allows the differential effect of Tier I/II versus Tier I services to be estimated for males. Despite the higher costs of Tier II services (which were almost exclusively classroom training), the evidence suggests that essentially no additional gains accrued from adding Tier II services to job search assistance.

The selection of classroom training curriculums was carried out much less systematically in the Buffalo and Texas WAD projects than in the Downriver program. Corson, Maynard, and Wichita (1984, pp. 75-77) point out in their overview report on all six displaced worker demonstration sites (including Buffalo) that the one-year duration of the project severely limited both the careful selection of high-growth occupations and the assessment and testing required to insure that participants possessed the motivation and academic skills to benefit from formal classroom training. In general, CT was restricted to those occupations and training deliverers amenable to short-duration, high-intensity courses developed on short notice. Similarly, Bloom (1990, p. 139) points out that the disappointing results obtained for Texas WAD Tier II services do not necessarily demonstrate that supplementing JSA with occupational training cannot be an effective adjustment assistance strategy. Rather, he suggests that the blue-collar orientation of Tier II training curriculums available from a local community college was not well matched to the backgrounds and interests of the mostly white-collar participants in the Houston WAD project.

The New Jersey UI Demonstration

All eligible claimants assigned to the three treatment groups in the New Jersey project were offered a common set of reemployment services early in their UI claim period. The first of these services was an orientation session followed sequentially by testing, a job search workshop, and finally an individual counseling session. The purposes of the job search workshop were to help claimants deal with the loss of their jobs, to make self-assessments and develop realistic employment objectives, and to organize effective job search strategies, including effective job application and interviewing techniques. Counseling was intended to help each claimant develop a realistic reemployment plan. Following their counseling session, claimants in the JSA-only group were free to begin their job search subject to the expectation that they were to maintain periodic contact with the demonstration, either directly with individual staff members or by using a resource center located in each demonstration office. Resource centers contained job listings, telephones, and occupational and training literature.

Claimants in the JSA/retraining group were offered the opportunity to enroll in a classroom training or OJT program. Acceptable CT programs—which were offered by a wide range of public and private training providers—were subject to the restrictions that their expected duration not exceed six months and that remedial education be offered only if necessary to enable claimants to progress to vocational training. Finally, claimants in the JSA/reemployment bonus group were informed of the specifics of the bonus program and turned lose to begin job search.[5]

Corson et al. (1989) present net impact estimates of treatment effects for the first year following the date of filing the initial UI claim. Table 3.2 indicates that by the second quarter after filing, workers offered the JSA-only and JSA/reemployment bonus treatments enjoyed quarterly earnings that are significantly higher than the earnings of the control group. By the fourth quarter, however, the earnings effect of both treatments had tailed off to essentially zero. Looking at UI benefits, the difference between the JSA-only and JSA/reemployment bonus estimates is positive ($83) and statistically significant indicating a sizable incremental effect of the bonus in speeding up reemployment. For JSA plus skill training, nevertheless, there is no evidence of either a permanent increase in earnings or expedited reemployment. (Estimated net effects on earnings are even smaller in quarters 3 and 4.) The authors caution that this conclusion may be misleading because of the low take-up rate (15 percent) among treatment group members offered JSA/training. That is, any positive effect of training for claimants who actually received training services would be substantially diluted, because the vast majority of workers assigned to this treatment chose not to enroll in a training program.

The follow-up study of the New Jersey program by Anderson, Corson, and Decker (1991) is useful because of its longer postprogram observation period and more detailed look at the JSA/training treatment, including separate net impact estimates for CT and OJT. Focusing only on claimants who actually participated in a skill training program (as opposed to the random sample of all claimants offered skill training), classroom training is seen in table 3.3 to significantly reduce earnings in the initial two quarters. This result is expected since training is likely to be ongoing during these quarters. But in quarters four through ten, CT increases earnings by as much as $582 per quarter relative to the earnings of claimants receiving JSA-only. Even larger and highly significant incremental effects are observed for OJT trainees. The authors explain that the primary reason for these very large OJT estimates is that by the third quarter after the claim date, OJT trainees were employed for almost 11 of 13 weeks in that quarter as compared to less than 7 weeks of employment for JSA-only claimants. It must also be noted that only forty-five individuals actually received OJT services.

Table 3.3 Estimated Incremental Effects of Classroom Training and OJT on the Quarterly Earnings of Training Recipients in the New Jersey UI Reemployment Demonstration

Quarter	Classroom training	OJT
1	–$458**	$1,469***
2	–635***	2,347***
3	–314	2,632***
4	195	2,995***
5	384	3,174***
6	191	2,480***
7	323	2,652***
8	505**	2,681***
9	409*	2,932***
10	582**	3,005***

SOURCE: Anderson, Corson, and Decker (1991, table III.4).
NOTE: Estimates are relative to those for claimants who received JSA-only services.
***, **, and * indicate significance at the 1 percent, 5 percent, and 10 percent levels, respectively.

These results for skill training are clearly much more favorable than the evidence presented in the evaluations of the other three demonstration projects. Nevertheless, Anderson, Corson, and Decker (1991, pp. 37, 51) suggest two reasons for caution in basing policy on their results. First, since claimants receiving training are self-selected, the evidence cannot be used to argue that training will increase earnings for a randomly chosen group of UI claimants. Second, evidence obtained for subgroups of claimants indicates that JSA/training has its largest impact for the same subgroups (such as high school graduates) that are affected to the greatest extent by the JSA-only treatment. That is, retraining has a larger impact for claimants who already possess marketable skills than for claimants who are less market-ready. This reason for caution is not particularly surprising, since the relatively low-cost classroom training courses provided in New Jersey were designed to upgrade claimants' existing skills rather than to provide training for a totally new occupation (see Corson et al. 1989, pp. 109-11). An example of skill upgrading cited in the evaluation report is that an individual with accounting skills might be trained to use a spreadsheet package on a personal computer.

The TAA study

In the context of the short-duration training offered in New Jersey, results obtained in the TAA study are especially relevant, since TAA funds longer-term retraining programs intended to equip displaced workers to enter entirely new occupations or industries. TAA participants also clearly exhibit the characteristics associated with displaced workers, namely, they are in most cases permanently separated from their prelayoff employers, typically because of a plant closing.

Drawing cases from ten states, the TAA evaluation study by Corson et al. (1993) is based on interviews with nearly 4,800 sample members broken down into three groups: (1) recipients of TRA income-maintenance benefits; (2) TAA trainees, nearly all of whom were receiving TRA benefits; and (3) a comparison sample of UI exhaustees. Further disaggregation occurs for training received in 1987-88 and 1988-89. TAA trainees typically enrolled in programs intended to develop specific job skills in occupations different from the occupations of their prelayoff jobs. Most of these programs were supplied by either a vocational training center or a local community college, and mean length of training exceeded one year for both the pre-1988 and post-1988 TAA trainee samples. A majority of TAA trainees failed to begin training until after they had exhausted their 26-week UI entitlement period. Thus many TAA trainees chose to enter training only after they were jobless for a substantial period of time, suggesting that entrance into a retraining program became an option only after workers recognized that finding a job in their old industrial sector was very unlikely. A $12,000 voucher allowed trainees to choose their own training program with the assistance of Employment Service staff. While over half of TAA trainees had been machine operators in their prelayoff jobs, fewer than 5 percent pursued training in that occupation. The occupations most frequently selected by trainees were technical, mechanical/repair, managerial/professional, and administrative support.

Table 3.4 presents net impact estimates for the twelfth quarter following the initial UI claim calculated for both the pre-88 and post-88 samples and controlling for a variety of personal and predisplacement job characteristics. The first two rows of the table indicate that there

Table 3.4 Estimated Effects of TAA Program Services 12 Quarters After the Initial UI Claim

Program service and sample	Outcome variables[a]		Comparison group
	Quarterly earnings	% of time employed	
TRA benefits:			
Pre-88 sample	–$408	–3.13	Matched sample of UI exhaustees displaced from mfg. jobs
Post-88 sample	24	3.6	
Training:			
Pre-88 sample	–$416**	–1.83	TRA recipients only
Post-88 sample	152	4.88	

SOURCE: TRA benefits: Corson et al. (1993, tables IV.5-IV.8) and training: Corson et al. (1993, tables VI.1 and VI.2).
a. Estimates are regression adjusted.
**Indicates significance at the 5 percent level.

are no significant differences between TRA recipients and the comparison sample of UI exhaustees in either quarterly earnings or the proportion of time employed. A comparison of unadjusted means of the outcome variables over the twelve-quarter observation period suggests that TRA recipients lagged UI exhaustees in terms of earnings and employment through quarter 4, after which they gradually began to catch up. The fourth quarter was a period in which most UI exhaustees could no longer receive UI benefits, but most TRA recipients were still receiving TRA benefits.

Figure 3.1 Mean Quarterly Earnings for the TAA Trainee and TRA Recipient Post-88 Samples of the TAA Evaluation, 12 Quarters

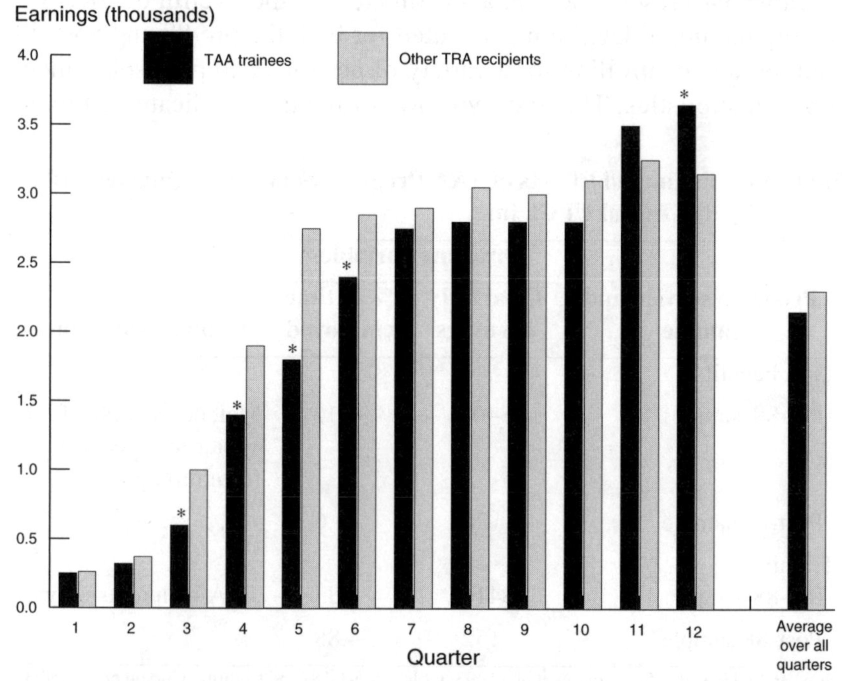

SOURCE: Corson, Decker, Gleason, and Nicholson (1993, figure V1.2).
*Indicates a significant difference at the 5 percent level.

The lower half of the table reports net impact estimates for the same two outcome variables obtained comparing TAA trainees to all other TRA recipients. (Corson et al. 1993 suggest that the appropriate comparison group for TAA trainees is TRA recipients rather than UI exhaustees.) These results for the twelfth quarter indicate considerable convergence of TAA trainees to the labor market performance of other TRA recipients, especially for the post-88 sample. As shown in figure 3.1, mean earnings of post-88 TAA trainees fall below those of TRA recipients in quarters 3 through 6; this would be expected since trainees were more likely to participate in long-term training, which would keep them out of the labor force longer. Thereafter, however, trainees' earnings rise faster than those of TRA recipients. This result is noteworthy because TAA trainees are more likely to have moved to a new occupation or industry in the job they held three years after their initial UI claim. It might be recalled from chapter 1 that a common finding in the displaced worker literature is that workers who changed industrial sectors to find new jobs typically suffer greater earnings losses than the displaced who did not change industries. Thus, one interpretation of table 3.4 and figure 3.1 is that TAA training had a positive effect in the sense of causing the earnings of industry- and occupation-switchers to converge to the level of earnings of displaced workers less likely to have been obliged to make such switches. It may also be worth noting that some post-88 TAA trainees may have chosen to enter a training program to extend their benefit entitlement period rather than to build up their stock of human capital.

UI Reform Experiments

Supplementing the results obtained for job search assistance in the displaced worker demonstration projects is evidence gathered from experimental evaluations of proposed reforms of the UI system. The proposed reforms all have the dual purposes of speeding up the reemployment of UI claimants and reducing the budgetary costs of UI. One set of reforms focuses on enhanced services to improve the job search skills and employment opportunities of UI claimants and on stricter enforcement of the work search rules that determine continuing eligibility for benefits. A second set examines the reemployment effects of cash payments to UI recipients who find jobs quickly and keep them for a specified time period. The final reform tests the effectiveness of self-employment as an alternative reemployment strategy.

The Job Search Experiments

Evaluation results are available for six random-assignment job search experiments.[6] In addition to the New Jersey UI Demonstration discussed earlier, the experiments are the Nevada Claimant Placement Program, the Charleston Claimant Placement and Work Test Demonstration, the Nevada Claimant Employment Program, the Washington Alternative Work Search Experiment, and the Reemploy Minnesota Project. Except for the Charleston and New Jersey projects, the experiments are similar in focusing on a cross section of UI claimants. (Charleston excludes victims of mass layoffs and New Jersey excludes those under age 25 with less than three years of tenure.) Some of the basic design features of the six experiments are presented in table 3.5. As seen in the table, all of the experiments seek to intervene reasonably early in the unemployment spell. The projects also all emphasize in varying degrees enhanced JSA services including job search workshops and resource centers, more frequent checks of claimant eligibility, and better coordination between Job Service personnel of the Employment Service (ES) and UI staff in providing services and monitoring eligibility. A novel aspect of the Washington State experiment is that one of its treatments eliminates all checks on work search activity, while the other two tailor claimants' work search requirements to their individual circumstances and local labor market conditions. (The traditional program requires three employer contacts per week for continued receipt of UI benefits.)

For each of the six experiments, table 3.6 reports estimates of treatment effects on weeks of UI benefits received. Estimates in the first column are simple treatment group/control group differences in means, while the second column presents estimates adjusted for differences in individual characteristics using regression analysis. The two Nevada experiments and the Reemploy Minnesota program provided the most intensive services and had the largest impact in reducing UI duration. Results shown in the table for these three experiments suggest that the enhanced JSA services and improved ES/UI coordination reduced UI duration by between 1.6 and 4.3 weeks. Given the moderate cost of JSA services, these experiments have very favorable ratios of benefits to costs.

Table 3.5 Major Design Characteristics of the Job Search Assistance Experiments

Project	Enrollment period	Treatment(s)	First contact
Nevada Claimant Placement	February 1977 to March 1978	One treatment: more intensive services, weekly interviews and eligibility checks, all services from same ES/UI team	After third UI payment
Charleston Claimant Placement and Work Test	February 1983 to December 1983	Three treatments: (1) strengthened work test, enhanced placement services and a 3-hour job search workshop; (2) strengthened work test and enhanced placement services; and (3) strengthened work test	After first UI payment
New Jersey UI	July 1986 to June 1987	One JSA treatment: required follow-up contacts with ES staff, access to job search materials at resource centers	Apprximately 5 weeks after claim filed
Nevada Claimant Employment	July 1988 to June 1989	One treatment: higher quality ES and UI services, all services from same ES/UI team	4 weeks into benefit year
Washington Alternative Work Search	July 1986 to August 1987	Three treatments: (1) elimination of all work search requirements, (2) individualized work search requirements, and (3) individualized work search requirements plus attendance at a 2-day job search workshop	At interview following claim filing
Reemploy Minnesota	July 1988 to June 1990	One treatment: intensive personalized JSA, all services from same staff person	At claim filing

Table 3.6 Estimated Effects of the Job Search Assistance Experiments on Weeks of UI Benefits

Project and treatment	Net impact: Without regressors	Net impact: With regressors	UI benefits measured over[a]
Nevada Claimant Placement	–3.90***		First spell of UI (12.4)
Charleston Claimant Placement			
1. Strengthened work test, enhanced placement services, and workshop	–0.70*	–0.76**	First 6 months of claim (15.5)
2. Strengthened work test and enhanced placement services	–0.50	–0.61*	
3. Strengthened work test	–0.50	–0.55	
New Jersey UI	–0.50**	–0.47**	Benefit year (17.9)
Nevada Claimant Employment			
Including trainees	–1.60***		Not specified (14.5)
Excluding trainees	–2.10***		
Washington Alternative Work Search			
1. No search requirements		3.35***	Benefit year (16.0)
2. Individualized work search		0.17	
3. Individualized work search plus job search workshop		–0.47*	
Reemploy Minnesota	–4.32**		Not specified (not available)

SOURCE: Meyer (1992, table 4).

a. Control group mean shown in parentheses.

***, **, and * indicate statistical significance at the 1 percent, 5 percent, and 10 percent levels, respectively.

Unfortunately, Meyer (1992, pp. 35-38) raises several concerns about the Nevada and Minnesota experiments involving weaknesses in their experimental designs and the completeness of their evaluations. In the Nevada experiments, large estimated effects may be partly the consequence of differences in the ability of Job Service personnel rather than the effect of the JSA services provided. In Minnesota, randomization may have been compromised by the inclusion in the control group of a substantial number of individuals with separation issues relating to the reason they left their last job that would lead to an administrative hearing. If these individuals tended to have longer spells of unemployment, they would account for some part of the over four-week difference in mean weeks of UI receipt.

The other three experiments appear to be more methodologically sound. Table 3.6 shows that for both the Charleston and New Jersey experiments, treatment services reduced UI receipt by about half a week. The combination of additional services and tightened eligibility checks in the New Jersey demonstration makes it difficult to determine which aspect of the program induced the reduction in UI duration. Results for the Charleston demonstration indicate, however, numerically small incremental effects above that of the strengthened work test (treatment 3) for enhanced placement services and the job search workshop (treatments 1 and 2). Corson, Long, and Nicholson (1985, pp. 106-108) conclude in their evaluation report that there is no strong evidence that the treatments affected the reemployment success of Charleston claimants by either encouraging more active job search or helping claimants to find jobs more rapidly. Rather, it appears that the reporting requirements, coupled with the cessation of UI payments for failure to report, are the most important reasons why the treatments led to a reduction in UI expenditures. Claimants in Charleston tended to leave UI rolls either because they were formally denied benefits or they simply stopped claiming benefits.

Results shown in table 3.6 for the Washington State experiment indicate that, compared to standard work search requirements, the suspension of search requirements (treatment 1) increased length of UI payments by over three weeks. At the same time, individually tailored job search requirements combined with a job search workshop (treatment 3) produced a small but still statistically significant reduction in UI duration of about half a week, while individualized work search alone (treatment 2) had no effect. Johnson and Klepinger (1994) suggest that the effect of treatment 3 on UI benefits might have either of two explanations: (1) the job search workshop made claimants more efficient in their job search, or (2) required attendance at the workshop acted as a deterrent to continued receipt of UI benefits by raising the perceived cost of remaining on UI. Hazard function estimates provided by the authors (not shown) are useful in distinguishing between these explanations. Consistent with the conclusion reached for the Charleston demonstration, the hazard function estimates point quite clearly to the second explanation as the more important mechanism through which treatment 3 produced the observed decrease in UI benefits. That is, treatments providing more intensive JSA services that include a job search workshop reduce UI payments primarily by raising the costs of remaining on UI rather than by enhancing job search skills.

The Reemployment Bonus Experiments

To encourage active work search by UI claimants, an alternative to stricter monitoring of claimant search efforts is a reemployment bonus. To date, four random-assignment reemployment bonus experiments have been carried out. The first is a state-funded program in Illinois conducted between mid-1984 and mid-1985. Two reemployment bonus treatments were implemented as part of the Illinois program. The first paid a cash bonus of $500 to a random sample of new UI claimants who found a job within 11 weeks of the initial claim (the qualification period) and held that job for at least four months (the reemployment period). In the second treatment, another random sample of new UI claimants was told that, once a hiring commitment was made, the employer of each newly hired claimant would be eligible for a $500 cash bonus. Here the intent of the subsidy was to test the effect of a marginal wage-bill subsidy (or training subsidy) in reducing the duration of insured unemployment. The qualification and reemployment periods are the same for the employer bonus as for the claimant bonus.

As reported by Woodbury and Spiegelman (1987), large positive effects are found for the claimant bonus treatment but not the employer bonus treatment. The program's take-up rate is very high (84 percent) for those eligible for the claimant experiment, and the treatment is found to reduce UI benefits by $158 and UI duration by 1.15 weeks, where both outcome variables are measured over the benefit year. These estimates are obtained for all workers assigned to the claimant treatment, whether or not they agreed to participate and whether or not they actually received the bonus payment. Woodbury and Spiegelman calculate that UI benefits were reduced by a striking $2.32 for every $1 paid out in bonuses to claimants. The authors also provide evidence that the favorable effect on UI duration is not due to participating claimants accepting a less favorable job match (thereby sacrificing earnings) in order to qualify for the bonus. On the other hand, the program participation rate is considerably lower in the employer bonus treatment at 65 percent; and there is no significant treatment group/control group difference in either UI benefits or duration of UI payments.

The very favorable results obtained for the Illinois claimant reemployment bonus experiment led to USDOL funding for three additional random-assignment experiments in New Jersey, Pennsylvania, and Washington State. These experiments were designed to provide evidence on how to fine-tune the reemployment bonus concept by introducing more variation in the amount and timing of bonus payments to claimants. In the New Jersey UI Reemployment Demonstration, the maximum reemployment bonus was specified to be one-half of the claimant's total UI entitlement, where UI entitlement was defined as the lump-sum payment capturing the stream of benefit payments to be received over the remaining weeks of UI eligibility. The maximum bonus could be collected by accepting a job during the first two weeks after agreeing to participate in the program at the assessment/counseling interview. After these two weeks, the size of the bonus decreases by 10 percent per week, reaching zero at the end of the eleventh week after the assessment/counseling interview. To qualify for the bonus, the claimant's new job must be more than part time and the employer other than the previous employer. The Pennsylvania and Washington experiments offered two and three levels of bonus payments, respectively, expressed as multiples of average weekly benefit amounts, combined with two levels of the qualification period. The reemployment period is about four months in all three post-Illinois experiments.

The New Jersey, Pennsylvania, and Washington experiments are all found to have much smaller effects on UI expenditures than the Illinois claimant experiment. In New Jersey, the incremental effect of the reemployment bonus above that of JSA-only is 0.50 weeks less in UI duration and, as shown in table 3.2, \$83 less in UI payments.[7] In Pennsylvania and Washington, similarly, the estimated effects of different combinations of bonus payments and qualification periods cluster around one-half of a week of UI payments.[8] As pointed out earlier in table 3.6, this is about the same effect achieved by more closely monitoring work search behavior in the Charleston and Washington State job search experiments, but at a much higher cost due to the bonuses. There is also a tendency for the larger bonuses and longer qualification periods to be associated with larger estimated effects, but these relationships are not strong. In the Washington experiment, for example, the high bonus payment level together with a long qualification period reduced UI receipt by 0.76 weeks and UI benefits by \$138, both measured over the benefit year. Consistent with the Illinois results, finally, an encouraging aspect of the other three experiments is that there is no evidence that rate of pay on the new job is adversely affected by an earlier return to work.

Following a flurry of excitement generated by findings of the Illinois claimant experiment, the less favorable results reported for the subsequent experiments caused an abating of labor economists' interest in the reemployment bonus concept. Nevertheless, a reemployment bonus was included among changes in the UI system recommended by the Clinton administration in its proposed Reemployment Act of 1994 (see U.S. Department of Labor 1993, p. 9).

Davidson and Woodbury (1991) attempt to provide an explanation of why the three later experiments obtained significantly smaller bonus impacts than were observed in Illinois. Their analysis indicates that the key factor in understanding this difference is that the reemployment bonus effect in Illinois combines a very large estimated impact for workers eligible for 12 weeks of federally funded extended UI benefits and a rather small impact for workers eligible for the regular 26 weeks of state-funded benefits. Workers eligible for extended benefits are expected to search less intensively than workers eligible for regular benefits because the additional period of benefits reduces the financial pressure to find a new job quickly. What seems to have happened in Illinois is that the reemployment bonus caused workers eligible for extended benefits to disproportionately increase their search effort relative to those not eligible. The result is that the greater relative increase in the search effort of extended benefit recipients led to a reduction in UI duration in comparison to what it would have been had the extended benefit program not been available. In terms of policy implications, Davidson and Woodbury suggest a possible role for the reemployment bonus in Canada and in Western European countries where, as noted in chapter 2, workers are typically entitled to one year or longer of unemployment compensation benefits, rather than just six months as is standard in the United States.

One final issue that may be addressed in the context of the reemployment bonus experiments is termed the "displacement effect" in the labor economics literature. The basic problem is that even if a labor market intervention like the reemployment bonus enhances the reemployment prospects of program-eligible workers, it will have no effect on total employment if each new job offered is at the expense of a job opportunity not available to ineligible workers. Davidson and Woodbury (1993) explore the likely size of the displacement effect of a reemployment bonus program using a partial equilibrium matching model of the labor market. Workers potentially subject to displacement fall into two categories: (1) UI-eligibles who fail to find a job in time to qualify for the bonus (including workers who have exhausted their UI benefits), and (2) UI-ineligible workers.

The authors proceed by making use of data gathered in evaluating the Illinois experiment to infer values for unobservable parameters of their search model. The model is then solved to yield estimates of the displacement effect. Results reported indicate that overall unemployment falls in response to the bonus program; that is, the positive effect of bonus payments on the reemployment opportunities of program-eligible workers more than outweighs possible displacement effects for ineligibles. Nevertheless, the unemployment of UI-ineligible workers is found to rise in the one case (out of three the authors consider) in which assumed parameter values are characteristic of a recession. The magnitude of the displacement effect is small, since it never exceeds 1.9 displaced workers per thousand. But even so, Davidson and Woodbury (1993, p. 601) suggest that the effect is large enough that 30 to 60 percent of the gross employment effect of the bonus is offset by displacement of UI-ineligibles. As they note, the finding that displacement is greatest under conditions characteristic of a recession substantially weakens the attractiveness of the reemployment bonus as a policy alternative.

The Self-Employment Demonstrations

In the late 1980s, the USDOL initiated two demonstration projects to test the effectiveness of self-employment as an alternative reemployment strategy for UI claimants.[9] The Washington State project began in September 1989 and supplied program services through March 1991. The Massachusetts project began in May 1990 as a three-year demonstration project. Both projects are early intervention programs designed to encourage new UI claimants to start up their own small businesses. Program services offered in both projects included twenty hours of training in basic business skills, counseling, and financial assistance. The financial assistance available in both projects included bi-weekly UI benefits. In addition, participants were exempt from the regular UI work search requirement while enrolled in the demonstrations.

Along with these similarities, the projects differed in two important respects. First, the Massachusetts project was targeted to unemployed workers judged likely to exhaust their UI benefits. The Washington project did not impose this targeting restriction. Second, the Washington project provided, in addition to regular UI payments, a lump-sum payment equal to remaining UI benefits to those who completed five project "milestones."[10] These were defined as completing a set of four business training modules, developing an acceptable business plan, opening a business bank account, satisfying all licensing requirements, and obtaining adequate funding.

Both of the self-employment demonstrations were formally evaluated using a random-assignment methodology. But in addition to the net impact estimates, an important finding reported in the Abt Associates evaluation is that interest in the self-employment projects was not strong among UI claimants. Of those invited to participate in the programs, only 7.5 percent of Washington claimants and 3.8 percent of Massachusetts claimants were interested enough to attend an orientation session. And of those who attended the orientation sessions, less than two-thirds filed an application (which had to include a new business idea). Thus, program take-up rates were very low at about 4 percent for Washington and 2 percent for Massachusetts. In their report,

Benus, Wood, and Grover (1994, p. ii) comment that "while many profess an interest in self-employment, relatively few choose to pursue self-employment when the opportunity arises." Acceptable applicants were assigned randomly to treatment and control groups. Total sample sizes are about 1,500 claimants for Washington and 521 claimants for Massachusetts.

Labor market outcome estimates were obtained over follow-up periods averaging 21.3 months in Washington and 18.9 months in Massachusetts. The most favorable of the net impact estimates reported are that the programs in both states sharply increased the likelihood of self-employment and accelerated the start of self-employment. In Washington, for example, 52 percent of the treatment group had at least one self-employment experience during the observation period, as compared with 27 percent of the control group. This difference in self-employment experience is only somewhat smaller in Massachusetts at 47 percent and 29 percent for the treatment and control groups, respectively. Benus, Wood, and Grover (1994, p. 39) suggest that the larger impacts in Washington reflect the financial incentives provided by the state's lump-sum payment.

Other program net impact estimates tended to show smaller effects and less consistency across the two projects. With respect to self-employment earnings, a positive effect was obtained for Washington, but the program had no effect in Massachusetts. The authors of the evaluation report also suggest that program services might affect wage and salary earnings as well as self-employment earnings.[11] Taking both categories of earnings into account, the Washington program is found to have no effect on combined earnings (a positive effect, as noted, is obtained for self-employment earnings and a negative effect for wage and salary earnings); while the Massachusetts program increased combined earnings (no effect on self-employment earnings coupled with a positive effect on wage and salary earnings). Excluding the lump-sum payment in Washington, both projects reduced the dollar amount of UI benefits received during the first benefit year. Including the lump-sum payment, however, the Washington demonstration increased total UI payments to participants. From the perspective of generating employment for others, finally, neither program is found to significantly affect the employment of nonparticipants.

Selected Studies of Disadvantaged Worker Programs

The economically disadvantaged differ from displaced workers in the barriers they face in overcoming joblessness. One of the most important of these barriers for disadvantaged workers is lack of work experience. Nevertheless, useful evidence on some of the displaced worker issues raised thus far is available from recent evaluations of disadvantaged worker programs. Examined in this section is evidence on the effectiveness of classroom and on-the-job training in the National JTPA Study and of job search assistance in California's multicounty Greater Avenues for Independence (GAIN) program. The highly successful GAIN program in Riverside County is highlighted in the discussion.

Readers may also have noted the absence of information on basic education programs in this chapter. The reason is that basic education was not included in the mix of services provided in the five displaced worker projects discussed earlier. At the same time, national commissions frequently suggest that strengthening basic skills is essential to allow American workers to cope with rapid technological change and increased international competitiveness (see, for example, U.S. Department of Labor 1986, pp. 33-34); and the third program evaluation criterion listed in chapter 1 argues that basic education should be part of a comprehensive displaced workers program. The four demonstration projects funded by the Rockefeller Foundation as part of the Minority Female Single Parent Demonstration provide important information on how to go about structuring basic education programs.

The National JTPA Study

In 1986 the USDOL commissioned a study to measure the impact of programs funded by Title II-A of JTPA, which is targeted to serve economically disadvantaged Americans. Using data for over 17,000 JTPA applicants scattered across sixteen locally administered sites, the evaluation report by Bloom et al. (1992) provides net impact estimates for four target groups—adult women and men (ages 22 and older) and female and male out-of-school youths (ages 16 to 21). Sample members are assigned randomly to either a treatment group or a control group.[12] But before random assignment, individuals were classified into three service strategy subgroups based on the services recommended by program intake staff. The CT subgroup consists of individuals recommended for classroom training in occupational skills and basic education.[13] Next, members of the OJT/JSA subgroup were recommended for either on-the-job training or job search assistance or for both (treatment group members recommended for OJT typically were enrolled in JSA while searching for an OJT position or an unsubsidized job). Finally, members of the other services subgroup were recommended for services including JSA, basic education, and work experience—but not classroom training in occupational skills or on-the-job training.

Bloom et al. (1992) point out that adult treatment group members in both the classroom training and OJT/JSA service subgroups were much more likely than control group members to have received the recommended service.[14] Over an 18-month period following random assignment, estimated earnings effects of JTPA services are shown for adults in table 3.7. For women, the classroom training results follow the expected pattern; that is, earnings losses occur in the first quarter or two, representing an initial investment of time in training, followed by earnings gains increasing in size over the remaining quarters. The positive effects measured for the last two quarters are statistically significant. For men, on the other hand, none of the estimated effects is significantly different from zero. Note that these estimates are obtained for sample members assigned to the service subgroup, not for those who actually enrolled in a CT program.

The OJT/JSA treatment has a more immediate and sustained positive impact on the earnings of both adult women and men than does classroom training. This would be expected for a service strategy that emphasizes immediate placement in either an on-the-job training slot or an unsubsidized job. Women in the OJT/JSA subgroup enjoyed positive and statistically significant earnings impacts of from $109 to $144 per quarter in five of the six quarters. Estimates for men are of similar magnitude in all but the first quarter, although estimated impacts are less often statistically significant.

Evidence recently made available for an additional 12 months of follow-up is important for understanding whether the classroom and on-the-job training effects shown in table 3.7 persist beyond the initial 18 months. For adults engaged in OJT, Bloom et al. (1994) report estimates obtained for months 19-30 of the 30-month follow-up period that are larger for both men and women than the corresponding estimates for months 7-18. In particular, OJT is found to increase annual earnings in months 19-30 by $1,021 (or 17 percent) for women and $1,125 (or 13 percent) for men. Both of these estimates are statistically significant.

Table 3.7 Estimated Impact of JTPA Title II-A Programs on Quarterly and 18-Month Earnings, by Gender and Service Strategy

Service strategy and time period	Adult women	Adult men
Classroom training		
Quarter 1	–$70*	–$101
2	5	126
3	52	213
4	79	50
5	144**	151
6	188***	–21
All quarters	398	418
OJT/JSA		
Quarter 1	$144***	$54
2	81	135
3	129**	164*
4	109*	94
5	142**	133
6	138**	201**
All quarters	742**	781*

SOURCE: Bloom et al. (1992, exhibit S6).
***, **, and * indicate significance at the 1 percent, 5 percent, and 10 percent levels, respectively.

The sustainability of the positive earnings effect of classroom training is not as clear. Bloom et al. (1994) find that for adult women the impact of CT drops from $434 to $365 per year moving from months

7-18 to months 19-30 of the follow-up period. For men, on the other hand, an increase from $632 to $910 annually over the same two periods is reported. Although neither is statistically significant, the estimates for months 19-30 represent substantial gains in annual earnings on the order of 7 percent and 11 percent, respectively, for women and men.

These results for disadvantaged adult workers provide evidence for randomly selected subgroups of the labor market effectiveness of on-the-job training and, to a lesser extent, of classroom training. As such, they support the results shown in table 3.3 for displaced workers in New Jersey who were self-selected in the sense that they opted to undertake the offered services. The JTPA and New Jersey findings indicating a strong positive effect of on-the-job training are especially important given the unexpectedly ambiguous OJT results in table 3.2 for the Buffalo displaced workers program. Nevertheless, there are two important caveats to the JTPA findings. First, Bloom et al. (1992) suggest that the earnings gains under JTPA are due primarily to increases in hours worked, rather than to higher hourly earnings while employed. Second, the authors (1992, p. 14) mention that program staff members tended to recommend the most job-ready applicants for the OJT/JSA service strategy.

As noted in the context of criterion 2 in chapter 1, a fundamental problem in implementing OJT programs is recruiting a sufficient number of employers willing to offer OJT slots. Evidence on this problem is provided by Bishop and Montgomery (1986), who examine employer familiarity with and participation in four targeted employment subsidy programs in operation in 1980. Using a USDOL survey of nearly 6,000 employers, the authors find that participation rates in these programs are very low, primarily because firms lacked knowledge about the existence and rules of the programs. Bishop and Montgomery also report, however, a strong effect of establishment size on the likelihood of both familiarity and participation, and that employer usage can be increased by vigorous promotion by local program administrators.

The Riverside GAIN Program

Under the federal Omnibus Budget Reconciliation Act (OBRA) of 1981, states were given the authority to design their own programs to improve the labor market prospects of welfare recipients. One of the series of OBRA-related state programs is California's GAIN program, which was implemented between 1988 and 1990 in six counties. A key feature of GAIN that distinguishes it from most other welfare employment programs of the 1980s is its emphasis on up-front basic education. Welfare recipients who do not possess a high school diploma (or its equivalent), who do poorly on a math and literacy test, or who are not proficient in English are deemed by GAIN to be "in need of basic education." These individuals can choose either a basic education class or a job search activity, but if they choose JSA and fail to obtain employment they must enter basic education. Recipients judged not in need of basic education begin by participating in job search. GAIN participants in either of these sequences who fail to obtain employment after completing their initial activities move on, after undergoing an employability assessment, to a next level of activities including skills training, vocationally oriented postsecondary education, on-the-job training, or unpaid work experience.

Using a random assignment experimental design, the GAIN evaluation carried out by the Manpower Demonstration Research Corporation provides net impact estimates for both heads of single-parent families and heads of two-parent families. Estimated program effects for single parents (who represent about two-thirds of welfare recipients in the study) are found to vary substantially across counties. The cross-county range of these estimates is from -8 percent to 59 percent for earnings and from 2 percent to -12 percent for welfare benefits measured during the first year of the follow-up period. Similar variation in the outcome variables with a greater overall increase in earnings and decrease in welfare payments occurs in year 2. For both years, the largest positive estimates for earnings and the largest negative estimates for welfare payments are found for the Riverside County program.

Friedlander, Riccio, and Freedman (1993, ch. IV) carefully discuss the factors that make Riverside different from the other five GAIN programs. The conclusion they reach is that Riverside's most distinctive feature is its "message" to all welfare registrants, even those in basic education classes, that employment is central, that it should be sought expeditiously, and that low-paying job opportunities should not be routinely turned down. The program's management underscored this message to staff members by establishing job placement standards as one of several criteria for assessing performance. For program clients, the centrality of employment is reinforced by Riverside's rigorous use of sanctions to secure the participation of all mandatory registrants (those with children older than age 6) in recommended program services. Riverside also implemented a strong job development component to insure that jobs were indeed available to registrants. It is important to note, finally, that the Riverside program clearly benefited from a local economy that grew faster than any of the other county economies, even though Riverside's unemployment rate was not the lowest of the six counties.

The Minority Female Single Parent Demonstration

Between 1982 and 1988, the Rockefeller Foundation provided funding to community-based organizations located in Atlanta, Providence, San Jose, and Washington, D.C. to operate comprehensive welfare employment programs for low-income minority single mothers. The Minority Female Single Parent projects in Atlanta, Providence, and Washington followed either of two conventional approaches to providing services. In Atlanta and Providence, a "sequential" approach was used in which women with poor basic skills were enrolled initially in remedial education courses and only later placed in job skills classes after they attained academic prerequisites. The Washington project emphasized a "general employability" model that included instruction on motivation, basic reading and math, and job search skills. A course for better-prepared trainees augmented these general classes with instruction in the basic concepts of electricity, mechanics, and tools as preparation for further training or employment in nontraditional jobs.

The San Jose Center for Employment Training (CET) program differed from the other three Minority Female Single Parent projects and from most OBRA-based programs in seeking to integrate basic education with job skills training. Three features of the CET program combined to make it unique. First, low-income single mothers entering the program did not receive initial assessment and referral services but were instead placed immediately, regardless of their formal educational deficiencies, in an open-entry, self-paced, job training curriculum. Curricula were developed or dropped in response to changes in local labor market demand as indicated by an industrial advisory board composed of employers and by the efforts of CET job developers. Second, basic educational skills were taught concurrently with skill training as they pertained to the job skills being learned. This allowed program participants to acquire essential basic skills while still progressing toward the ultimate goal of a job. Finally, training was provided in-house using experienced instructors drawn from local firms. Since curricula were self-paced and competency-based, instructors had the time to provide participants with individual attention.

The evaluation report by Mathematica Policy Research provides dramatic support for the "integrated" program model used in the San Jose CET program. Measured over a 30-month follow-up period, the sequential and general employability approaches used in Atlanta, Providence, and Washington are found to have essentially no effect on earnings and employment using a random-assignment evaluation design. In striking contrast, the CET program is estimated to increase employment and total earnings by about 14 percent and 22 percent, respectively, above control group means (see Burghardt et al. 1992, table IV.1). The larger estimated impact on earnings than employment implies that hourly wages as well as hours of work increased under CET, and the Mathematica researchers report a direct CET effect on average hourly earnings of nearly 11 percent. On the cost side, it is interesting to note that cost per CET treatment group member is about $3,600 per year, which is in the middle of the range for Minority Female Single Parent demonstrations of between $2,700 to $4,800.

Summary

The United States clearly leads the world in the quantity and sophistication of its program evaluation research. This chapter reviewed the evidence available for government-supported evaluations of the reemployment services offered in five displaced workers projects carried out during the 1980s and into the 1990s. Two of these evaluations made use of a random-assignment evaluation design, while the other three used a treatment group/comparison group design. Considered in turn in this concluding section are the reemployment services provided in the displaced worker demonstrations, namely, job search assistance, classroom training, and on-the-job training.

This evidence for displaced workers was supplemented by results obtained from studies of proposed UI system reforms in six job search experiments, four reemployment bonus experiments, and two self-employment demonstrations. (The New Jersey UI Reemployment Demonstration project is included among both the displaced worker and UI reform studies.) Also considered in this chapter were findings obtained from three studies examining for the economically disadvantaged the labor market effectiveness of job search assistance, classroom training, on-the-job training, and basic education services. Basic education is not included in the mix of services supplied in the displaced worker demonstrations.

Beginning with job search assistance, evidence provided by the displaced worker demonstration projects indicates quite clearly that JSA services speed up the reemployment of displaced workers. It appears that many displaced individuals possess sufficient marketable skills that they can find new jobs with limited, relatively low-cost assistance. JSA allows for quick intervention before workers disperse after layoffs and plant closings; and, given its modest cost per worker, the evidence suggests that JSA services are cost effective.

The job search experiments provide additional evidence to support the effectiveness of job search assistance, indicating, in particular, that more stringent monitoring of the job search activity of UI claimants can pay off in reduced UI expenditures. Estimated program effects in these experiments tend to cluster around one-half of a week less of UI benefits. After an initial flurry of interest stimulated by the Illinois reemployment bonus demonstration, findings from the three subsequent reemployment bonus experiments in New Jersey, Pennsylvania, and Washington State indicate only modest potential for speeding up the reemployment process above the effects of much cheaper JSA services. Evaluation results from the self-employment demonstrations in Washington State and Massachusetts suggest a similarly cautious conclusion. While this evidence indicates that the self-employment programs did accelerate the reemployment of UI claimants as self-employed entrepreneurs, the impact of these programs on earnings is ambiguous. It is also important to note that only very small fractions of eligible claimants turned out to be interested in participating in the programs.

Results from the displaced worker demonstrations are more mixed for classroom training in vocational skills. Only the follow-up study of the New Jersey UI Demonstration focusing specifically on individuals who actually received classroom training services (as distinct from the random sample of all eligible individuals offered CT) yields evidence of a positive incremental effect of CT above that of JSA-only. It is worth noting that the short-term, low-cost training provided in New Jersey was designed to upgrade workers' existing skills rather than to furnish training for a new occupation. In contrast, TAA participants received longer-term training intended to equip them to enter a new occupation or industry. Evaluation results for the TAA program are positive in the sense that the longer-term investments in classroom training allowed the earnings of TAA trainees—most of whom were obliged to change occupation or industry to obtain reemployment—to reach the level of earnings of a comparison group of displaced workers who were more likely to have been industry and occupation stayers. (Displaced workers reemployed in the same occupation and industry typically suffer smaller earnings losses than occupation and industry switchers.) Moderately favorable results for classroom training are also obtained for economically disadvantaged adult workers in the random-assignment JTPA Title II-A evaluation.

The authors of these evaluation reports take considerable care in interpreting their inconclusive and often negative results for classroom training. Caveats mentioned include the difficulty of drawing reliable inferences from small sample sizes and low take-up rates for classroom training programs; the problem that program participants in limited-duration experiments have relatively little time left to receive job placement assistance; the scarcity of training providers capable of putting together high-quality, short-duration training courses on short notice; and the very real possibility that the classroom training provided is either not marketable in the local labor market or not of particular interest to the client population.

Although a substantial body of evaluation evidence on the effectiveness of classroom training is now available, it is difficult to draw policy conclusions from this evidence on how to design permanent, nationwide retraining programs. At present, it seems prudent to conclude only that classroom training should be restricted to carefully selected workers who can be offered training curricula tailored to their backgrounds and to the needs of local employers. Exactly how to anticipate the needs of employers in designing classroom training curricula is an open question, although considerable experience has been gained, most notably in the JTPA program, on the use of performance standards to increase the incentive of training providers to supply job-ready program graduates. JTPA performance standards are discussed in more detail in chapter 4. It should also be noted that the evaluation studies examined in this chapter do not provide evidence on the effectiveness of certification systems indicating mastery of particular occupational skills.

Even though the Buffalo displaced worker project provided surprisingly mixed evidence for on-the-job training, results from the New Jersey program for treatment group members who actually received on-the-job training are highly favorable, indicating incremental effects on earnings of as much as $3,000 per quarter relative to earnings of the JSA-only treatment group. A note of caution regarding this very positive result is that it is based on a small number of on-the-job training recipients who are undoubtedly highly self-selected. Nevertheless, the on-the-job training treatment is also found in the National JTPA Study to have an immediate and sustained positive impact on the earnings of both adult women and men. An issue that has yet to be successfully addressed in on-the-job training programs is how to successfully interest American employers in providing a sufficient number of on-the-job training slots.

As noted earlier, basic education services were not offered participants in the displaced worker demonstrations. Yet evidence yielded by a welfare employment program located in Riverside county in California indicates that a basic education program closely linked to job placement assistance can sharply increase earnings while decreasing welfare payments. Also discussed in this chapter was a second highly successful welfare employment program in San Jose, California that teaches essential basic skills concurrently with skill training as the basic skills pertain to the job skills being learned.

NOTES

1. The Buffalo program was one of six dislocated worker demonstration projects scattered across the nation that received USDOL funding. Due to cost considerations, it was decided that the impact analysis should be limited to one site. The Buffalo project was chosen as that site because of its size, a comprehensive mix of services, and the random selection of workers recruited for the program from six "target" plants.

2. In addition to assessing the effectiveness of alternative packages of reemployment services, the second major objective of the New Jersey project was to examine the possible use of the UI system to identify early in the claim period unemployed workers likely to face prolonged spells of unemployment and exhaust UI benefits. The approach used in New Jersey to distinguish the displaced from other UI claimants was to apply five screens during the fourth week of claiming benefits. The cumulative effect of these screens is the restrictions stated in the text.

Based on the New Jersey experience, 1993 federal legislation authorizing extended UI benefits (the Emergency Unemployment Compensation Amendments of 1993) requires the U.S. Secretary of Labor to establish a program for encouraging the implementation of a system for "profiling" new claimants for regular UI payments (see Runner 1994). The profiling system is intended to identify those claimants who are likely UI exhaustees and who may require adjustment assistance services to make a successful transition to new employment.

3. If longitudinal data are available for program participants and nonparticipants, a third "difference-in-differences" econometric approach is available to control for the selection bias that would arise if unobserved person-specific factors affect both earnings and program selection. This approach is used in an evaluation of the Canadian Employability Improvement Program discussed in chapter 5.

4. Standard references are Heckman (1978 and 1979).

5. The reemployment bonus is directed at the problem that the reemployment of displaced workers may be delayed, not by inadequate job search skills, but by a lack of motivation to engage in search or by the natural reluctance to accept a new job offering considerably lower wages and benefits than the prelayoff job. Evidence for New Jersey and three other reemployment bonus demonstration projects is discussed in more detail later in this chapter.

6. The discussion in this section borrows heavily from the comprehensive survey by Meyer (1992).

7. Using data from the New Jersey experiment, Anderson (1992) reports hazard function estimates also indicating modest incremental effects of the reemployment bonus on the probability of reemployment.

8. Evaluation results for these two experiments are reported by Corson et al. (1992) for Pennsylvania and by Spiegelman, O'Leary, and Kline (1992) for Washington State.

9. The discussion in this section is based on the Abt Associates evaluation report authored by Benus, Wood, and Grover (1994).

10. The lump-sum design used in Washington is patterned after the French Unemployed Entrepreneurs Program which provides a lump-sum payment received after the registration of the new firm. In contrast, the Massachusetts design of a steady flow of UI payments over a fixed time period is based on the British Enterprise Allowance Scheme (now called the Business and Enterprise Services program). Both of these well-known self-employment programs are discussed in Bendick and Egan (1987) and Leigh (1989, ch. 5).

11. Benus, Wood, and Grover (1994, p. 44) outline the following reasons for expecting that a self-employment program might affect wage and salary earnings: (1) self selection causes less capable treatment group members to remain unemployed or to become employed in wage and sal-

ary jobs, (2) participation in the demonstrations causes some treatment group members to delay their search for wage and salary employment, and (3) demonstration services (especially counseling) provide treatment group members with increased awareness of their marketable skills and an enhanced self-confidence in their employability. The first two of these factors would cause the demonstrations to have a negative effect on wage and salary earnings, while the third would be expected to have a positive effect.

12. In his critique of the National JTPA Study, Hotz (1992) argues that the study does not produce net impact estimates that are valid for the entire JTPA system because the 16 sites studied (out of over 600 sites nationally) are not representative of the system as a whole. The problem is that many sites made the decision not to participate in the study because of concern that assignment of applicants to control groups would harm their ability to meet recruitment goals and performance standards, and the ethics of denying services to members of the control groups during the follow-up period. Thus Hotz suggests that the estimates obtained are valid only for the sites that volunteered to participate in the study.

13. Basic education includes Adult Basic Education providing basic communications and mathematics training, high school or General Educational Development (GED) preparation, and English as a Second Language.

14. For the CT subgroup, 49 percent of the adult women treatment group received classroom training in occupational skills, as compared to 29 percent of the control group. These rates were 40 percent versus 24 percent among adult men. For the treatment groups in the OJT/JSA subgroup, 29 percent of both adult women and adult men received OJT, compared to less than 1 percent of the corresponding control groups.

4
Retraining Workers in Marketable Skills

This chapter addresses several of the policy issues raised in chapters 2 and 3 regarding classroom and on-the-job training. In chapter 2, it was pointed out that during the latter half of the 1980s the Swedish government spent nearly twice as much per dollar of Gross Domestic Product on adult training than did the governments of any other of the nations considered. The first of the three main sections of this chapter explores the nature of the services Swedes receive for this extraordinary commitment of resources to adult training. Of particular interest is the 1986 reorganization of the Swedish training system carried out to decentralize decision making and increase responsiveness to market forces.

Governments of other nations have recently sought to decentralize the provision of training services with the objective of better matching services provided to the needs of local employers and workers. But at the same time these governments step back from directly supplying training, they usually seek to make local program providers accountable for meeting policy goals established at the national level. The second section of this chapter examines the 1988 reform decentralizing Britain's training system and reviews available evidence on the role of performance standards in ensuring that efforts of local service providers are consistent with national policy goals.

In contrast to the government training system in place in Sweden and the employer-led/school-based system in the United Kingdom, still another training model is a system based largely on the firm. The third section, which is the longest section of the chapter, focuses on firm-based training systems. This section begins with discussions of features of the highly regarded German and Japanese models that appear to contribute to their success. Of special interest is the issue of how to ensure that employers supply enough in-house training slots to satisfy the demand of workers who would benefit from on-the-job training. Considered next is the payroll training tax recently enacted in Australia—called the Training Guarantee—which is intended to increase the incentive of employers to meet their own training requirements. The discussion of the Training Guarantee is supplemented by evidence for the French payroll training tax first imposed in 1971. The final part of this section briefly describes the national skill certification system existing in the United Kingdom and presents evidence, using British data, on the role of skill certification in indicating to potential employers that apprenticeship program graduates possess nationally recognized levels of occupational skills.

How It's Done in Sweden

Characteristics of the Swedish System

It is useful to discuss the Swedish training system in terms of the first four criteria of the evaluation framework sketched in chapter 1. These criteria are the following:

- Program services should facilitate the transition of displaced workers to jobs in growing industries and growing sectors within existing industries.
- Program activities must meet the needs of displaced workers.
- Programs must serve the entire spectrum of displaced workers, not just those easiest to place.
- Training must supply marketable skills to program graduates.

The Swedish government has a long-term commitment to adjustment assistance programs that satisfy the first criterion. As described in chapter 2, the Rehn-Meidner model implemented in Sweden in the mid-1950s explicitly emphasizes the role of active labor market programs in equipping laid-off workers to locate and qualify for new jobs in growing industries. In particular, adult training is intended to supply the enhanced skills required for displaced workers to move between occupations or industries. The nearly forty-year commitment of national resources made by Swedish society indicates a level of satisfaction with their adult training system that warrants study.

Prior to 1986, adult training in Sweden was administered jointly by the Ministries of Labor and Education. Operating under the Ministry of Labor, the National Labor Market Board established policy with respect to the quantity, quality, and location of training programs. The Ministry of Education was responsible for operating the system of 100 skill centers scattered across Sweden and employing the staff of the skill centers.

The reorganization of 1986 created the National Employment Training Board (AMU), which took over responsibility for operating the skill centers. The AMU is composed of a national board and 25 county boards, each board consisting of employer, union, and government members. Decision-making authority resides in the county boards, with these boards responsible for the implementation, evaluation, and maintenance of financial records for the training activities in their own counties. Duties of the national AMU board in Stockholm are limited to developing central curricula and overseeing the financial records of county boards. The national AMU board has just 26 employees.

The AMU training system offers about 450 general curricula available in all 100 skill centers, and each of the 25 regions may further develop additional curricula of its own. Most training courses are vocationally oriented and aimed at the upper secondary school level, with some programs reaching university levels. Courses are predominantly intended to provide skills in manufacturing, health care, office and computer occupations, and hotel and restaurant administration (Trehörning 1993, p. 62). However, there are also basic education courses in Swedish, mathematics, and English. (Displaced workers in Sweden are frequently immigrants.) Courses may last up to a year or more.

The discussion of the second criterion in chapter 1 pointed out that adult training programs that meet the needs of displaced workers should be designed with the following goals in mind: (1) program entry should be flexible and length of courses variable, (2) programs should demonstrate to trainees a clear connection between skills learned and employment opportunities, and (3) trainees should be provided with a form of income maintenance during their training period. The Swedish training system is designed to meet each of these goals. With respect to the first, since layoffs can occur at any time it is important that retraining programs permit immediate entry and are flexible enough to accommodate substantial variation in formal educational backgrounds. To this end, AMU programs are not organized around semesters beginning in the fall and winter and courses of fixed length. Rather, admission to skill centers is open, and trainees receive individual study plans and work with self-instructing materials to a large extent. After completing a training program, graduates are given a diploma, which conveys to potential employers precise information about the curriculum the worker has successfully completed and the skills he or she possesses.

A key aspect of AMU training is its modular system. For example, curricula in the mechanical engineering area are built around fifty-one different modules. Subsets of these modules taken sequentially comprise six different occupational specialties within mechanical engineering (i.e., lathe operator, milling operator, NC-operator, grinding operator, tool grinding, and grinding for tool work). The least intensive of these curricula (NC-operator) requires the completion of just one module, while the most intensive (milling operator) requires completing fourteen modules.[1] The modular system thus allows flexibility in individualizing study plans for trainees.

The modular system also extends to workers who are deficient in basic reading, communication, or computational skills. Basic education modules are available to those requiring basic skills upgrading in one or more areas, but the curriculum is restricted as much as possible to those skills directly required for vocational training or for adequate job performance. Bendick (1983, p. 217) notes that the system resists the temptation to include materials that would fill significant gaps in a worker's education but which are not directly related to employment.

Concerning the connection between training and job opportunities, AMU skill centers are staffed by well-paid, experienced instructors who provide in-depth instruction utilizing modern equipment and state-of-the-art technology. But since the atmosphere in training centers is intended as much as possible to resemble a work environment rather than a school, instructors relate to trainees less like teachers to students than like supervisors to employees. Most instruction is one-on-one or in small groups rather than lectures in a classroom setting.

Participation in adult training is heavily subsidized by the state. Training programs are provided tuition-free. In addition, unemployed workers eligible for unemployment compensation who are undergoing training received a training grant in 1992 ranging up to SEK 564 per day, five days per week. To put this number in perspective, SEK 564 is about 86 percent of the daily earnings of an average industrial worker (Trehörning 1993, p. 63). Workers who are not eligible for unemployment compensation received from SEK 239 to SEK 338 per day in training grants.

Moving to the third evaluation criterion, an important feature of AMU training is the broad mix of clients passing through the system. The same training system serves not only displaced and economically disadvantaged workers, but also currently employed workers interested in enhancing their skills to qualify for a promotion or to make the transition to a job in a shortage occupation. Since AMU training is the most common way for Swedish workers to upgrade their vocational skills, employers are more willing to consider job applications from graduates of the public training system and to evaluate each applicant on his or her own merits rather than on a prejudged notion of what all graduates of a publicly sponsored program are prone to be like. Narrowly targeted employment and training programs, such as those common in the United States, frequently run into the problem that graduates are difficult to place, despite adequate job qualifications, because association with the public program itself stigmatizes them.[2]

The 1986 Reorganization

The fourth of the evaluation criteria listed at the beginning of this section raises the issue of how to guarantee that classroom training programs supply marketable skills. Berit Rollén (1988), Director General of the AMU, points out that prior to 1986, major decisions involving adult training had to be made by the Ministries of Labor and Education in Stockholm. This highly centralized decision-making process was slow and cumbersome, and civil servants in neither ministry had a strong incentive to see that skill centers delivered high-quality training at a reasonable cost. The demands placed on training centers by the recession of the early 1980s made it clear that reorganization was necessary to increase flexibility and control costs in meeting the needs of the labor market. In response to these demands, the AMU was created in 1986 with the mandate to operate the system of skill centers in a more flexible and cost-conscious manner. Flexibility in the new agency was assured by decentralizing decision making to the county level. The tripartite organization of county AMU boards ensures close cooperation with employers in overseeing the quality of services and developing new curricula.

To make the AMU more cost effective, the radical decision was made to terminate direct funding by the central government. Instead, the AMU was designed to be financially self-supporting in the sense that the agency must set prices for training services that cover costs. Rollén (1988) comments on the dramatic adjustment faced by 5,700 agency employees forced to shift from a bureaucratic culture to a free-enterprise way of thinking. To obtain funding, it was no longer necessary to develop skills in convincing central government ministries of the needs of the skill centers. Instead, funding required an ability to listen to customers and respond accordingly. It is interesting to note that this change in cultures required the establishment of training programs in economics and marketing for AMU employees.

The AMU's biggest customers are the National Labor Market Board's regional boards, which operate the Employment Service. The National Labor Market Board receives funds from the central government to buy training services, but these services need not be purchased from the AMU. Other suppliers of training services in Sweden are the municipal adult education authorities, upper secondary schools, universities, folk high schools, adult education associations, and private companies. Rollén (1988) states that during its first year of operation, the AMU obtained 95 percent of its revenues from the sale of training services to the National Labor Market Board. The other 5 percent resulted from sales to private-sector companies. Training programs sold to a particular company can be tailored to meet the specific needs of that company.

Before leaving this discussion of the Swedish system, the handful of quantitative evaluation studies surveyed by Björklund (1991) should at least be mentioned. Björklund provides an overview of eight evaluations, which includes one study each of mobility grants and temporary relief work, two studies of intensified employment services, and four studies of skill training. The evaluations of skill training yield generally negative results. The one study that does show significantly positive effects of training on earnings indicates that foreigners benefit from training to a much greater extent than native-born Swedes—a result that leads Björklund to question the author's model specification, since many trainees of foreign citizenship had unusually low registered incomes in the initial year of the study.

Of the remaining four studies, the most favorable results were obtained for the two evaluations of intensified employment services. One of these studies showed that intensified services in the town of Eskilstuna increased employment, reduced weeks of unemployment, and improved monthly earnings for those who found jobs. The other JSA study found a positive effect of employment services on spells of unemployment for laid-off mining workers.

British TECs and Performance-Based Contracting

While Sweden operates an adult training system independent of the educational infrastructure, it is more common for national governments to subsidize existing educational institutions to supply training services to targeted groups of workers. A case in point is Britain. Continuing to focus on the issue of how to ensure that training programs supply marketable skills, this section begins with an overview of the 1988 reform of Britain's training system. As with Sweden's 1986 reorganization of its adult training system, the primary objective of Britain's 1988 reform was decentralization in the provision of training services.

An essential part of the 1988 reform in Britain is the requirement that payments to local service providers be linked to achieving specified national goals; that is, service providers are to be subjected to performance standards. The fifth of the criteria included in the evaluation framework outlined in chapter 1 states that training programs should effectively utilize existing educational and training institutions. With this criterion in mind, the second part of this section examines available evidence on the labor market impact of performance standards. This evidence relates to the U.S. experience with JTPA Title II-A programs targeted to disadvantaged workers.

Overhauling Britain's Training System

In 1988, the British government presented to Parliament a White Paper, *Employment for the 1990s,* outlining what it termed a radical reform of the nation's training system (Department of Employment 1988). As noted earlier, the training of redundant workers in a particular British industry had been the responsibility of employers in that industry through industry-specific Industrial Training Boards. The 1988 reform makes training locally based rather than industry-based. The rationale for this policy decision is presented in the following passage from the White Paper (Department of Employment 1988, p. 29):

> Several countries, notably Germany and the United States, also have more locally based training systems with the close and continuous involvement of employers and employer institutions. Such systems are much more likely to be attuned to the shifting pattern of employer needs, and to individuals' requirements, than the more inflexible arrangements at national and industry levels. It is at the local level that jobs and the need for particular skills arise. It is at the local level that people live and work and would wish to be trained for new or changing jobs.

The authors of the White Paper are also explicit in their assumption that small businesses will be the primary source of new jobs during the 1990s.

The key element in the 1988 reform is the establishment of a national network of Training and Enterprise Councils (TECs) to plan and deliver training services and promote small business development at the local level. A TEC is created when a group of local employers enters into a contract with the national Department of Employment. The Department of Employment provides funding, while each TEC is responsible for (1) assessing skill needs within the local labor market, (2) developing a plan to provide training tailored to satisfy these local needs, and (3) contracting for training services. Actual training programs are typically provided by local educational and training institutions serving as TEC subcontractors.

TECs are given wide-ranging responsibility for operating the plethora of training initiatives developed at the national level during the 1980s. Out-of-school youth who are jobless are currently guaranteed a training slot in the Youth Training program and an allowance for the duration of their training. Unemployed adults are eligible for three programs. The Employment Training program offers adults who have been unemployed for six months or longer a training allowance equal to their weekly unemployment compensation benefits plus £10 per week. In addition, temporary public service employment is available to adults unemployed for six months or longer through the Employment Action program. (These two programs have recently been combined into the Training for Work program.) Finally, unemployed workers desiring to start up and run their own small businesses are eligible for counseling on business planning, formal courses in business skills, and financial assistance as part of the Business and Enterprise Services program. (This program replaces the earlier Enterprise Allowance Scheme.)[3] To oversee all of these initiatives, the 1988 White Paper envisioned a national network of approximately 100 TECs covering the whole of Great Britain.

The contracts entered into by TECs and the Department of Employment obligate each TEC to meet the guarantees given by the government to young people and the long-term unemployed. In addition, these contracts include performance management standards that specify quantitative outcome measures. Outcome measures mentioned by the Department of Employment (1988, p. 42) relate to target groups served, qualifications to be achieved, acceptable job placement rates, business support activities, and unit cost requirements. In turn, the contracts between TECs and local institutional training providers link provider payment to the achievement of specified targets, presumably targets similar to the performance standards TECs themselves are subject to.

The TEC approach to delivering training services has at least two desirable features. The first is that the existing educational and training infrastructure is used to supply skills training tailored to meet local demand. Second, access to training of employees of small firms should increase because the fixed costs of training programs can be spread over the greater number of workers included in the geographic region covered by a TEC. As discussed later in this chapter in connection with firm-based training, a major policy issue involved with adult training is how to go about increasing the incentive of small and medium-sized firms to provide their employees with training opportunities.

The primary question raised to date about the operation of the TEC network concerns funding. Dolton (1993, p. 1265) expresses the opinion that there is little hope TECs will solve the chronic British problem of underinvestment in skills training. As amplified by Lynch (1993a, p. 39), the limited government funding available must be used to meet income support guarantees of Youth Training and the multiple adult training programs. Additional funding to support actual training initiatives must come from private-sector employers, but they have little incentive to make substantial investments in their local TECs. As a consequence, at least some local business representatives on TECs are frustrated because they do not feel that they should be administering what is in effect an income-maintenance program.[4]

A related problem noted by Lynch (1993a, p. 39) involves large, multisite firms that find themselves dealing with many different local TECs over training policies covering the communities in which they own facilities. In this situation, substantial variation may exist in the training of workers across local labor markets, leading some large firms to leave the TEC network. Unfortunately, these are often the very firms with sufficient resources to make a difference in the adequacy of TEC funding.

Effectiveness of Performance Standards

Barnow (1992) emphasizes that the application of performance standards to employment and training programs—often termed "performance management"—needs to be carefully distinguished from the evaluation of such programs as described in chapter 3. Performance management is an ongoing process that provides continuous feedback to program managers and the agencies responsible for monitoring programs. Its objective is to make program managers accountable for achieving readily measurable program goals such as job placement rate, wage rates at placement, and per participant cost. In contrast, programs are typically evaluated only infrequently; and evaluators seek to measure the market value of the skills added by the program.

To solidify the distinction between performance management and program evaluation, suppose that a program goal is the achievement of a high postprogram job placement rate. In this case, program managers would receive the same performance management credit in either of two quite different situations: (1) the program is restricted to individuals judged to be nearly job-ready at admission, or (2) individuals with low initial qualifications are admitted into a program that successfully increases skills through retraining. Nevertheless, program evaluation should reveal that only in the second case does the program have a positive impact measured in terms of what it added to participants. The most common criticism levied against performance management is that it encourages "creaming" in the selection of program participants; that is, participants are enrolled who are likely to do well in the labor market even without program services. To counter this incentive, a performance management system must take appropriate account of participant characteristics.

The 1988 reform in Britain creating the nationwide system of TECs is based on the Private Industry Council (PIC) model established in the United States as part of the Job Training Partnership Act of 1982. As described in chapter 2, the poor public image of the Comprehensive Employment and Training Act program in the late 1970s and early 1980s led to the design of a new training program emphasizing greater delegation of authority from Washington, D.C. to the state and local levels, more involvement by private-sector employers, and greater accountability throughout the system. The resulting JTPA divides up the nation into more than 600 local areas called Service Delivery Areas (SDAs). Funding is passed through from the federal government to the states and then on to the local level by formula. Each SDA is overseen by a PIC, which may either run the local JTPA program itself or act as a board of directors to the program. A majority of the PIC membership must be members of the local business community, and SDAs generally contract with local institutional training providers to deliver training services. JTPA also established a formal performance management system to focus the attention of local programs on labor market outcomes and to monitor success.

The performance standards system is more highly developed for JTPA Title II-A programs directed at disadvantaged youth and adults than for the other JTPA titles.[5] For adults, the statute specifies goals to be achieved in terms of placement and retention in unsubsidized employment, increases in wage rates and earnings, and reductions in the number of families receiving welfare and in the payments received. For youth, performance goals include attainment of "employment competencies" established by the PIC; completion of elementary, secondary, or postsecondary education; and enrollment in other training programs, apprenticeships, or the armed forces. In addition, standards relating to costs are to be considered.

It is the task of the U.S. Department of Labor to establish performance measures capturing the basic goals of the statute and to issue national standards that governors may adopt. Because of the difficulty and expense of collecting preenrollment information on applicants, it was natural for the USDOL to specify performance standards based on absolute levels rather than gains in wages and employment and reductions in welfare receipt. But since PICs are penalized for not meeting performance standards and rewarded for keeping their cost per trainee low and their job placement rate high, there is a strong incentive for them to cream in the selection of trainees and to provide low-cost, quick-fix services such as job search assistance.[6] As a possible offset to this incentive, the JTPA statute authorizes the USDOL to issue "optional adjustment models" that governors may use to adjust the expected performance of SDAs for variation in participant characteristics and local labor market conditions. Barnow (1992, p. 299) observes that in recent years, the USDOL has made a strong effort to reduce creaming and the provision of quick-fix services through policy directives and speeches, elimination of cost criteria from national performance standards, and addition to optional adjustment models of explanatory variables that better reflect improvements in earning capacity.

There are presently only a handful of empirical studies examining the significance of creaming in JTPA Title II-A programs. Barnow (1992, pp. 297-99) reviews a study by Dickinson et al. (1988) in which the authors conclude that SDAs vary significantly in the degree to which they balance the requirement of meeting performance standards with other objectives. SDAs that place primary emphasis on achieving high scores in the performance standards system are likely to engage in creaming. On the other hand, SDAs that emphasize other objectives (i.e., commitments to serving certain types of clients and responding to local employer needs and interests) found the performance management system to be of little hindrance in achieving their goals because most SDAs have little trouble meeting the standards.

Two additional studies have become available. In the first, Anderson, Burkhauser, and Raymond (1993) use data collected for disadvantaged adults in Tennessee who were first enrolled in a Title II-A program in 1987. A unique feature of this state-sponsored data set is that it includes detailed information on the personal characteristics of JTPA trainees that can be linked to program information. To determine whether the difficult-to-train are underrepresented in the trainee population, the March 1986, 1987, and 1988 Current Population Surveys are used to obtain a random sample of the entire economically disadvantaged population of Tennessee.

The authors test the importance of creaming by jointly estimating a two-equation model of JTPA trainee selection and the probability of their job placement. The JTPA statute defines the economically disadvantaged to include individuals who are receiving welfare or food stamps, members of families with income below the poverty line, foster children receiving government assistance, and the handicapped. PICs are also permitted to assist those facing significant barriers to employment, including high school dropouts and drug addicts. Explanatory variables specified for the right-hand sides of the two equations include most of the JTPA-specified characteristics, including receipt of welfare (AFDC), Supplemental Security Income (SSI), and unemployment insurance benefits. The dependent variable measuring job placement is whether the trainee was placed in a job within three months of successfully completing training. Anderson, Burkhauser, and Raymond note that this standard is used by Tennessee to evaluate the performance of PICs.

Table 4.1 summarizes results obtained when the two equations are estimated jointly, thus controlling for both measured and unmeasured influences on the dependent variables. Beginning with the job placement column, the estimate -15.53 is read as saying that SSI receipt reduces the probability of a successful job placement by over 15 percentage points.[7] Other negative predictors of job placement are receipt of AFDC, urban residence, high school dropout, female, and age. (Age, education, and unemployment rate are all measured as continuous variables.) Better-educated individuals are more likely to be placed in jobs, as are UI recipients;[8] and a black skin color has no effect.

The selection equation shows a quite different pattern of results. Among the negative predictors of job placement, only SSI receipt and urban residence are found to negatively affect selection; and SSI has a much smaller estimated effect on selection than it does on placement. The AFDC, high school dropout, and female variables—all of which lower placement success—are found to have no statistically significant effect on selection. On the other hand, increased schooling, which increases placement success, also has a positive impact on the chance of selection into a JTPA program. The authors conclude (1993, p. 621) that if one's concept of creaming is underrepresentation of subgroups within the eligible population with lower expected job placement rates, then creaming does not seem to be as much of a problem as critics would suggest. Only people with physical handicaps (SSI recipients) and those handicapped by poor education are significantly less likely than others in the eligible population to be both placed in a job and served by JTPA.

Table 4.1 Marginal Impacts of Individual Characteristics on JTPA Program Selection and Subsequent Job Placement (percentage point changes at variable means)

Variable	Job placement	Selection
SSI	–15.53**	–3.16**
AFDC	–13.85**	0.85
Urban	–11.63**	–10.38**
High school dropout	–8.26**	–0.40
Education (1 year)	1.20**	0.76**
UI	5.98**	0.79
Female	–5.89**	–0.54
Age (1 year)	–1.03**	–0.28*
Black	–0.48	0.35
Unemployment rate (1 point)	–0.21	--

SOURCE: Anderson, Burkhauser, and Raymond (1993, table 3).
**and * indicate statistical significance at the 1 percent and 5 percent levels, respectively.

A second study (Craig 1993) proceeds by linking a 1986 survey carried out by the National Commission on Employment Policy (NCEP) to a random sample of young adults taken from the National Longitudinal Survey of Youth (NLSY). NLSY data include detailed information on participation in government training programs, and the longitudinal character of the data permits measurement of earnings changes.

From the NCEP survey, Craig specifies the following four policy variables:

AWARDSIZE = fraction of the maximum 6 percent of the state budget dedicated to incentive awards.

CARROT = number of performance standards that must be passed to qualify for an award.

STICK = number of standards that may be failed before sanctioning is required.

ADJ = whether a state has a procedure to allow a SDA to apply for an adjustment in USDOL performance standards for unexpected difficulties associated with clients served, services offered, or economic conditions.

Controlling for variation in local labor market conditions and differences in personal characteristics, effects of the policy variables are analyzed using two models. The first model assesses whether higher incentives lead to more creaming in the enrollment process, while the second investigates whether change in average earnings measured before and after training is larger in states where there are greater incentives.

Beginning with the enrollment model, the test of the creaming hypothesis involves coefficient estimates on the interaction terms between work experience (defined as fraction of time spent working since the respondent left school) and the four policy variables. This test produces a number of estimates to be assessed and reconciled with each other, but the results seem to suggest that only specifications involving CARROT and ADJ are statistically significant. In particular, the interaction between CARROT and work experience is positive, indicating that in states with greater risk of not meeting performance standards there is a tendency to select more job-ready individuals. The interaction between ADJ and work experience is negative, suggesting that in states with an adjustment policy less-experienced individuals are selected. Both of these results are consistent with creaming.

Nevertheless, Craig comments that these results for enrollment might be interpreted as suggesting that higher incentives induce SDAs to provide services to those for whom value-added is higher and who might in fact be more-experienced individuals. The earnings change model is intended to test whether JTPA incentives increase value-added performance and not just creaming. Again, the number of coefficients estimated and the imprecision of the estimates make the results difficult to assess. Craig consequently provides simulation results for a variety of scenarios. Two patterns that emerge from the simulations are that (1) higher incentives lead to a rise in the value-added from training programs, even though the incentives are based on post-training outcome measures, and (2) states with adjustment policies have a higher value-added than those without. Consistent with the results of Anderson, Burkhauser, and Raymond (1993), Craig's findings appear to suggest that performance standards need not lead to creaming by program managers.

Firm-Based Training

Numerous studies estimating earnings functions for American workers have shown that firm-based training has a higher return than other forms of postschool training. Presumably this is because the training is linked more directly to skills needed in the workplace. An important issue in the provision of firm-based training is that a firm investing in training risks having skilled employees hired away by other firms that have not shared in the cost of training. This problem is commonly known as "pirating" or "poaching"; the consequence is that private-sector employers will underinvest in worker training. Underinvesting in training is especially likely to be the case for small and medium-sized firms.[9] Lynch (1992) presents evidence for young noncollege graduates that employer-provided training in the United States is limited to quite firm-specific skills, since such training from a previous employer never significantly affects current wages.

This section begins by examining two countries—Germany and Japan—in which firm-based training is much more prevalent than it is in the United States. The discussion in chapter 1 of the final criterion in the evaluation framework sketched the argument that it is increasingly important for American workers to be able to think creatively and solve problems, work effectively in teams, adapt flexibly to rapid shifts in product demand, and engage in lifetime learning. Germany and Japan are often presented as being far ahead of the United States in developing these productive characteristics in their workers. This section also discusses the training tax recently enacted in Australia to stimulate firm-based training. Using British data, the final part of the section presents some empirical evidence on the importance of formal skill certification in firm-based training programs.

German Apprenticeship Training

Chapter 2 provided a brief overview of the German dual system of apprenticeship training. As described there, the dual system is based on a partnership between schools, trade unions, employers, and the government. At the federal level, the government establishes guidelines for standard-setting, training regulations, and curricula for off-the-job training. These guidelines are translated by individual states (or *Lands*) into specific regulations and course curricula, which in turn are implemented in light of regional needs by self-governing Chambers of Industry and Commerce. German Chambers are organizations of employers. Unlike the voluntary promotional organizations we are familiar with in this country, however, German Chambers are quasi-public agencies that firms must join and to which they must pay dues. Chambers play the critical roles of accrediting firms to provide training and of assessing the qualifications of program graduates to receive vocational certification. There is no national system for assessing apprentice qualifications, but Harhoff and Kane (1993, p. 11) point out that examinations developed by Chambers focus on general skills, and that firms with consistently low pass rates may have their accreditation removed.

In 1988, about 72 percent of all school leavers entered the dual system to acquire training in 378 classified occupations (Her Majesty's Inspectorate 1991, p. 9). Length of apprenticeship training varies from two to three and one-half years, and apprentices complement their training in employers' workplaces with one or two days a week of off-the-job training at state-funded vocational schools or *Berufsschules*. Up to 40 percent of vocational school classwork is intended to develop a broad range of skills including mathematics, politics, languages, and communications. A good grounding in basic education curricula is viewed as important in helping apprentices develop skills that go beyond those required for a specific job or task. The remaining 60 percent or more of classwork provides theoretical education to complement the practical training provided by training firms.

The 378 classified occupations include many that Americans consider unskilled. Using retail shoe sales as an example, Hamilton (1990, pp. 143-44) argues that the German shoe salesperson who is "overtrained" from a U.S. perspective is not only quite competent in selling shoes, but he or she also has the basic qualifications to operate a shoe store and is prepared to take this step if the opportunity should arise. In contrast, he suggests, the American propensity to undertrain sales and clerical workers devalues work done by people without college degrees and leaves most of them with few options for upward occupational mobility. On this theme, Marshall and Tucker (1992, p. xviii) write that

> [Americans] who do not have and are not on their way to getting a baccalaureate degree—more than 70 percent of the population—are held in low regard, have little claim on the nation's goods and services, and are in no position to make the contribution at work of which they are capable. . . . In comparing our human-resources system for our front-line workers point for point with that of our competitors, we find a staggering cumulative deficit.

Although the Vocational Training Act of 1969 guarantees training to young Germans accepted into an apprenticeship program, it does not ensure permanent employment with the training employer at the end of the apprenticeship. About 59 percent of apprentices leave the employer with whom they trained and seek employment elsewhere. Since employer participation in the system is voluntary and trained apprentices are not bound to training firms, an important question concerns the incentive for firms to provide training. After all, there are no direct financial incentives for firms to offer training, and apprenticeship training is costly since employers pay trainees an allowance and bear the direct costs of training. Hamilton (1990: 35) reports that in the early 1970s, the net expense of an apprentice after subtracting his or her productive work is as much as $3,000 annually for large industrial and commercial firms, somewhat less for smaller firms, and half as much or less for craft firms. Prewo (1993) calculates that in 1991 German firms spent $10,500 per apprentice after netting out the trainees' contribution to output. Detailed calculations provided by Harhoff and Kane (1993, p. 8) indicate that as of 1980 the net cost of training an apprentice was about $5,991 and $9,381, respectively, in the craft and industrial sectors (in 1990 U.S. dollars). Soskice (1994, p. 36) reports net annual apprenticeship costs (in 1980 Deutschmarks) of DM 14,310 and DM 10,963, respectively, for industrial/commercial-sector firms of more than 1,000 and less than 1,000 employees and of DM 7,248 for smaller craft firms.

The report of Her Majesty's Inspectorate (1991, p. 13) indicates, in fact, that most German firms choose not to be training firms. Soskice (1994, pp. 35-37) adds the information that the probability a firm offers apprenticeship training is directly related to its size measured in terms of number of employees. In particular, a large majority of firms with less than 10 employees do not provide apprenticeships, while fewer than 1 percent of firms with more than 500 employees fail to train apprentices.

Among those firms that do provide training, small *Handwerk* establishments located largely in the crafts sector can be distinguished from large *Industrie* firms in the industrial and commercial sectors by the share of training costs borne by employers. Steedman (1993, pp. 1287-88) points out that in *Handwerk* establishments, trainees bear a large share of training costs by accepting a wage well below the full value of their marginal product.[10] These establishments provide about a third of all apprenticeship slots. In larger capital-intensive *Industrie* companies, on the other hand, she suggests that it can safely be assumed that there is a substantial net cost to the firm.

So why do *Industrie* firms pay for what appears to be transferable training? Her Majesty's Inspectorate (1991, p. 3) points out several reasons for companies to become accredited to offer training, and several other authors have also recently attempted to come to grips with this question (see Bishop 1994, pp. 19-26; Harhoff and Kane 1993; Lynch 1994; Soskice 1994; and Steedman 1993, pp. 1287-88). The reasons discussed in the literature appear to boil down to essentially four factors.

The first concerns turnover. Employers will not invest in training unless they believe that trained workers will remain with the firm long enough for them to recoup their investment. Bishop (1994, pp. 20-21) reports that from the mid-1980s to the early 1990s, only 38 to 41 percent of American workers had been on their current job for more than five years. The percentages for German workers for about the same time period are substantially higher at between 59 and 63 percent. (The percentages for Japanese workers are higher still at from 63 to 67 percent.) Clearly contributing to the longer job tenure of German workers relative to Americans are the greater legal and contractual obstacles to layoffs and dismissals in Germany. Also potentially important is the role of the German apprenticeship system in generating information that reduces the importance of job shopping and tryout hiring in the youth labor market.

A second factor involves screening. Only accredited training firms can accept apprentices, and firms with an established reputation for training receive many more applications for apprenticeship positions than they can accommodate. This puts training firms in a position to select those applicants who appear to be the most trainable and motivated. In addition, many firms train more young people than they plan to hire, allowing them to engage in a second round of screening by choosing the most qualified of program graduates for permanent employment. Deciding not to hire an apprentice is much cheaper than dismissing a regular employee, which allows apprentices to serve as a buffer for adjusting employment levels to short-term fluctuations in demand (Harhoff and Kane 1993, pp. 16-17). Since the national system of wage determination keeps wage differentials small, the chance that a trained worker will be bid away by a competing firm is minimal. Indeed, Soskice (1994, pp. 35-37) argues that an employer seeking to expand its workforce by hiring away skilled workers trained by other firms runs the considerable risk that the pool of available workers will be largely limited to "lemons," that is, workers the training company did not wish to retain.

A third reason firms seek accreditation as training employers stems from the value German society attaches to having a highly skilled workforce. As described by Hamilton (1990, p. 34), Germany's prosperity depends heavily upon the ability to export; and Germany competes successfully with the United States and Japan for world leadership in the export of industrial products with a third of the U.S. and half the Japanese population. Since apprenticeship training is widely regarded as the source of Germany's international competitiveness, a company's public image is enhanced by being accredited as a training firm. In effect, a company that trains apprentices is certified as producing a high-quality product because the public is aware of the machinery for controlling the quality of apprenticeship training. Hamilton (1990, p. 36) makes this point in the following description of a full-page ad for Lufthansa Airlines in the popular magazine *Der Spiegel*:

> [The ad] shows four apprentices clustered around a jet engine attending raptly to an adult worker's instructions. Lest there is any doubt about what is happening, the words "Lufthansa Training" are visible on the fuselage in the background. The caption reads, "Whoever wishes to go high needs a solid foundation." The double meaning is obvious to any German reader: (1) These young men, who wish to make something of themselves as airplane mechanics, need the solid foundation of apprenticeship training; (2) You, the airline passenger, who wish to fly, need the solid foundation provided by Lufthansa's high-quality aircraft maintenance, which is assured by first-rate training.

Finally, important institutions that make up Germany's industrial relations system may also play a role in accounting for employers' willingness to pay for general training. Lynch (1994, pp. 66, 79) suggests that local Chambers use moral suasion within the business community to protect firms that train a large number of workers from excessive poaching. In addition, Harhoff and Kane (1993), Rogers and Streeck (1994, pp. 111-12), and Soskice (1994, pp. 42-43) point out that, among other functions, works councils monitor employer compliance with Germany's system of apprenticeship training. This responsibility includes checking employers to make sure that nationally standardized curricula have been implemented in the workplace, that apprentices are not used unduly for production, that the skills taught to apprentices are portable and not primarily workplace-specific, and that competing firms are prevented from poaching workers trained elsewhere.

Before turning to the Japanese model of firm-based training, two additional issues regarding the German apprenticeship system remain to be considered. The first concerns a principal criticism of the system—its rigidity. Rigidity in the German system is manifest in the large number of finely divided occupational specialties and the resistance to change inherent in the complex system regulating apprenticeship training. Hamilton (1990, pp. 148-49) illustrates both of these points using the example of metalworkers' training. He reports that some forty-two different metal-working occupations were recently consolidated into just six broadly defined training fields. This consolidation had the desirable impact of increasing both the universality of training and the flexibility of trained workers. Nevertheless, the consolidation took place only after eight long years of negotiations among employers, unions, and the government.

Considered at greater length is a second issue involving the transferability of the German apprenticeship system to the United States. Harhoff and Kane (1993) are not optimistic on this issue, taking the position that deeply rooted labor market institutions rule out the possibility that U.S. employers would be willing to accept part of the cost of general training. In particular, they suggest that relative to German firms, the incentive for American employers to invest in worker training is low because (1) unions cannot be counted on to restrict poaching by competing firms, (2) American wages are more flexible and firing costs are low, and (3) mobility costs are lower in the United States.

On the other hand, Hamilton (1990, p. 152) comments that the replacement of the traditional German model of full-time workplace training at age 15 or 16 with the modern dual training system makes some form of apprenticeship training a much more viable option for American workers. The reason is the strong commitment of American society to universal schooling; and Lynch (1993b, p. 1301) notes that community colleges, in particular, are increasingly linking up with local employers to develop technical courses designed to equip students with appropriate vocational skills.

Indeed, available anecdotal evidence suggests that German firms are successfully establishing transplant facilities in the United States and employing American workers. What appears to have happened is that ten years of sustained growth, continuing through the 1991-92 global recession, left Germans in the enviable position of enjoying shorter workweeks and more holidays and vacation days per year than workers in any other industrialized country in the world (see Benjamin 1993). At the same time, Germany has the less enviable status of being among the world leaders in average labor costs per hour. Rapidly rising labor costs have provided German employers with a strong incentive to overcome their traditional reluctance to transfer production abroad. Examples include the highly publicized expansions of BMW and Mercedes-Benz in South Carolina and Alabama, respectively.

Writing in *The Wall Street Journal*, McCarthy (1993) reports that more than 200 German companies have established facilities in North and South Carolina. These two states are the leading magnets for German industrial firms. As he notes, the Carolinas are not an international transportation hub, and they lack the concentration of research universities that exist in New England and California. Nevertheless, German firms apparently find that high-quality vocational/technical schools and community colleges and malleable southern workers more than compensate for higher transportation costs and the absence of close proximity to research universities. Osterman and Batt (1993) provide a useful description of the extensive and accessible community college systems in both North and South Carolina and the long-term commitment of the systems in both states to vocational training programs tailored to specific employers.

An interesting example of the transferability of the German dual system to this country is the apprenticeship program first developed in 1980 by the German-owned Stihl Incorporated, a manufacturer of chain saws and lawn trimmers and blowers (see Salwen 1993). Located in Virginia Beach, Virginia, Stihl established a dual system apprenticeship program after it was unable to hire skilled craftsmen to build the precision machines needed to make finely tuned parts for its motors. Over time, the Stihl program has evolved into an 8,000-hour apprenticeship combining shop-floor training with a twenty-eight-credit curriculum at the local Tidewater Community College that ranges from blueprint reading to industrial mathematics. As is common in German apprenticeship programs transplanted to the United States, Stihl managers worked with community college teachers to design course content to meet Stihl's requirements. Admission to the program requires that trainees pass a basic mathematics test, followed by interviews with company officials and a manual skills examination.

Lifetime Learning in Japan

While a German-style apprenticeship training system fosters the identification of workers with a particular occupation, the organization of work in Japan depends on the attachment and loyalty of workers to employers. The description in chapter 2 emphasized five main features of the Japanese firm-based training model:

- Close coordination with the education system facilitates a continuous flow of workers who possess solid basic skills and a willingness to work together and learn on the job.
- Life-long training achieved primarily by rotating workers through various jobs within the firm. This training produces skills that are intrafirm-general but interfirm-specific.
- Senior workers play a major role in training younger, less-experienced workers.
- Workers share information and responsibility within work teams.
- Broadly trained workers are retained on payrolls in times of declines in demand, especially by large firms. Breadth of training makes it possible for employers to shift redundant workers to jobs in another department, a subsidiary, or even another firm.

In a recent study, Hashimoto (1994) offers a useful theory that serves as an organizing framework for understanding Japanese firm-based training. The theory focuses on the practices of Japanese firms that lower the costs of investment in technical skills and, of equal importance, in employment relations. It is training in employment relations that allows Japanese workers to communicate effectively with co-workers and to share information rather than to hoard it to their own individual benefit (a problem known as "opportunism"). Hashimoto (1994, p. 125) contrasts the attitudes of Japanese and American workers toward sharing information and responsibilities in the following passage:

> Imagine a situation, for example, in which a supervisor asks a subordinate worker to fix a glitch in the production process. A Japanese worker would see such a request as an opportunity to prove his value to the firm. He would take it upon himself to ask all conceivable parties for advice and information, and those asked, in

> turn, would be trained to provide help willingly on the spot. Should he fail to come up with a solution, he would not be penalized. Instead, if he solves, say, eight of ten problems, he will gain respect and his prospects of promotion are improved. In turn, others depend on him, when called on, to provide help. In contrast, an American worker is said to be reluctant to seek advice unless his superior specifically requests such action, and many of those contacted would be equally reluctant to cooperate by providing help and advice.

Key to this theory is the linkage between schools and firms. The production of graduates who are homogeneous in terms of mastery of basic academic subjects allows the firm to concentrate on providing firm-specific technical training in the workplace. Indeed, solid basic education permits self-study to play an important role in imparting technical training; that is, workers can be expected to study manuals or books on their own. In the hiring process, schools further reduce employer costs by performing much of the screening function through "semiformal" relationships between firms and specific high schools.

Likewise, training in employment relations received in school provides the basis for workers' ability to function in a team-production setting and to teach technical skills to younger, more junior employees. Hashimoto notes that the Japanese tradition of hierarchical teaching has carried over to modern industrial training. Employers can count on the cooperation of senior employees in training subordinates because of this tradition, which is reinforced by making a worker's ability to instruct more junior co-workers a key criterion for promotion. An environment of "lifetime" employment guarantees the senior worker that the newly trained worker will not be a threat to the trainer's job security. In turn, a lifetime employment commitment is rational for employers because broadly trained workers do not defect to other firms, and the training provider is allowed to capture the returns on even general forms of training. Brown et al. (1993, p. 433) add that the linking of pay to tenure, skills, and performance rather than job categories, coupled with a well-developed promotion ladder within nonmanagement ranks, gives rise to a steeper age-earnings profile for frontline Japanese workers than exists in most other industrialized countries.

To summarize, the essence of Japanese firm-based training is that homogeneity in basic skills, willingness to learn and to teach others, and the ability to function as part of a team all have the effect of lowering training costs. How transferable is this model to an American workforce, whose basic academic and technical skills are much more diverse and generally lower than those of the Japanese? Hashimoto (1994) examines this question in the context of Japanese automobile transplants in the United States. Transplant firms studied are Diamond-Star Motors (a joint venture between Mitsubishi Motors and Chrysler), Honda, Mazda, Subaru-Isuzu, and Toyota. Nissan refused to be interviewed.

Hashimoto found that the first problem transplant firms faced was assembling their workforces. Because the American educational system could not be relied upon to perform much of the screening function, firms had to develop their own screening procedures. These procedures usually were based on a high school diploma or its equivalent and made use of a battery of tests intended to measure mechanical aptitude, facility in assembling and disassembling simple mechanisms, and ability to work cooperatively with others. Young persons with no previous experience in the auto industry were preferred for assembly-line jobs because of transplants' desire to train, rather than to retrain, workers in their own ways of operating.

Once hired, employees of transplant companies received on-the-job training supplemented by formal courses which, in the case of Honda and Toyota, were taught at training centers located adjacent to the plants. Formal training included courses in employment relations as well as technical skills. One difference from the firm-based training model developed for Japanese workers is that greater heterogeneity in basic skills means that self-study is not as practical for Americans. Instead, Hashimoto notes that training at transplants made extensive use of videos and pictures, as opposed to written materials, combined with a great deal of hands-on training.

Japanese automobile transplants are still young in the United States. To date, however, Japanese firms appear to have successfully overcome the different constraints involved in hiring and training American workers. For example, Dertouzos, Lester, and Solow (1989, p. 20) conclude that Japanese transplants in the United States have come close to the quality and productivity of the best plants in Japan. In a recent article, titled "For Japan's Economy, a Call to Arms," Ohmae (1994) suggests that Japanese transplant operations in the United States produce goods of the same quality as in Japan but 30 percent cheaper.

The Australian Training Guarantee

In 1990, Australia adopted for the first time a training tax imposed on employers called the Training Guarantee. All Australian firms with payrolls greater than $200,000 (Australian) were required to spend 1.0 percent of their payroll on structured training programs in 1991, with the tax rate rising to 1.5 percent beginning in 1992. A program qualifies as a "structured" training program if (1) its objectives are clearly defined before the program begins, and (2) the skills to be acquired are clearly identified, as are the means of imparting these skills. The focus of the Training Guarantee is on formal training. For on-the-job training to qualify, there must be a period of instruction followed by a period of closely supervised work.

Firms that fail to spend the required percentage of their payroll on structured training must forfeit the difference between 1.5 percent and what they spent to the government, which, in turn, uses the tax revenues to finance additional training activities. The basic rationale for the training tax is the perception that employers needed to take greater responsibility for meeting their own training requirements. As noted by Osterman and Batt, (1993, p. 469), increased training provided by firms for whom the training tax constraint is binding has the desirable impact of enlarging the overall level of training received by the nation's workers without the problems inherent in designing and delivering government programs.

Lynch (1993a, pp. 33-37) summarizes the major arguments leading to the passage of the Training Guarantee. The first is the reluctance of Australian employers to invest in training because of binding minimum wages and other rigidities established in centralized collective bargaining contracts. These rigidities make it difficult for firms to share the costs of general and specific training with their employees. In addition, Australian employers had the usual concern about competing firms poaching skilled workers in whom they had invested. At the same time, relatively flat wage profiles imposed by collective bargaining reduce the returns to training from the worker's perspective, thus weakening his or her incentive to invest in training off-the-job.

Two important policy questions associated with a training tax are (1) how to specify in practice the training expenditures that meet the fixed percentage requirement and monitor this requirement, and (2) whether the tax increases training provided by small firms and the access to training of unskilled workers. Concerning the first issue, Lynch (1993a, pp. 36-37) describes how Australia has implemented a 50 percent rule in deciding whether a particular expenditure should be allowed to count toward the 1.5 percent requirement. That is, eligible training programs must have at least 50 percent of program expenditures devoted to training, as opposed to pure productive work or social or recreational activities. For example, firms may hire eligible trainers or train their own trainers. In either case, the entire salary of a trainer can be counted as a training expenditure if he or she spends 50 percent of his or her time doing training. Important outstanding questions include how to define the qualifications of trainers whose salaries count toward the fixed percentage requirement, and how to restrain firms from overstating the training component of a particular program or activity. Lynch (1993a, p. 37) mentions that the government is currently in the process of establishing nationally recognized standards and certificates to eliminate the use of trainers approved through disreputable mail-order firms. Clearly, there is the potential for the government to feel obliged to create a sizable bureaucracy to monitor employer compliance. The alternative is to stimulate creative tax avoidance on the part of employers.

Evidence on the bureaucracy issue as well as on the incidence of training by firm size and skill level is available for the French training tax imposed on all firms with more than 10 employees.[11] Enacted in 1971, the training tax obligated every French employer to spend 0.8 percent of its payroll on continuing education and training of its employees or to pay a tax equal to the difference between its mandated and actual training expenditures. The tax rate was raised to 1.0 percent in 1974, to 1.1 percent in 1977, and to 1.2 percent in 1987. Since January 1993, the mandated spending rate has been 1.4 percent. This tax rate is applied to expenditures on formal training programs provided either directly by the firm or by a postsecondary educational institution. Bishop (1993b, p. 286) notes that the bureaucracy needed to monitor compliance has been kept to a minimum, adding that the auditing of company reports of training expenditures requires a staff of only 120 controllers for the entire nation.

The French experience relating to the distribution of training is less encouraging. Bishop (1993b, table 1) reports that regardless of occupation, the incidence of training increases with firm size. In 1990, training incidence ranged from 8 percent of all employees of small firms of 10-19 employees up to 53 percent of all employees in the largest firm size category (2000+ employees). Within each firm size category, in addition, unskilled operatives received the least training. Among firms in the 500-1999 size category, for example, the incidence of training ranged from 15 percent for unskilled operatives to 55 percent for supervisors and technicians and 62 percent for managers and professionals. Bishop (1993b, p. 290) explains that the training tax creates a strong incentive for companies to substitute formal training for informal training such as that acquired through the Japanese *kaizen* process. The kind of informal training that small employers excel at providing—close supervision and informal training by the owner—is not eligible for the subsidy. Thus small firms must join together in cooperative efforts to achieve the economies of scale necessary to make formal training feasible.

There appears to be a social consensus in France favoring the training tax. This includes a lack of vocal employer opposition. In Australia, on the other hand, the Training Guarantee has turned out to be generally unpopular. Employers dislike the paper work and threat of government interference. There is also resentment that the levy must be met even by unprofitable firms. Unions have become disillusioned because the training mandate has failed to provide the hoped for enhancement of the skills of production workers. And there is the continuing concern that too many employers are meeting their Training Guarantee requirements with expenditures on executive training programs that often have a large recreational component. Although there appears to be considerable sentiment to abolish the levy, major provisions of the 1994 amendment to the 1990 Training Guarantee Act are limited to (1) extending the ability of a group of firms to be treated as a single entity for the purpose of defining a training employer, (2) expanding the per apprentice allowance that may be treated as an allowable training expenditure, and (3) allowing an excess in Training

Guarantee expenditures in one year to offset a shortfall in expenditures the next year.

Evidence on Skill Certification in Britain

Earlier discussion in this chapter of the Swedish adult training system and German apprenticeship training mentioned the role of skill certification in conveying information to potential employers on the skills possessed by program graduates. Nationally recognized credentials should have the advantage of enhancing the transferability and hence the value to the individual of vocational training. In addition, Baily, Burtless, and Litan (1993, pp. 126-28) note that a national system of skill certification might also allow the government to insist that before any training provider—whether private-sector employers or nonprofit and for-profit training institutions—is compensated, their graduates be required to meet certification standards. As described by Heckman, Roselius, and Smith (1993), however, a disadvantage of a formal testing system is that teaching in training programs might rapidly become directed toward performing well on a general standardized test rather than toward specific job-related skills needed in the local labor market or by the firm providing the training.

Blanchflower and Lynch (1994) furnish empirical evidence for American and British youth on the labor market impact of apprenticeship training and, for British youth, of nationally recognized skill certification. But before delving into their results, some additional background information on British youth training programs and the vocational qualification system is helpful. Chapter 2 noted that during the 1970s, the principal institutional sources of training for British youth were apprenticeships and company-sponsored training organized under the Industrial Training Board structure. Although apprenticeship training was not as widespread in Britain then as it is in Germany today, it was distinctly more common than in the United States. Most apprenticeships in Britain provided a mix of training in the workplace and day release programs operated at local colleges. On average, apprenticeships lasted 43 months for males and 34 months for females. Company-sponsored training programs were typically split between colleges and employer training centers and usually involved the full-time participation of trainees. These courses were much shorter in duration than apprenticeships, and well over half were completed in under six months.

A strong link existed between British apprenticeship training and further qualifications attained by passing an examination. Blanchflower and Lynch (1994) report that approximately nine out of ten workers who completed an apprenticeship also obtained some kind of skill certification during or at the end of their program. Two types of certification—Cities and Guilds-Craft and Cities and Guilds-Advanced—account for nearly 60 percent of all those obtained by apprentices. These are qualifications typically obtained by craft workers. Females were less likely than males to obtain apprenticeship training and, among apprenticeship program graduates, females were less likely to obtain skill certification. Apprenticeship training for females tended to be concentrated in hairdressing.

The National Council for Vocational Qualifications (NCVQ) was established in 1986 with the objective of rationalizing the existing diverse set of vocational qualifications. Within each major industry, the NCVQ encouraged representatives of employers, unions, and professional groups to establish standards of workplace competence. NCVQ accreditation is based on these competency standards, subject to the requirement that training be of sufficient breadth to be the basis of further skill development (Department of Employment 1988, pp. 32-33). The National Vocational Qualification (NVQ) standard established for each occupation is structured as a hierarchy of five levels of performance. At the low end, Level 1 measures competence in the performance of a range of work activities, most of which are routine and predictable. At the high end, Level 5 requires competence in applying a range of fundamental principles and complex techniques in a broad and unpredictable set of workplace contexts. Substantial personal autonomy is often a feature of Level 5 skills, along with significant responsibility for the allocation of resources and personal responsibility for the design, planning, execution, and evaluation of workplace tasks. One application of the NVQ structure is that employer-led TECs may use NVQs to contract out training programs to institutional training providers and to measure the performance of these subcontractors.

As described in chapter 2, the apprenticeship training system in place under the Industrial Training Board structure was dismantled by the Thatcher government during the 1980s and replaced by the government-sponsored Youth Training Scheme. YTS, in turn, was later replaced by the current Youth Training program. Blanchflower and Lynch (1994) argue, nevertheless, that YTS was introduced with limited empirical information for British youths on the impact of traditional apprenticeship and employer-provided training programs that were replaced. They also suggest that the recent surge in interest in apprenticeships among U.S. policy makers can be informed by the British apprenticeship experience, even though it is less well known than the German system, because of the greater similarity of the institutional structures of the two countries.[12]

In their empirical analysis, Blanchflower and Lynch (1994) make use of two large microeconomic data sets gathered for American and British youth. The data sets are the U.S. National Longitudinal Survey of Youth and the British National Child Development Survey (NCDS).

Table 4.2 Estimated Impact on Hourly Earnings of Apprenticeship Training in the U.K., Noncollege Graduates, 1981 (*t*-statistics in parentheses)

Training variables	All workers	Males	Females
In an apprenticeship	–0.128	–0.093	–0.192
	(1.94)	(1.19)	(1.44)
Completed apprenticeship:			
No qualifications[a]	0.023	0.018	0.018
	(3.79)	(2.26)	(1.70)
City & Guild Craft	0.042	0.044	–0.109
	(2.12)	(1.95)	(1.57)
City & Guild Advanced	0.072	0.072	0.027
	(3.75)	(3.30)	(0.27)
Training with current firm	0.024	0.018	0.026
	(2.97)	(1.51)	(2.26)

SOURCE: Blanchflower and Lynch (1994, table 8.6).

a. Includes those with all other qualifications escept City & Guild Craft and City & Guild Advanced.

U.S. data show that apprenticeship training has a large impact on earnings, especially for males. Using the NCDS sample, table 4.2 presents estimates of the impact of training on 1981 wages controlling for a number of factors that might also affect earnings, including ability test scores. The negative sign of the estimates in the first row suggests that British apprentices share in the cost of their training with employers. Completion of an apprenticeship is seen in the next row to raise earnings by about 2 percent for both males and females. (The "no qualifications" category includes all other qualifications apart from the City & Guild categories.) At least for males, however, the wage gain to successful apprentices is even higher when the gains associated with skill certification are added. Among males, a City and Guild Craft certificate conveyed a further gain of 4 percent, while a City and Guild Advanced certificate added a 7 percent gain. In contrast to the apprenticeship results, the impact of firm-sponsored training shown in the last row is larger for females than males.

Blanchflower and Lynch conclude from their results that if the current Youth Training program is to serve as an adequate replacement for apprenticeship training in terms of meeting the skill needs of employers, then a nationally recognized system of certifying skills should be implemented as part of it. Similarly, they recommend that nationally recognized qualifications should be part of any program intended to expand apprenticeship training in the United States.

A related study by Dolton, Makepeace, and Treble (1994) examines the effect of government-subsidized training provided through the Youth Training Scheme. Using data for about 10,000 16-to-19-year olds between 1985-86 and 1988-89, the authors estimate an earnings equation in which YTS participation is interacted with apprenticeship training, off-the-job training, and no training. Keeping in mind that the data allow only the short-run effects of training to be measured, their results are not particularly supportive of the YTS program. On-the-job training is found to increase the earnings of both males and females relative to youth who received no training at all, but only for those respondents who did not participate in YTS. In contrast to the findings of Blanchflower and Lynch, apprenticeship training appears to *lower* earnings, particularly for respondents who received apprenticeship training under the YTS program. The authors (1994, p. 269) remark, however, that this result is not unexpected, because many apprentices had not completed their training by the time earnings were measured. Finally, YTS training not accompanied by apprenticeship or off-the-job training decreases the earnings of women and has no statistically significant effect for men. It is also interesting to note that receipt of a vocational qualification certificate is found to have no statistically significant effect on the earnings of either young men or young women.

Summary

This chapter discussed three models of the provision of adult training services in terms of the criteria sketched in chapter 1, with special attention given the criterion that training must provide marketable skills. Considered first was the government training model in place in Sweden. The Swedish adult training system is well known for the breadth of its curricula, its open entry, the flexibility of its modular system in individualizing study plans, the quality of its instructors and its modern equipment, and the large fraction of the adult population it serves. Participation of Swedish employers and union officials in overseeing program quality and developing new curricula has traditionally focused the attention of program managers on providing job-ready graduates. Even so, the 1986 reorganization of the training system created a new agency—the National Employment Training Board—with the mandate to operate Sweden's nationwide system of skill training centers on a financially self-sustaining basis.

The second training model discussed in the chapter is characterized by local employer leadership in utilizing community educational institutions to provide training within a decentralized decision-making system. This employer-led/school-based model was implemented in Britain in a fundamental reform of that nation's training system in 1988. At the heart of the 1988 reform is the mandate given to groups of local employers organized into Training and Enterprise Councils to plan and deliver training services. To ensure accountability in meeting national policy goals, TECs are subject to performance standards; and available evidence on the effectiveness of performance standards obtained for the JTPA Title II-A program in the United States is reviewed. Despite the common criticism that performance standards lead to creaming in the selection of program clients, the JTPA evidence suggests that the incentive of program operators to cream can be controlled by careful specification of the clients to be served.

Finally, the firm-based training model was described as it has evolved in the German dual system of apprenticeship training and the Japanese lifetime employment system. In both nations, a tradition emphasizing the importance of a highly skilled workforce reinforced by the requirements of export-led economies has resulted in systems that provide workplace training opportunities to substantial fractions of the working populations. Youth are the primary beneficiaries of in-house training in Germany, while on-the-job training is more likely to continue over the working lifetime in Japan. Careful attention was paid to the incentive structures existing in each country to induce employers to provide workplace training.

A tradition of firm-based training does not exist in this country. Nevertheless, anecdotal evidence on the experience to date of German and Japanese transplant firms in the United States suggests that the basic approaches to training of both countries are applicable to American workers. To increase the incentive for U.S. employers to supply training to their employees, a possible policy intervention is the imposition of a mandatory training tax on company payrolls. The training levy idea was discussed in this chapter in the context of the Australian Training Guarantee enacted in 1990, supplemented by experience gained over a longer time period for the French training tax. Another policy intervention considered in the context of firm-based training is a national system of certifying worker skills, such as the British National Vocational Qualification system. Recent empirical evidence relating to British apprenticeship training during the 1970s indicates that nationally recognized credentials signaling mastery of occupational skills substantially enhanced the 1981 earnings opportunities of young workers.

NOTES

1. This example is provided in Rollén (1988).

2. A well-known paper by Burtless (1985) provides evidence of a stigma effect in the context of a targeted wage-subsidy program carried out in Ohio during 1980-81. His results suggest that rather than indicating that targeted workers could be employed at attractive government-subsidized wage rates, program vouchers were used by employers as a labor market signal of potentially poor job performance.

3. Bendick and Egan (1987) provide a useful qualitative evaluation of the British Enterprise Allowance Scheme (EAS) along with the French Unemployed Entrepreneurs program. The French program provides a lump-sum payment to the unemployed entrepreneur, which is received

about two months after the new firm has been registered, while the EAS supplies the entrepreneur a weekly allowance for a maximum of 52 weeks. An important conclusion of the authors' analysis is that the initial capitalization and proprietors' credentials needed to ensure that a newly created small business will survive and possibly create jobs for other individuals means that unemployed entrepreneur programs should be at most a minor component of the package of services intended to promote employment opportunities for the displaced. See also Leigh (1989, ch. 5).

4. *The Economist* (1994a) recently characterized as "fundamental flaws" in the present operation of the TEC network the problems that (1) TECs are being asked to concentrate on the delivery of welfare rather than training services, (2) central government mandates prevent them from adopting to local conditions, and (3) TECs are caught up in the competition between separate central government agencies responsible for administering a fragmented group of programs.

5. The JTPA Title III program for displaced workers includes one performance standard (entered employment rate) and an optional goal (average wage at placement) for use in judging performance, but the USDOL has not implemented a rewards/sanctions system for Title III programs.

6. The reward for exceeding performance standards is additional funding, while failure to meet standards results in a reorganization of the SDA and restrictions on which training providers may be retained in the future.

7. Since members of the eligible population and the JTPA sample are required to be under age 60, all SSI recipients are significantly limited in their ability to work and have work histories that are insufficient for eligibility for regular Social Security disability benefits.

8. This result is understandable since eligibility for UI benefits requires recent work experience and hence a closer tie to the labor market than those whose benefits have run out or whose work history does not qualify them for benefits.

9. There are several reasons why smaller firms are less likely to be able to internalize the benefits from training than larger firms. One is that smaller firms tend to pay lower wages, and thus they are more likely to be constrained by minimum wage restrictions from passing on part of training costs to trainees. In addition, as noted earlier in the text, smaller firms often find that the average costs of training workers are much higher than those incurred by larger firms, because small firms have fewer workers over whom to spread fixed costs. Finally, small firms are more vulnerable to production losses associated with workers learning rather than producing, and they are less able to offer an internal career ladder to retain workers within their organizations.

10. Lynch (1994, pp. 76-77) links nationally recognized skill certification to the willingness of German apprentices in general to work for lower wages during their period of training. Contrasting German apprentices who earn about one-third of the adult unskilled wage with British apprentices who typically earn 60 percent or more of the adult rate, she suggests that the Youth Training Scheme introduced in Britain during the 1980s implemented a skill certification system in which standards are low, certificates are too industry-specific, and exams fail to reliably measure an individual's actual skills. According to Lynch, the consequence is that British trainees are not willing to accept the same wage reductions as German apprentices, who can be confident that their greater skills will be rewarded in the post-training period. British employers, in turn, provide both less training and training that is more firm-specific than that supplied by German firms.

11. This discussion of the French training levy is largely drawn from Bishop (1993b and 1994, pp. 57-61).

12. Compared to those in the United States, Blanchflower and Lynch (1994) suggest German institutional structures differ in terms of the long-term relationships between banks and firms, a greater link between schools and postschool training, and a strong influence of local Chambers of Commerce on the number of apprenticeship positions offered.

5
Assisting the Unemployed in Job Search

The first criterion of the evaluation framework outlined in chapter 1 specified that the services provided in active labor market programs should facilitate the transition of displaced workers to jobs in expanding industries and growing sectors within existing industries. Of the categories of active labor market programs indicated in table 2.1, the two designed to assist displaced workers in making the transition from distressed to expanding industries and industry sectors are adult training programs and employment services. Adult training programs were examined in the previous chapter. This chapter, which is divided into four main sections, focuses on the efficient provision of employment services to displaced workers. The first section relates employment services traditionally provided by most OECD countries to the more proactive job search assistance (JSA) services introduced in chapter 3 in the context of the U.S. displaced worker demonstration projects.

The second section of the chapter examines the limited empirical evidence available on the effectiveness of existing employment services in Canada and the United States. Agencies responsible for providing employment services in the two countries are the Canadian Employment Centre (CEC) system and the U.S. Employment Service (ES). Both agencies were created during the 1930s to function as federally funded but state- or province-operated labor exchanges. The discussion of limitations of the CEC and ES systems in this section lays some groundwork for a consideration in the third section of the highly regarded Swedish Employment Service and the Canadian Industrial Adjustment Service.

Most industrialized nations make eligibility for unemployment insurance benefits at least nominally conditional on some form of active job search.[1] At the same time, an issue of concern in many nations is the increasing incidence of long-term unemployment among the unemployed. The final section of the chapter examines policies recently implemented in Britain, Canada, and Australia to maintain the work incentives of the unemployed by more closely linking receipt of unemployment compensation benefits to active job search coupled with enhanced employment services.

Components of JSA Programs

Employment services are usually divided into core and support services. The core labor exchange service is intended to lower transaction costs involved in matching job seekers to job vacancies in the local labor market. This function typically includes applicant screening and job placement. Beyond this core service, public employment agencies often play the supportive roles of (1) acting as a "gateway" for access to retraining services and transitional employment opportunities, and (2) validating the job search requirements of unemployment insurance programs.

Neither of these core or support services may be directly relevant to a displaced worker whose job search skills are rusty from disuse or whose primary employment opportunities are either not listed by employers with the public employment service or lie beyond the geographic boundaries of the local labor market. As described in chapter 3, the U.S. displaced worker demonstration projects were designed, among other reasons, to test the labor market effectiveness of an expanded menu of employment services. Termed "job search assistance," these services go beyond the traditional labor exchange function of public employment agencies in terms of reaching out to the unemployed, improving their job search skills, and assisting them to locate jobs that are not listed or advertised by employers. To provide an overview of the range of possible JSA services, this section briefly outlines the services supplied across the Downriver, Buffalo, Texas WAD, and New Jersey UI Reemployment demonstration projects. JSA services are discussed in roughly the sequential order in which they might be offered.

1. *Outreach.* The first problem is to make known to displaced workers the services offered by a JSA program. With respect to workers affected by a plant closing or mass layoff, the surest means of making contact is to offer assistance at the plant site before layoffs begin and

workers disperse. Clearly, advance notification of layoffs and plant closures would increase the chance of effective outreach to workers about to be laid off. For other unemployed workers, outreach depends more on media campaigns, word-of-mouth, and referrals by staff members in unemployment insurance offices.

2. *Orientation.* Orientation plays the key role of informing prospective participants about the range of services offered by the program, what these services can and cannot be expected to deliver, and what is expected of participants themselves. The objective is to help unemployed workers arrive at a sensible decision regarding program participation. In particular, unemployed workers anticipating recall and those who can reasonably be expected to find satisfactory jobs without assistance should be discouraged from continuing further. On the other hand, other jobless individuals may be unrealistically clinging to the hope of being recalled. Orientation services for these workers should include assistance in correctly assessing their recall prospects.

In approaching workers who appear to be good candidates for JSA services, it is important for program staff members to clearly acknowledge that there is no guarantee that jobs available to program graduates will offer prelayoff levels of pay and benefits. Potential participants should especially be cautioned that not everyone benefits from relatively costly and time-consuming retraining programs.

3. *Assessment and testing.* The next service offered in many JSA programs is an assessment session intended to determine whether a participant already possesses locally marketable skills or whether retraining is a necessary precondition for reemployment. Formal testing is often used to determine the participant's vocational interests and his or her aptitude for undertaking particular retraining programs. In some cases, testing may reveal that remedial education is a prerequisite for retraining. A frequent outcome of an assessment and testing session is a written agreement between the client and a program staff member outlining a viable back-to-work strategy. The written agreement is often called an "employability plan."

4. *Job search workshops, resource centers, and job clubs.* Based on the assessment results, participants are typically placed in either a classroom training or on-the-job training program or enrolled in a job

search workshop. Job search workshops in the displaced worker demonstrations generally lasted about twenty hours spread over several days. Workshop content usually consisted of two primary elements. First, specific job search skills were taught, including resume preparation, techniques for locating job leads, and effective application and interviewing practices. Second, motivational activities and exercises were provided to raise the low self-esteem that many displaced workers suffer after being laid off.

Following the job search workshop, most programs channeled participants into either a resource center or a job club. Resource centers provide participants a base of operation for their self-directed job search in a central facility typically outfitted with a telephone bank, telephone and business directories, newspaper help-wanted ads, and listings of job openings from the public employment service. An important objective of resource centers is to create an atmosphere of mutual encouragement and support by encouraging job seekers to operate out of a common location.

Batt (1983) comments that few experiences in life are as isolating as looking for a job. Job clubs are designed to deal with this feeling of isolation. Meeting on a regular basis to follow up on job leads, job clubs allow for the supervised application of recently acquired job search skills while offering the opportunity for developing a group support system during the search period. Corson, Maynard, and Wichita (1984, pp. 132-34) describe a successful implementation of the job club concept in the Lehigh Valley program of the Dislocated Worker Demonstration projects. A key feature of this program is a fixed membership per club of about fifteen participants that was unchanged until all club members were able to find employment. The reduction in the number of club members as placements occurred had a positive rather than negative effect on remaining members and project staff, since job club moderators took pride in watching the club "close out." The authors caution, nevertheless, that because of the highly personal interaction likely to be generated in job clubs, they may not be appropriate for all clients in all areas.

5. *Follow-up counseling.* Most JSA programs provide some form of follow-up counseling ranging from informal, occasional counseling, which consists largely of job interview advice, to sophisticated case-

management systems, which assign clients to particular counselors who have full responsibility for their progress through the program. Whatever form counseling takes, its primary goal is to ensure that participants are making satisfactory progress in their job search. Particular services a counselor can provide include serving as a "sounding board" for participants, supplying job information and arranging for support services, urging clients to make use of resource center facilities, and encouraging participants to persevere in their search.

6. *Job matching and job development.* As noted, public employment agencies have traditionally offered the service of matching job vacancies listed with the agency by local employers to individual job applicants, making use of a core of resume information provided by the job seeker. Resume information typically includes the applicant's vocational interests, formal education, and work history, supplemented, if available, by vocational test scores.

Beyond the job vacancy information furnished by employers, some JSA programs also offer the service—called job development—of utilizing the informal contacts of staff members to turn up job openings that are not advertised or listed with the public employment service. In other words, the function of a job developer is to uncover job vacancies that would be unlikely to come to the attention of a displaced worker searching on his or her own. Job development is successful when job developers establish a reputation with local employers by carefully screening workers to ensure that referrals satisfy the employer's hiring requirements.

Evidence for the Canadian and U.S. Employment Services

Table 2.1 indicated that Canada ranks along with Sweden and Germany in having the highest public expenditure ratios on employment service programs of the seven countries considered. At the other extreme, the United States and Japan rank lowest on employment service spending. This section begins with a consideration of available evidence on the labor market impacts of employment services provided in Canada. Examined in detail is a recent study by Osberg (1993) of the role of Canadian Employment Centres in assisting jobless Canadians to find employment during the 1981-86 period. The second part of this section surveys available evidence for the United States. A well-known article by Johnson, Dickinson, and West (1985) evaluates whether workers who received Employment Service job referrals obtained better jobs sooner than those who did not. In addition, Bishop (1993a) examines the impact of ES referrals and other job finding methods on employers' assessments of the productivity of new hires. Finally, Jacobson (1994) reviews other recent studies evaluating the effectiveness of ES services.

Canadian Evidence

In Canada, as in the United States, there are a variety of job search methods available to jobless individuals; and public employment agencies are just one of these methods. While high-paying jobs are usually found through informal information networks involving personal contacts, public employment agencies typically list jobs paying below-average wages. Osberg (1993) notes that the average wage of jobs listed at CECs was $6.24 in 1986-87, whereas the average wage of all workers in similar industries was $11.24 and the average wage of new hires was $7.91.[2] Consequently, the choice of a job search strategy by jobless workers is simultaneously a choice of the wage offer distribution, implying that users of public employment agencies are not a random sample of all jobless individuals.

Osberg's empirical analysis is based on 1981, 1983, and 1986 data drawn from the Canadian Labour Force Survey of inhabitants of a large random sample of dwelling units. A two-stage procedure is utilized to control for sample selection. The first stage of this procedure involves estimating a probit model of CEC use by jobless workers. Statistically significant determinants of CEC use are found to vary over the business cycle. In all three years studied, however, the probability of using the CEC system rose as duration of unemployment spells increased, suggesting that the jobless turn first to other job search methods. In addition, CEC use is found to be higher for those who lost their last job (as opposed to those who left their last job for other reasons) and for those eligible for unemployment insurance.

Controlling for sample selection, the second stage of Osberg's analysis estimates the impact of CEC use on job-finding success. His results are mixed. Stratifying the data by year, gender, and duration of unemployment (spells less than or greater than three months), in none of the six regressions reported for the short-duration unemployed does CEC use have a statistically significant effect on the probability of finding a job. The CEC appears to be of little assistance in placing workers who turn out to have relatively short spells of joblessness. This finding is consistent with Osberg's (1993, p. 360) remark that the CEC is criticized in Canada for inadequate screening of referrals, slow service, and irrelevance to most recruitment decisions.[3]

Among the six regressions estimated for the long-duration unemployed, a significantly positive effect of CEC use on job-finding success is found in only two equations—the equation for females in 1986 and the equation for males in 1983. Indeed, CEC use has a significantly *negative* estimated effect in 1981 for long-duration unemployed males. In interpreting these results, it should be noted that 1981 was a period of relatively low unemployment (8.3 percent), 1983 was a high unemployment (13.7 percent) year, and 1986 was somewhere near the midpoint of the cycle. Osberg (1993, p. 366) concludes from his results that the CEC is not of much help at the peak of the business cycle, even for the long-duration unemployed, since jobs are relatively plentiful and job seekers tend to find them on their own. Nevertheless, he suggests that the CEC provides a valuable safety net function for the long-duration male jobless who have exhausted their usual job search methods during the trough of a recession. The CEC also seems to provide significant assistance to long-duration jobless women at the midpoint of the business cycle.

Osberg's analysis is one of ten studies commissioned in 1986 by the Canadian government as part of an effort to rigorously evaluate and revitalize the national employment service. Of particular concern to government officials was the apparent decline during the 1970s and early 1980s in the CEC's labor exchange role indicated by a downward trend in the volume of its job placement activity measured relative to labor force growth. Trebilcock (1986, p. 46) comments on the poor job placement record of the CEC, pointing out that most employers do not list job openings with the system because they view job applicants referred to them by CECs as generally people with poor work histories.

The commissioned studies are particularly useful in gaining an understanding of three JSA-related issues: (1) the effectiveness of a universal screening interview followed by employment counseling targeted to the non-job-ready, (2) the labor market impact of computer-assisted job search, and (3) the potential of privatization in revitalizing Canada's employment service.

A key element in the revitalization strategy for the national employment service is the introduction of Service Needs Determination interviews. The purpose of these short (typically about 11 minutes) interviews is to allow CEC staff members to distinguish clients who are already job-ready from those who appear to have severe barriers to overcome before they can be said to be job-ready. Job-ready clients are routed to self-service facilities such as Job Information Centre display boards and group information sessions. Six out of every ten Service Needs Determination interviews conclude with clients being referred to a self-service facility. Clients determined not to be job-ready are scheduled for employment counseling sessions at their local CEC office. Through the counseling process, these clients are assisted in establishing employment goals, resolving employment-related problems, and implementing their plans to enter or stay in the labor force. A survey of CEC staff members funded by Employment and Immigration Canada (EIC) finds that over two-thirds of respondents indicated that Revitalization affected positively the quality of counseling services (see EIC 1989b, p. 70). Major factors correlated with the improvement in counseling services are improved identification of target groups, more effective management of counselor time, more manageable caseloads, and greater focus on clients' needs.

Turning to computer-assisted job search, those CECs that offered jobless workers the National Employment Services System (NESS) were subjected to evaluation. NESS is a computerized on-line system of processing job orders and maintaining data on worker clients. EIC (1989b) summarizes a survey of CEC staff members in which they were asked to assess the impact of NESS on the quality of job matching services provided. Some 83 percent of respondents cited improvements in the quality of services to worker clients. These improvements included (1) faster and wider exposure of job orders, (2) easier access to information, (3) more effective identification of target group clients, (4) ability to spend more time with clients, and (5) ability to refer clients to more vacancies (EIC 1989b, pp. 55-56). Some 76 percent of CEC respondents also felt that NESS helped to improve quality of services to employers, primarily because of greater speed in making referrals, availability of more up-to-date information, and more efficient monitoring of job orders (EIC 1989b, p. 46). Consistent with this qualitative evidence are the results of multivariate regression analyses indicating that NESS speeds up the time it takes for CECs to make their first referral to a job order and reduces the number of days required to fill a vacancy (EIC 1989b, pp. 34-36).

Concerning the potential for privatizing employment services, finally, an important constraint in Canada is that private-sector employment agencies cannot charge job seekers for placement services; that is, only employers may be billed for successful job placements. A study of private-sector labor market intermediaries (private employment agencies and temporary help services) suggests that private-sector firms, subject to this constraint, will concentrate, quite understandably, on labor markets in which profit potential exists. These labor markets tend to be limited to highly skilled positions, standardized occupations such as word processing, and large urban areas. Employment and Immigration Canada (1989b, pp. 99, 129) concludes that private-sector firms are not a practical substitute for the CEC, except possibly in large urban areas and for some occupational categories.

U.S. Evidence

Sponsored by the U.S. Department of Labor, the Employment Service evaluation by Johnson, Dickinson, and West (1985) is based on data collected for approximately 8,000 new applicants for ES services in thirty Job Service offices in twenty-seven states between July 1980 and May 1981. The net impact of ES services on earnings and other labor market outcomes is measured by comparing the labor market experiences following application to the ES of individuals who received job referrals with the experiences of those who did not. Thus, the CEC study by Osberg and the ES evaluation examine the impact of public employment agencies at two different stages in the job search process. Osberg investigates job seekers' use of the CEC (which may or may not lead to a job referral), while the ES evaluation by Johnson,

Dickinson, and West focuses on the impact of actual job referrals for workers who chose to apply to their local Job Service office.

Clearly, Employment Service applicants receiving a referral need not be a random sample from the pool of new applicants, because ES staff members may either cream in making referral decisions or emphasize assistance to hard-to-place clients. In either case, it is critical to consider whether individuals selected for job referrals differ systematically from those not selected. Results of a careful comparison carried out by Johnson, Dickinson, and West indicate that the referred and not-referred groups are generally comparable on measured characteristics, and that the not-referred group may be somewhat more advantaged on unmeasured characteristics. If anything, therefore, net impact estimates could slightly underestimate the impact of ES job referrals.

Table 5.1 presents the main evaluation results reported by the authors broken down by gender. Shown in the table are means for the referred and not-referred groups adjusted using ordinary least squares regression to control for differences in demographic characteristics, work histories, characteristics related to the provision of ES services (dummy variables for job attachment, union membership, and veteran status), measures of applicants' motivation to find work, and site and other environmental characteristics. Differences in the adjusted means represent the net impact of an ES referral.

For men, the table shows the surprising result that receipt of an ES referral does not result in a significant impact on any of the measures of labor market performance. In particular, during the six-month period following application to the ES, men who did *not* receive a referral and located a job on their own found their job six-tenths of a week sooner and earned $98 more than those who did receive a referral. Neither of these small negative estimates is significantly different from zero.

In contrast, an ES referral has positive and statistically significant effects on a number of the labor market outcome variables for women. Women who received a referral earned on average $325 more (a 23 percent increase in earnings) than women in the comparison group during the six-month observation period. The major factor in accounting for this earnings gain is the reduction of almost three weeks in the length of time necessary to find the first job. Wage rates earned by the referred group are no different from those earned by the not-referred group. Johnson, Dickinson, and West (1985, p. 136) conclude that at least part of the reason ES assistance is more effective for women than men is that women have less labor market experience and less access to the traditional network of job-finding methods. The authors also note that the cost per individual referred is minimal, ranging from just $30 to $80.

Table 5.1 Estimated Impact of ES Referrals on Labor Market Outcomes for Men and Women

Labor market outcome	Referred group	Not-referred group	Difference
	Men		
Earnings in 6 months	$2,564.33	$2,662.79	–$98.46
Weeks to first job	12.73	13.37	–0.64
Percent of 6-month period:			
Unemployed	49.48	48.11	1.36
Out of labor force	7.58	9.10	–1.51
Employed	42.94	42.79	0.15
Hours worked in 6 months	420.46	427.94	–7.48
Wage rate	$6.10	$6.22	–$0.12
	Women		
Earnings in 6 months	$1,725.03	$1,399.93	$325.10*
Weeks to first job	12.90	15.69	–2.79*
Percent of 6-month period:			
Unemployed	46.25	47.40	–1.14
Out of labor force	10.74	17.87	–7.13*
Employed	43.00	34.73	8.27*
Hours worked in 6 months	397.86	309.54	88.31*
Wage rate	$4.34	$4.52	–$0.18

SOURCE: Johnson, Dickinson, and West (1985, table 3).
NOTE: Group means are regression adjusted.
*indicates significance at the 1 percent level.

Bishop (1993a) uses data collected from employers in a recent survey carried out by the National Federation of Independent Business on the experience of about 1,600 firms with new hires. Among his results is the finding that new hires referred to employers by public employment agencies generally perform poorly. Holding constant worker and job characteristics, referrals from public agencies (the ES, vocational rehabilitation agencies, JTPA, and community-based organizations) are found to be significantly less likely to be perceived by employers as willing to work late and to contribute to the firm's profitability, both initially and after six months on the job. When separate dummy variables for ES referrals and for referrals by other government agencies replace the single public employment agency dummy, both types of government referrals had similar negative coefficients.

To summarize, the empirical results reported in this section for the United States, as well as for Canada, are clearly mixed. The conclusion that emerges from this evidence is that if public employment agencies have any potential at all, this potential is largely unrealized. It follows to many observers that the ES should either be radically restructured or abolished.

Among the many critics of the U.S. Employment Service, Baily, Burtless, and Litan (1993, pp. 136-39) argue that there are two main problems facing the agency. First, the ES does not know where job vacancies are, since employers are under no obligation to list their vacancies. As a consequence of not having good information on the occupational demand for labor, the agency is in a weak position to direct the unemployed to appropriate vocational training programs such as those funded by JTPA.

Second, the ES has been weighed down over the years by the obligation to help the most disadvantaged class of job seekers—UI recipients, persons subsisting on welfare, and poor teenagers seeking access to targeted employment and tax-subsidy programs. A bit of historical background would be helpful on this point. During the 1950s and early 1960s, the ES sought to serve all job seekers by establishing one-on-one relationships between ES staff members and employer personnel representatives. As noted earlier, these relationships are a key aspect of what is known as job development. Bishop (1993a, p. 380) notes that ES referrals during this period accounted for nearly 20 percent of the nation's new hires. Beginning in the mid-1960s, however, political priorities shifted and the ES was made responsible for the placement of targeted populations, including welfare recipients and other disadvantaged workers. At the same time, individual ES staff member control of job orders began to decline, weakening the working relationships that had been established between agency staff and employers. ES referrals fell to about 8 percent of all new hires in 1971 and remained low throughout the 1970s and 1980s.

Baily, Burtless, and Litan argue that this obligation to the disadvantaged gives rise to a problem of adverse selection. As the clientele of the Employment Service became younger, poorer, and less skilled as the result of new government regulations, employers searching for good workers began to look elsewhere. And as more attractive employers shied away from Job Service offices, average workers had less reason to apply for agency services, further reducing the average quality of ES clients. Marshall and Tucker (1992, p. 223) add that the dynamics of adverse selection led to a social underinvestment in employment services with the result that, because it is starved of resources, the ES has not computerized many of its offices and does not do a serious job of counseling. In fact, Bishop (1993a, p. 381) observes that without support from its traditional constituencies (i.e., employers, voters, and nondisadvantaged workers), the ES was unable to fend off substantial budget cuts during the 1990-91 recession, and it began to lose even its ability to serve the disadvantaged.[4]

Given this generally quite pessimistic assessment of the Employment Service, it is interesting to note the much more positive view appearing in Jacobson's (1994) recent literature review prepared for the U.S. Advisory Commission on Unemployment Compensation. Beginning with a critique of the Johnson, Dickinson, and West (1985) analysis, Jacobson suggests, particularly for males, that the relevant follow-up period for measuring labor market outcomes is not the first six months following application to the ES, as shown in table 5.1, but rather the first six months following referral. His argument is that unemployed males are more likely than unemployed females to be UI claimants, and that the incentive for UI claimants to return to work increases substantially after the six months of UI benefits are over. From this perspective, the Johnson, Dickinson, and West study is likely to understate ES effects on labor market outcomes for males, since it ignores the potential effectiveness of ES services in aiding UI claimants after their benefits have been exhausted.

Jacobson also reviews an as yet unpublished series of analyses of Pennsylvania administrative data for UI claimants carried out by Arnold Katz and himself. Recognizing that the ES is often turned to only after other job search methods have failed or are unavailable to searchers, Jacobson and Katz find that the ES is effective in reducing the joblessness of UI claimants, particularly for UI exhaustees and women. Direct placements, as would be expected, have by far the largest positive effects on reemployment, but referrals that do not lead to placements also appear to provide useful information about available jobs that shortens the period of joblessness. Jacobson (1994, p. 30) concludes from this evidence that the direct placement services provided by the Employment Service reduce the duration of joblessness and have a small positive effect on earnings. Because the cost of its services is low, the ES is cost effective.

The second half of Jacobson's survey examines studies of the ability of the Employment Service to make job placements. These studies include a series of GAO reports based on data from individual ES offices and an unpublished study by Jacobson of administrative data collected for individuals registered with the Pennsylvania ES between 1978 and 1987. Using detailed data on management procedures in ES offices, the GAO reached a number of provocative conclusions including the following:

- Offices in states subjected to measurable performance standards reinforced by awards for obtaining favorable outcomes had placement rates double those of offices in other states.
- Offices with a self-service system placed 20 percent more applicants in permanent jobs compared with offices where job seekers could only see job lists with the help of ES staff.
- Offices serving relatively small populations and those facing low applicant-to-labor-force ratios were far more effective than offices serving large populations and facing high applicant-to-labor-force ratios. This provides strong support for the view that the ES is more effective when it has the flexibility to provide personalized services to voluntary applicants.

- Local offices that spent time communicating with employers had a 12 percent higher permanent placement ratio compared with offices that did not communicate with employers. It is clear that ES offices able to devote resources to job development are much more effective in obtaining permanent job placements.
- Offices that held individual intake interviews had placement rates 24 percent higher than offices that used group intake.
- More ES involvement with other placement or job training programs (such as JTPA) was associated with better performance.

Jacobson (1994, p. 39) summarizes the GAO's studies as indicating that (1) reductions in resources have played a major role in reducing the effectiveness of the ES, and (2) the ES is charged with many activities that detract from the performance of its labor exchange function. Despite these disadvantages, the GAO evidence suggests that marginal changes in management procedures and funding could dramatically improve performance. Jacobson's own study also concludes that most, if not all, of the observed decline in the ES placement rate in Pennsylvania can be accounted for by shifts in the proportion of hard-to-place registrants and structural changes in the industrial mix of available jobs.

"Best Practice" Employment Service Programs

Following up on this discussion of criticisms and proposed changes in public employment agencies in Canada and the United States, it is useful to look in some detail at examples of "best practice" employment service systems. Two long-standing and highly regarded employment service programs currently in operation on a nationwide basis are the Swedish Employment Service and the Canadian Industrial Adjustment Service.

The Swedish Employment Service

It was noted in chapter 2 that the focal point of Swedish labor market policy is its nationwide system of 360 employment exchange offices. In addition to the 360 regular offices, the Employment Service has 60 specialized placement offices staffed by personnel specially qualified to assist job seekers to find jobs in specific fields such as technology and accounting and finance. In some major urban areas, the Employment Service also operates a drop-in placement service called Expo that provides quick information about job vacancies (Trehörning 1993, p. 61). No registration of job seekers takes place at Expo centers. Finally, since August 1991, the Employment Service has operated a special office in central Stockholm for international job placement. It provides referrals for jobs outside the Nordic countries and helps Swedes living abroad who will be moving home and are seeking employment.

For the late 1980s, the OECD (1990, pp. 31-32) reports that Sweden ranked highest (at 1.0) among nineteen countries in employment office staff members per thousand persons aged 15 to 64. These countries include Britain, Germany, Australia, and Canada. Similarly, Sweden ranked lowest (at 14) in average number of unemployed persons per employment office staff member in 1988.

It is clear that the Swedish Employment Service is much more than a labor exchange. Key aspects of the Swedish system include the following:

- Immediate provision of services
- A permanent case manager assigned to each client
- Near-universal listing of job vacancies by employers
- A computerized system for matching job vacancies and job seekers
- Attention to the needs of individuals who are not immediately job-ready

Beginning with the first aspect, the Employment Service takes the position that immediate involvement of laid-off workers in the service delivery system is important to prevent a period of idleness that is destructive to workers' motivation and effectiveness in seeking reemployment. Indeed, mandatory advance notice of mass layoffs and plant closures allows services to begin in many cases before workers' current jobs actually end.

Clients of the Swedish Employment Service are assigned a case manager who remains responsible for the case until the worker becomes reemployed. Even though the case manager may refer the client to specialists within the system for assessment and testing or for training, the case manager is the continuing point of contact between the client and the system. A primary task of the case manager is to select the appropriate set of services to be provided each client. Three groups of clients may be distinguished: the job-ready, those with an appropriate vocational objective but lacking the required training, and those who need assistance in selecting a vocational objective.

A job-ready client may proceed directly to job search, relying on the Employment Service's listings of job vacancies. Swedish law requires employers to list with the public employment service all jobs lasting more than ten days, while forbidding the operation of private employment agencies.[5] Insistence that employers list their job openings at the public employment service tends to eliminate the adverse selection problem noted in connection with the public employment services in the United States and Canada. That is, possession of information on the full range of available employment opportunities and on the qualifications needed to fill them makes it attractive for Swedish job seekers to visit the Employment Service to get good job leads. At the same time, employers can be confident that workers referred to them are not limited to the lower end of the skill distribution. Bendick (1983, p. 221) reports that as of the early 1980s, job vacancies were listed on weekly newspaper-like sheets, which were available at all Employment Service offices. By the late 1980s, a fully computerized job placement system provided each employment office with on-line access to information about job seekers and job vacancies. Baily, Burtless, and Litan (1993, pp. 138-39) make the common-sense argument that jobless workers in areas with high unemployment in the United States often find that access to better employment opportunities requires a geographic move. But long-distance job seekers are forced to invest in costly and often fruitless in-person searches. These costs would be substantially reduced if local employment service offices, as in Sweden, could provide information on job vacancies in labor markets around the country.[6]

Beyond supplying information on job vacancies, the Swedish Employment Service provides assistance in locating jobs not listed or advertised by employers. A first source of information on these jobs results from the job development activity of placement staff and training staff members. In addition, rising unemployment during and immediately after the 1990-91 recession caused the Employment Service to expand its job search training activities to include the formation of job clubs. In Sweden, job clubs are groups of unemployed job seekers who meet every day at their local employment exchange office to obtain information on the overall state of the labor market and to be trained in how to engage in job search, reply to help-wanted advertisements, fill out job application forms, and interview effectively. Trehörning (1993, p. 62) refers to a recent Employment Service follow-up survey indicating that nearly half the positions filled by job club participants had not been advertised or listed in the Service's own vacancy lists.

A second group of Employment Service clients are those who have already selected an appropriate vocational objective but who lack the required qualifications. These clients are referred to a training program offered by a skill center. The system of skill centers operated by the National Employment Training Board was discussed in some detail in chapter 4.

Finally, clients who need assistance in selecting a vocational objective can be referred to specialists who provide vocational testing and assessment. Vocational testing and counseling may last several weeks. In his evaluation of Sweden's employment and training system, Bendick (1983, pp. 215-16) comments that

> . . . in no part of its services is this lavishness [in the level of resources invested] more striking than when a client is attempting to select an occupation (for example, prior to entering training). The availability of specialized counseling and testing services has been mentioned earlier. Additionally, the case manager can arrange short visits to training classes or to typical job sites or even short-term trial placements in typical jobs and will himself participate in what strikes an American observer as an amazingly patient process of thought and discussion.

Job seekers who, in addition, require rehabilitation can obtain testing and assessment services at an employability institute.

The Canadian Industrial Adjustment Service

Undoubtedly the best-known public employment service agency specializing in job development is Canada's Industrial Adjustment Service (IAS). Established in 1963, the IAS is a federally funded agency intended to serve as a catalyst in bringing together local labor and management officials to locate job opportunities for workers displaced by economic and technological change. IAS assistance is also available to companies or communities facing labor shortages. This additional responsibility of the agency helps it avoid the possible stigma of only being associated with layoffs and plant closings.

The IAS is very small in terms of number of employees and size of budget. During the middle 1980s, its staff consisted of just sixty experienced professionals, with only three persons located in its headquarters office in Ottawa and the rest assigned to regional field offices. Its annual budget was between $6 and $8 million (in Canadian dollars).

As described in the Secretary of Labor's Task Force report (U.S. Department of Labor 1986, p. 21), the IAS program operates on five premises.

1. Reemployment services should be offered in advance of, rather than after, a plant closing or mass layoff.

2. Advance warning is essential to allow time for planning and implementing appropriate reemployment services.

3. Worker adjustment to displacement is best accomplished by the joint action of the parties directly involved.

4. The role of government is to encourage and support, not to supplant, the efforts of management and labor.

5. Program participation should be voluntary.

After learning that a plant closing is imminent, the IAS acts immediately to meet with labor and management representatives at the highest possible level and to offer its assistance in finding new jobs for laid-off workers. Early warning of a layoff is quite likely because six of the ten Canadian provinces have plant closing laws that require 8 to 16 weeks' advance notice of layoffs affecting fifty or more workers. In addition, a national advance notice law applies to government-regulated enterprises such as airlines and railroads.

If the IAS's offer of assistance is accepted, which is nearly always the case, the agency negotiates a brief formal agreement, which establishes an ad hoc labor-management adjustment committee consisting of an equal number of labor and management representatives. Labor representatives include prospective job losers wherever possible. The purpose of the agreement is to obtain from both the employer and the union (if a union is present) a commitment of time and financial resources to the adjustment process. The IAS provides a chairman, whom the adjustment committee may select from a roster of experienced people. In addition, it pays half of the committee's costs, with the company usually picking up the other half. Committees typically finish their work and disband in about one year. According to the Secretary of Labor's Task Force, the IAS arranges from 400 to 600 labor-management agreements per year.[7]

The basic thrust of the IAS is to place unemployed workers in jobs that are never publicly announced, but instead are filled by word-of-mouth. From this strategy follow several of the important features of the program. One of these is an emphasis on prompt placement rather than retraining, relocation, or counseling. Adjustment committees not only undertake to uncover job openings, but they also attempt to make it easier for prospective employers to consider client workers by assisting in the screening process. Workers who cannot be placed are referred to the CEC system for relocation or retraining assistance. When the committee has done all that it can in terms of placing displaced workers, it disbands and the chairman writes a final report documenting the work of the committee. Batt (1983, p. 5) comments that the final report includes a description of what happened to every laid-off worker, adding that

> [S]uch detailed reporting offers a refreshing contrast to what happens in the United States. As a general rule here, no one knows what has happened to the displaced people—not the company, not the union, not the employment service, not anyone. Nor does anyone appear to care enough to find out.

A second element of the IAS strategy is recognition that it is people with extensive experience in the industry and community—that is, the labor and management representatives on an adjustment committee—who are in the best position to use their informal contacts to engage in job development. Thus the IAS advisor to an adjustment committee keeps a low profile, and the committee itself is flexible enough to look at the individual needs of each worker. Worth emphasizing is the basic philosophy of the IAS that displaced workers are to be assisted individually by persons who know them personally.

The Secretary of Labor's Task Force (U.S. Department of Labor 1986, appendix A) comments favorably on the operation of the IAS. Noted in particular are the program's modest cost (about $171 per year for every worker served), reasonably good placement rates (about two-thirds of workers affected by plant closings are placed within a year), absence of bureaucratic red tape, contribution to improved labor-management relations, and favorable effect on reducing workers' resistance to technological change and relaxation of trade restrictions. The Task Force report also mentions that, according to a survey of displaced workers served during the 1982-83 fiscal year, IAS assistance reduced the length of unemployment spells by an average of two weeks. Thus the Task Force comments that the program virtually pays for itself by lowering UI outlays and accelerating the return of workers to tax-paying status.

As noted in chapter 2, the Task Force's favorable evaluation of the IAS formed the basis for its recommendation that federal funding should be provided states to develop rapid response units capable of reacting to major layoffs and plant closures with on-site offers of job search assistance and retraining. This recommendation was subsequently incorporated as a major element of the Economic Dislocation and Worker Adjustment Assistance act of 1988, which amended Title III of the Job Training Partnership Act.

A recent evaluation of the IAS by Employment and Immigration Canada (1993) concludes with what appears to be a less positive assessment of the program. The EIC evaluation is based on a survey of a random sample of almost 1,900 displaced workers, about 800 of whom were IAS participants. It should be noted that IAS participants enjoyed significantly higher earnings prior to being laid off than did the members of the comparison group. Comparing postprogram labor market outcomes for the two groups, the EIC concludes that laid-off workers who received IAS services took significantly longer to begin active job search and spent more time in job search. The longer period of job search means that IAS participants received four and one-half more weeks of UI benefits and nearly $1,700 more in UI payments.

A closer look at the evaluation results reveals, however, that the negative net impact estimates obtained for the program as a whole are mainly the consequence of particularly adverse outcomes for IAS participants who received two or more services. Take-up rates for program services are much higher for IAS participants than for nonparticipants, and it is this aspect of the IAS program that leads to the unfavorable net impact estimates. That is, there is no evidence that the negative impact of multiple services *per se* is greater for IAS participants than for the comparison group. Rather, the negative outcomes for the IAS program appear to be related to the fact that more IAS recipients participated in multiple services than is true for the comparison group.

Looking at the specific services offered by the IAS, it is clear that individual services differ substantially in their effect on reemployment opportunities. In particular, job placement assistance is found to be associated with less time looking for work, fewer weeks unemployed, a greater likelihood of finding a full-time job, and higher postprogram earnings. The evaluation report also notes that circulating resumes is the only other single service associated with positive labor market outcomes. On the other hand, participation in a retraining program is associated with a lower likelihood of finding a full-time job and with more weeks of unemployment. Similarly, career counseling appeared to do little except increase the total number of weeks unemployed, while what the report terms "job search counseling" delayed the initiation of the job search process but had no real impact on employment outcomes. These results seem to indicate that the IAS can provide a key labor market function by concentrating on its primary role as a job development agency. But its effectiveness appears to be seriously diluted when program participants are channeled into related services including retraining.

Maintaining the Work Incentive of the Unemployed

Unemployment insurance benefits provide a first line of defense for workers faced with involuntary job loss and increase the political sustainability of public policies that permit freer international trade and the introduction of new technology. At the same time, UI benefits have the effect of reducing the cost of job search, thereby lengthening the expected duration of search. Longer duration of job search is not a serious problem with respect to laid-off workers who can reasonably be expected to be recalled to their old jobs when the economy recovers (i.e., cyclical unemployment). It is clearly more of a problem in the context of the longer-term structural unemployment associated with industrial restructuring if, as might be expected, availability of UI slows the transition of displaced workers to jobs in growing industries by reducing incentives to widen the industrial scope of their job search and to engage in retraining.

An issue of increasing concern among policy makers in many industrialized nations is the rising incidence of long-term unemployment among the jobless. This section examines policies implemented during the late 1980s and early 1990s in Britain, Canada, and Australia intended to more closely link receipt of unemployment insurance benefits to active job search, coupled with improved JSA services. As described in chapter 2, all three of these countries provide unemployment compensation benefits for up to one year or longer (50 weeks in Canada); and it was noted in connection with table 2.2 that the United Kingdom and Australia face a relatively high level of long-term unemployment.

Britain's Scheduling and Programming Strategy

The basic employment service in the United Kingdom has traditionally been job matching provided by the Employment Service through a dense network of Jobcentres located on high (or main) streets throughout the nation. Job vacancies are displayed on cards, and a job seeker can drop by his or her local Jobcentre and select those that are of interest. A receptionist is available to furnish more information about each job and to set up interviews with employers. Despite the generally high marks given the Jobcentre system for the share of job vacancies it lists (OECD 1992, p. 141), concern increased during the 1980s regarding the ability of the system to keep the long-term unemployed in some form of contact with the labor market. The Department of Employment (1988, p. 55) comments that despite a decline in unemployment during the second half of the 1980s,

> . . . there is evidence that a significant minority of benefit claimants are not actively looking for work. Some are claiming benefit[s] fraudulently while working at least part-time in the black economy. Others seem to have grown accustomed to living on benefit[s] and have largely given up looking for work, . . . [Still] others believe, mistakenly, that they might be financially worse off taking a job or are reluctant to travel daily more than a short distance to where jobs are available.

Chapter 2 noted that British workers who are unemployed for longer than one year are eligible for income-maintenance benefits for an indefinite time period under the Income Support program. While Income Support originally played only a minor role in assisting the unemployed, the OECD (1992, p. 141) notes that currently about three-quarters of the unemployed rely exclusively on this means-tested benefit. During the 1980s, consequently, Britain's Employment Service was confronted with the problem of facilitating the reemployment of large numbers of unemployed workers with little recent contact with the labor market. The policy response to this problem, implemented during the latter half of the 1980s, is known as the "scheduling and programming strategy." Along with offers of information and assistance, this strategy emphasizes periodic interviews with unemployment compensation recipients designed to keep them in contact with the labor market.

Table 5.2 outlines the schedule of Employment Service interventions in the scheduling and programming strategy. Newly unemployed workers are expected to check in with their local Unemployment Benefit Office or Jobcentre to receive information on their rights to unemployment insurance benefits and their obligations to engage in job search. A New Client Adviser helps the client prepare a back-to-work plan. Financial assistance through the Travel to Interview Scheme is available to clients who must travel to job interviews beyond normal daily traveling distances.

After three months, workers who are still jobless are invited to meet with a claimant adviser who reviews their back-to-work plan and may refer them to either a Job Search Seminar or a Job Review Workshop. Job Search Seminars offer two days of assistance on how to search out and apply for jobs and on how to behave in job interviews, while Job Review Workshops are two-day workshops designed to help clients with professional and executive backgrounds who are exploring new career options.

Table 5.2 Schedule of British Employment Service Contacts in the Scheduling and Programming Strategy, by Duration of Unemployment Spell

Duration of unemployment	Employment Service action
Day 1	Basic check of entitlement; benefit forms issued.
First week	Explanation of "benefit contract" (i.e., claimant's legal rights and obligations); agreement on a back-to-work plan.
Week 13	Review back-to-work plan; claimants may attend a 2-day course on job search techniques or a 2-day workshop on alternative careers.
.Week 26	First Restart interview: review benefit contract; develop new back-to-work plan; access given to Jobclubs, Training for Work program, and the Job Interview Guarantee program.
Week 52	Second Restart interview: same actions as week 26 but required attendance at a Jobplan workshop if other options were not followed up on.
Week 78	Third Restart interview: same actions as week 26 plus warning that attendance at a Restart course could be mandatory.
Week 104	Mandatory attendance at a 1-week Restart course. Involves overcoming perceived barriers to employment, assessment of skills and experience, enhancement of job search skills, and designing a plan of action leading back to work.

SOURCES: OECD (1992, tables 3.8 and 3.9) and Employment Department Group (1991).

During the first six months of unemployment, most job seekers are viewed as being basically job-ready but in need of assistance in locating suitable employment opportunities. This attitude changes after six months, when the jobless become eligible for the Restart program. Restart is intended for the long-term unemployed who may have become convinced that they will never again be employed and have adjusted to a low standard of living. The program begins with an interview with a claimant advisor. These interviews are repeated every six months with the same claimant adviser, so that a good working relationship can be achieved between adviser and client. Depending on the needs of the client, the adviser can recommend a variety of services, including a slot in an adult skill training program, a place in a Jobclub, participation in a Jobplan workshop, access to the Job Interview Guarantee program, a temporary public-sector job under the Training for Work program, financial assistance to set up a small business, and a slot in a Restart course. Jobclubs, Jobplan workshops, and Restart courses are three of the most important of these programs.

Jobclubs in Britain feature many of the services described earlier for job search workshops in the U.S. displaced worker demonstration projects. More specifically, Jobclubs typically offer workers unemployed for at least six months two weeks of four half-day sessions per week of structured training on how to look for jobs, write more effective job applications, and come across well in interviews. Following these two weeks, clients are given access to "resource areas" (or resource centers) containing telephones and sources of labor market information. At this stage, which is limited to four to six months, there is more support from other club members and less from the Jobclub leader. Workers unemployed for a year who have not followed up on other options offered them at their Restart interview are required to participate in an one-week Jobplan workshop. Jobplan workshops offer participants an opportunity to take a fresh look at their situation with the objectives of clearly identifying their strengths and skills, setting new employment goals, and drawing up an action plan for getting back to work.

Attendance at a Restart course is mandatory after two years of receiving unemployment benefits for those claimants who have refused to participate in other programs. In addition to providing information on the range of available JSA options, Restart courses involve small groups of the long-term unemployed in exercises intended to overcome barriers to labor force participation, sort out career options, motivate the resumption of active job search, and produce an individualized plan of action for reemployment. Courses are typically five days in length.

The OECD (1992, annex 3.D) reports that as of 1989, more than 10 percent of claimants who were sent a letter inviting them to attend a Restart interview stopped claiming benefits rather than attend. More recently, about 9 percent of claimants scheduled to attend a Restart course stopped claiming benefits. Although these drop-out rates could be reflecting reemployment, the OECD suggests that it is more likely that many who dropped their claim for benefits have access to other income, in which case their Income Support claim (which is means-tested) could well be fraudulent. Tending to support this conclusion is U.S. evidence for the Charleston and Washington State job search experiments described in chapter 3. Evidence produced for these two experiments shows that strengthened reporting requirements and mandatory attendance at a job search workshop reduced UI payments by raising the costs of remaining on UI rather than by enhancing the job search abilities of claimants. Anderson (1992) also reports for the New Jersey UI Reemployment Demonstration that the positive effect of JSA activities on reemployment probability is due more to their effect on scaling down recall expectations than their effectiveness in enhancing job search skills.

Similar results are reported for a French program introduced in 1992, which was designed to combat long-term unemployment by evaluating, through individual interviews, the job prospects of workers unemployed for more than a year (see OECD 1993, pp. 108-10). As a consequence of the interviews, about 16 percent of the long-term unemployed were immediately dropped from UI rolls. Some of these individuals were dropped due to retirement and other special factors, but many others failed to fulfill mandated job search requirements. The program also appears to have produced a decline in long-term unemployment of about 5 percent. However, the desirable effect on unemployment due to increased hiring of the long-term unemployed was substantially offset by a reduction in the hiring of short-term unemployed workers, leaving total unemployment essentially unchanged. This evidence raises an important red flag that targeted programs intended to benefit a particular category of workers may operate as intended for the targeted group, but only at the expense of the job opportunities of nontargeted workers. This "displacement effect" was considered in chapter 3 in the context of the U.S. reemployment bonus experiments.

Canada's UI Initiatives

The discussion in chapter 2 commented on the generosity of Canada's unemployment insurance system. Indeed, among the seven countries included in table 2.1, only the United Kingdom reports a higher public expenditure ratio on passive labor market programs than Canada.

The relative generosity of the Canadian UI system during the 1980s stemmed from basically three factors. First, unemployed Canadians could qualify for UI on the basis of as little as 10 to 14 weeks of employment, depending on the unemployment rate in the region in which they lived. In contrast, Japan requires 26 weeks of work during the past year to qualify for UI, while Germany requires 30 weeks of employment during the previous year plus 52 weeks of work during the last three years. Second, Canadian workers who voluntarily quit their jobs may collect UI benefits following a disqualification period that averaged just two weeks. Most countries, including the United States, restrict UI benefits to the involuntary unemployed. Finally, unemployed Canadian job seekers were eligible for up to 50 weeks of UI benefits.

The Labour Force Development Strategy announced by the Canadian government in 1989 had the purposes of tightening up on UI eligibility while, at the same time, allowing a reallocation of UI resources from income maintenance to active labor market policies. A policy statement released by Employment and Immigration Canada (1989a, pp. 11-12) spells out the following changes in eligibility for UI benefits.

1. While retaining the UI program's sensitivity to differences in regional unemployment rates, a new UI benefit schedule increases the minimum weeks of employment required to become eligible for UI benefits in most areas of the country. For example, the minimum weeks worked requirement for workers in Saskatoon, Montreal, and St.

John's would increase from 10 weeks to 13 to 16 weeks under the new regulations.

2. The maximum period of UI entitlement is reduced except in those regions suffering very high unemployment rates. For example, claimants in regions with an unemployment rate of 11 percent who had worked for at least 30 weeks were entitled to 50 weeks of UI benefits. Under the new regulations, these claimants qualify for just 42 weeks of UI.

3. Workers who quit their jobs without just cause are still eligible to receive UI, but they face a 7- to 12-week delay before benefits commence, and the duration of their benefits is reduced. In addition, the replacement rate for insurable earnings is cut to 50 percent from 60 percent.

4. Penalties are significantly strengthened for fraudulent use of the UI program by claimants and employers.

The Labour Force Development Strategy also permits UI funds to be spent on active labor market programs. Prior to 1989, payment for the costs of training and other reemployment services came out of the budget of the Canadian Jobs Strategy (CJS), while income support for UI recipients was paid for from the UI account. (The comprehensive CJS program created in 1985 was outlined in chapter 2.) In 1989, Employment and Immigration Canada was permitted for the first time to use the UI account to fund training program costs, supplementary allowances, and associated income support payments. Employment and Immigration Canada's policy statement (1989a) projects for the early 1990s that reforms of the UI system will save $1.3 billion (Canadian) in UI expenditures per year. This represents about 10 percent of the UI program's total annual expenditures beginning in 1990. Of the $1.3 billion, approximately $500 million is projected to be spent on improved UI benefits for maternity, sickness, and parental leave, as well as for workers over the age of 65. The remaining $800 million is dedicated to raising the skills of Canadian workers and enhancing job placement and job development services. In particular, the IAS is to receive a more than doubling of its budget to $15 million, allowing program services to be made available to about 1,000 firms and their workers annually (in comparison to the 400 to 600 firms noted earlier). Legislation passed in 1990 authorized a greater percentage of UI funds to be earmarked for training.

In 1991 a restructuring of Canadian employment and training programs was carried out in which the Job Development, Job Entry, and Skill Shortages programs of the Canadian Jobs Strategy were incorporated into the new Employability Improvement Program. Added to this program, moreover, was the Feepayer option, which was previously outside the CJS. The Feepayer option permits UI-eligible workers to receive income support and an exemption from having to engage in job search while undergoing training. However, Feepayer option participants themselves, or a third party, are required to pay for training costs. Following 1989, as noted, the Labour Force Development Strategy made UI funds available to pay these costs. The overall objective of the Employability Improvement Program of 1991 was to decentralize decision making, allowing CEC counselors to work with UI clients to develop reemployment plans more closely attuned to the needs of the individual. This policy change resulted in increased use of the Feepayer option. Prior to 1991, the preferred approach was the Direct Purchase option under which workers eligible for CJS programs were assigned to program slots purchased from training institutions by the government.

An evaluation study commissioned by Employment and Immigration Canada recently examined the effect of UI-sponsored training on labor market outcomes for participants in the Feepayer, DIR, Job Entry, Job Development, and Skill Shortages programs (see Park, Riddell, and Power 1993). A brief description of each of these programs follows.

Feepayer clients must qualify for UI and must have been out of school for more than two years. Feepayers are eligible to enroll in any training program recommended by their CEC counselor, including, since 1991, basic skills training.

DIR clients either took training (often in the evening) that did not interfere with their job search or did not inform their local CEC office that they were enrolled in training while on UI.

Job Entry clients include women reentering the workforce after an absence of at least three years and out-of-school youths with little labor market experience.

Job Development clients must have suffered long-term unemployment defined as being unemployed for at least 24 weeks in the previous 30 weeks.

Skill Shortages clients are workers recommended by their CEC counselors for training in skills designated at the national level as being in short supply.

The Park, Riddell, and Power study is based on longitudinal data collected for UI trainees and nontrainees whose UI receipt began in 1988, 1989, 1990, or 1991. Training provided to workers participating in all five programs is classroom training. However, the average length of training courses differed significantly by program, with Feepayer program participants enrolled in the longest courses (33.5 weeks on average) and Skill Shortages participants enrolled in the shortest courses (19.2 weeks).

Availability of longitudinal data collected for trainees and nontrainees makes it possible to use a "difference-in-differences" econometric approach to controlling for the selection bias likely to be present because both observed and unobserved factors influence earnings as well as program selection. The key assumption underlying this approach is that there is an unobserved permanent component of earnings that varies across individuals but is fixed over time, and that this permanent earnings component also influences the program selection decision. Park, Riddell, and Power also estimate a two-stage model for controlling for sample selection, using a multinomial logistic model to form selection bias correction terms for each of the five training programs. However, the authors (1993, p. 124) argue that the difference-in-differences approach is more credible because it nets out the large differences observed between programs in preprogram earnings.

Table 5.3 presents net impact estimates for the five components of the Employability Improvement Program obtained using the differences-in-differences econometric methodology. Shown are estimated net impacts measured in terms of 1991 earnings for the 1988 and 1989 cohorts of UI claimants. For each cohort, estimates are calculated for base year earnings measured both two years and one year prior to initial receipt of UI benefits. The table indicates that the impact of UI-sponsored training depends strongly on the particular program studied. Across both cohorts, only the Job Entry program resulted in consistently positive and statistically significant impacts on earnings. In addition, the Skill Shortages program records very large and statistically significant estimated impacts for the earlier cohort and distinctly positive but not significant estimates for the later cohort. It is interesting to note that both the Job Entry and Skill Shortages programs provided trainees a much greater opportunity to combine OJT with classroom training than was possible in the other three programs (see Park, Riddell, and Power 1993, p. 29).

Table 5.3 Impact of Canadian UI-Sponsored Training Programs, 1991 Earnings, by Cohort of UI Recipients and Pretraining Base Year

	1988 cohort		1989 cohort	
Training program	**1986**	**1987**	**1987**	**1988**
Feepayer	4816***	3494***	–20	906
DIR	1981	2181	–1018	1013
Job Development	1531	2221*	–215	1291
Job Entry	4461***	4935***	4054**	6296***
Skill shortages	6188***	5429***	1965	1784

SOURCE: Park, Riddell, and Power (1993, table 5.12).
NOTE: Estimates are based on comparisons of average earnings.
***, **, and * indicate significance at the 1 percent, 5 percent, and 10 percent levels, respectively.

In contrast to these two Employability Improvement Program components, net impact estimates obtained for the Feepayer, DIR, and Job Development programs are only rarely positive and statistically significant and are occasionally even negative. All of the estimates shown in table 5.3 are based on a simple comparison of average earnings. Controlling for residence and a limited number of personal characteristics in a regression framework, program net impact estimates display the same general patterns seen in table 5.3, although the individual estimates tend to be smaller in magnitude.[8]

Australia's Newstart Program

While income support was commonly received by displaced Australians enrolled in a retraining activity, the government implemented in July 1991 a fundamental reform of its unemployment benefit program intended to make income maintenance more directly related to claimant self-help. Termed Newstart, the program was a response to a growing number of long-term unemployed Australian workers. Instead of providing unemployed workers with income support and leaving it up to them to conduct their own job search, Newstart is designed to diagnose the difficulty the unemployed are having in finding employment, and then to deal actively with their needs through retraining and other forms of active labor market assistance.

Like the British scheduling and programming strategy, Newstart treats the long-term jobless (defined as being out of work for more than 12 months) differently from those experiencing shorter periods of joblessness. In particular, the Newstart program creates two new payment schemes—the Job Search Allowance for the shorter-term unemployed (and those under age 18) and the Newstart Allowance for the long-term unemployed. The objective of the Job Search Allowance is to prevent long-term unemployment by early identification of clients likely to have difficulty obtaining reemployment. With this objective in mind, the Commonwealth Employment Service (CES) interviews all clients after three months of unemployment, and again if they remain unemployed after six months. If the CES determines that vocational training is needed to improve labor market prospects, Job Search Allowance participants receive a training allowance along with their Job Search Allowance. To ensure an adequate number of training slots, the government pledged to provide funding for additional active labor market services through the end of 1993-94.

A key feature of the Newstart program is the tailoring of assistance and program requirements to the individual needs and capacities of the unemployed. For workers unemployed longer than 12 months, continued receipt of income-maintenance benefits requires that an application be submitted for participation in the Newstart Allowance payment system. In turn, receipt of the Newstart Allowance is conditional on the working out of an Activity Agreement by the client and a CES staff member. This agreement outlines the steps that the individual will have to take to improve his or her employment prospects. Clients who fail to meet their obligations by refusing offers of assistance or by exerting insufficient effort themselves may have their payments suspended for a period or canceled entirely.

Summary

The core employment service provided in most industrialized nations, including the United States, is the traditional labor exchange function involving matching unemployed workers to job vacancies listed by employers in the local labor market. Beyond this core service, public employment services typically play the supportive roles of gatekeeper in allocating retraining and transitional employment opportunities and of enforcer of job search requirements imposed by unemployment insurance programs.

Following a brief overview of more proactive job search assistance services, this chapter began with a review of the limited empirical evidence available on the effectiveness of the U.S. and Canadian public employment services in matching the unemployed with vacant jobs. A favorable interpretation of this evidence is that the public employment agencies of both nations appear to have potential, but that this potential is largely unrealized. Particularly for the United States, the absence of consistently positive net impact estimates for public employment services is not surprising, given regulations targeting services to the disadvantaged, a sharp decline in federal funding, and the absence of universal listing of job vacancies by employers. The outcome of a process of adverse selection is that the U.S. Employment Service is basically limited to the referral of unskilled workers to low-paying and often temporary jobs. ES job matching services are consequently of little interest to many displaced workers. Nevertheless, ES job matching services are very low cost, and the argument can be made that the ES serves a valuable "backstop" function in aiding job seekers who lack good information about the pay and location of vacant jobs or have failed to locate jobs using other job search methods. There also appears to be considerable variation in efficiency across local ES offices, with offices subject to state performance standards and those engaging in job development with employers generally demonstrating higher placement rates.

Considered next was the operation of the highly regarded Swedish Employment Service. The Swedish government provides a highly efficient job matching service as well as a broad mix of more proactive job search assistance services. Key aspects of the Swedish system include (1) immediate provision of services to laid-off workers, (2) a permanent case manager assigned to each client, (3) near universal listing of job vacancies by employers, (4) a computerized system for matching vacancies with job seekers, and (5) attention to the needs of those not immediately job-ready through extensive vocational testing and assessment. A near universal listing of job vacancies and the highly computerized labor exchange system make it attractive for Swedish job seekers of all levels of job readiness, including the highly skilled, to visit their local employment exchange office to get leads on jobs available across Sweden. At the same time, employers are assured that workers referred to them are not limited to the lower end of the skill distribution.

Beyond its labor exchange function, the Swedish Employment Service provides a number of JSA services. One of these is the involvement of staff members in job development to help in locating jobs not listed or advertised by employers. The job development function of public employment services was considered in more detail in the context of the Canadian Industrial Adjustment Service. The IAS is a low-cost federal agency that serves as a catalyst in inducing local labor and management officials to work together to locate job opportunities for workers displaced by economic and technological change. A recent evaluation of the IAS concludes that job development, when not contaminated by the receipt of additional services, is associated with less time looking for work, a greater likelihood of finding a full-time job, and higher postprogram earnings.

Employment services are usually linked to unemployment benefits by requirements that UI benefit recipients engage in some form of active job search. The United States offers unemployed workers a UI program that is stringent, relative to the programs of most other OECD countries, in terms of eligibility requirements, wage replacement rates, and period of benefit eligibility. Other industrialized nations that offer more generous UI programs are typically faced with a more severe problem of long-term unemployment.

The final section of the chapter examined recent initiatives in Britain, Canada, and Australia to deal with the issue of long-term dependency on income-maintenance benefits. Canada's new approach is to limit eligibility and length of benefits and to shift a majority of the UI funds saved to active labor market policies. Canadian Employment Centre staff members are instructed to work closely with claimants in developing individualized reemployment plans. Britain and Australia are pursuing active labor market policies designed with two objectives in mind. The first is to decrease the likelihood that a recently laid-off worker will become a member of the long-term unemployed through increased access to training and job search assistance programs. (The long-term unemployed are defined as being unemployed for more than 6 months in Britain and more than 12 months in Australia.) Programs in both nations seek to identify early in the unemployment spell those claimants likely to have difficulty finding reemployment without assistance. The second objective is to increase the labor market contact of the long-term unemployed by making continued receipt of income-maintenance benefits more directly related to claimant self-help.

NOTES

1. In the United States, for example, the unemployment insurance system promotes the reemployment of claimants by imposing a set of work search requirements and referring claimants who are not job-attached and do not expect to be recalled to the Employment Service.

2. Osberg also comments that the wage of $6.24 overstates the wages actually available to CEC users because organizations such as the federal government and universities (who want to be seen as making jobs available to a broad range of Canadian applicants) may list jobs with the CEC without any real expectation that such listings will produce serious candidates.

3. Osberg's remark about the CEC is in the context of similar complaints he reports about public employment agencies in Australia, Britain, and the United States.

4. At current staffing levels, Bishop (1993a, p. 384) suggests that the ES appears to see its market niche as a highly automated, high-volume referral system. As part of its labor exchange function, Bishop also notes that the new referral system of the ES bases referrals on the General Aptitude Test Battery, which evaluates applicants' potential performance in a wide range of jobs.

5. Trehörning (1993, p. 59) notes that in December 1992 a government commission of inquiry presented draft legislation that would permit the establishment of private employment agencies as a supplement to the public employment service. As in Canada, it would be illegal to charge job seekers a fee, but employers who hire workers through the agency may be billed.

6. The authors add that these costs could be further reduced if innovations in telecommunications equipment could be exploited to permit face-to-face interviews with geographically distant prospective employers through teleconferencing.

7. A more recent estimate obtained from personal correspondence with Ging Wong, Director of the Insurance Programs Division of the EIC, is that the number of IAS agreements was 860 per year during the early 1990s.

8. Sample sizes for these regressions are 571 and 407, respectively, for the 1988 and 1989 cohorts. Park, Riddell, and Power (1993, p. 121) note that these sample sizes are somewhat lower than those used to calculate the estimates in table 5.3 because of missing observations for the control variables.

6
Conclusion

Chapter 1 described displaced workers as unemployed individuals with considerable work experience who lost their previous jobs because of a layoff or plant closing associated with widespread industrial restructuring. Industrial restructuring, in turn, is the consequence of substantial excess capacity in key industries resulting from fundamental technological, political, regulatory, and economic forces that are radically changing the global competitive environment. Michael Jensen (1994) of the Harvard Business School recently argued in *The Wall Street Journal* that today these forces are generating a "Third Industrial Revolution" comparable in scope to the previous two.[1]

Since their job losses follow from industrial restructuring, displaced workers face a low probability of being recalled to their old jobs or even to similar jobs in their old industries. And because of their considerable work experience, many displaced workers have not been obliged for perhaps many years to test the labor market by engaging in job search. Thus the job search skills of the displaced are likely to be rusty, and they are quite unlikely to possess up-to-date information about alternative job opportunities, particularly those in other industries.

Following immediately from this simple characterization of displaced workers are the following policy prescriptions:

- Training is likely to be necessary for at least some displaced workers to qualify for jobs in expanding industries. In this context, training should be defined broadly to include not only vocational skill retraining but also training in basic math and communications skills necessary for reemployment or as a prerequisite for skill training.
- Job search assistance (JSA) services are essential to enhance the job search skills of many of the displaced.
- Displaced workers will typically benefit from an efficient public employment service that furnishes job vacancy information not necessarily restricted to the local labor market.

The OECD includes both JSA and job matching services under the general heading of employment services. Employment services and adult training are major components of what are known as active labor market programs.[2]

A large literature exists indicating that displaced workers suffer sizable earnings losses associated with lengthy periods of postlayoff joblessness and lower wages upon reemployment. These earnings losses have been found to be especially large for displaced workers possessing lengthy job tenure with their prelayoff employers, those forced to change industry or occupation to find a new job, and residents of high-unemployment areas.

Using longitudinal data covering the 1980-86 period for high-tenure workers in Pennsylvania, a recent study by Jacobson, LaLonde, and Sullivan (1993a, 1993b) provides a comprehensive picture of earnings losses suffered by the displaced. The authors find that earnings losses of displaced workers average about $9,000 or 40 percent of prelayoff earnings in the year following displacement. The size of these losses declines somewhat over time, as almost all displaced workers find stable employment after six quarters of unemployment. But even during the fifth year after job separation, lower-wage reemployment jobs led to earnings losses that average approximately $6,500, or 25 percent of former earnings. Moreover, earnings losses associated with temporary layoffs and wage reductions began even before workers were permanently separated from their firms. Taking into account the prelayoff earnings dip, the period of postdisplacement joblessness, and lower reemployment wages, Jacobson, LaLonde, and Sullivan calculate that the present value of earnings losses for a typical displaced worker is on the order of $80,000. This is clearly a major financial setback for experienced workers. There is little wonder that labor unions and sympathetic policy makers object with such stridency to policies including trade liberalization and environmental protection that may lead to increased displacement. Farber (1993) presents evidence indicating that older and more educated workers were more vulnerable to job loss during the 1990-91 recession than during earlier recessions. Moreover, he suggests that the wage loss associated with displacement for the full-time reemployed was substantially larger for workers displaced in 1990-91 than it was for workers displaced earlier.

From a social perspective, the fundamental problem is that while all consumers benefit from the lower prices made possible by freer international trade and improved technology, the substantial labor market costs associated with industrial restructuring are concentrated on displaced workers. Recognizing this problem, the governments of all industrialized nations offer an array of labor market services intended, at least in part, to reduce the costs of displacement. These services are typically divided into active and passive programs. The primary passive program provided by all industrialized nations is an unemployment compensation system intended to help maintain the consumption of unemployed workers and their families during a temporary period of joblessness. But since the joblessness faced by displaced workers is not fundamentally cyclical, it is widely argued that more aggressive active labor market policies are required to assist the displaced in making the transition to new jobs in growing industries. The OECD has been instrumental in causing policy makers in many countries to redirect their focus from passive to active labor market policies.[3]

In comparison to most other industrialized nations, the United States devotes a small fraction of national resources to both active and passive labor market programs. Our active labor market programs, in particular, can accurately be described as fragmented and subject to dramatic fluctuations in funding and focus. The two areas in which the United States does lead the world are in its willingness to fund limited-duration demonstration projects and the technical sophistication with which the labor market effects of these projects are evaluated. Chapter 3 described the empirical evidence available for the Downriver, Buffalo, Texas WAD, and New Jersey UI displaced worker demonstrations. Also examined in chapter 3 was evidence on the impact of retraining services provided under the Trade Adjustment Assistance program. Despite this wealth of empirical evidence, the net impact estimates summarized in chapter 3 are subject to enough qualifications, particularly with respect to skill training provided in a classroom setting, that it is not easy to draw strong policy recommendations for the design of permanent, nationwide programs.

The thesis advanced in this monograph is that experience gained by other highly developed nations in the design and implementation of active labor market programs is worth considering by American policy makers as they contemplate new labor market policy initiatives. The six nations studied fall into two groups. The first group consisting of Sweden, Germany, and Japan provides their workers with a stable, nationwide employment and training system. Within this group, Sweden is well known for its comprehensive government training system operated in conjunction with an extensive network of employment exchange offices. Germany and Japan are best known for their firm-based training models, with the major difference between the two nations being that Germany's dual system of apprenticeship training focuses training opportunities on youth while workplace training in Japan continues throughout a worker's career with his or her employer.

The countries in the second group—Britain, Canada, and Australia—have in common recent major restructurings of their employment and training programs involving the shift of resources from passive to active labor market policies. Canada's strategy is to limit eligibility and duration of unemployment insurance benefits and to shift a majority of the UI funds saved to active labor market policies. Britain and Australia are attempting to deal with the issue of dependency on income-maintenance benefits with active labor market policies designed to prevent recently laid-off workers from joining the ranks of the long-term unemployed and to increase the labor market contact of workers already included among the long-term unemployed.

Because the labor market programs in all six of these countries have not typically been subjected to formal evaluation in which program costs and benefits are estimated and compared, chapter 1 outlined an informal evaluation framework against which the operation of active labor market programs in different nations may be consistently assessed. Viewed from the perspective of U.S. policy makers, the evaluation framework consists of the following six criteria:

1. Program services should facilitate the transition of displaced workers to jobs in expanding industries and growing sectors within existing industries.

2. Program activities must meet the needs of displaced workers—that is, programs should be flexible, job-oriented, and low cost to participants.

3. Programs must serve the entire spectrum of displaced workers, not just those easiest to place.

4. Training programs must supply marketable skills to program graduates.

5. Programs should effectively utilize existing education and training institutions.

6. A broadening of the concept of job skills should be encouraged—that is, restructured employers require workers who are retrainable and adaptable to new technologies and work organizations.

In line with criterion 1, the discussion in this concluding chapter focuses on what can be learned from the experience of these six nations with adult training and employment services, since these are the categories of programs intended to facilitate mobility between industries and sectors within industries. Adult training is considered first, followed by a discussion of employment services in the second section. The final section of the chapter outlines an agenda for assisting displaced American workers.

Adult Training

Chapter 4 examined the following three training models found in the countries considered: the government training model, the firm-based training model, and the employer-led/school-based training model. Of the six countries studied, the nations that offer stable, nationwide employment and training systems—Sweden, Germany, and Japan—are leading examples of the operation of the government training and firm-based training models. Building on the discussion in chapter 4, this section begins with a consideration of lessons that can be learned from the Swedish government training system. This is followed by an examination of firm-based training systems in Germany and Japan. Considered finally is the employer-led/school-based system recently implemented in Britain.

The Government Training Model

Sweden's government training model is implemented through the National Employment Training Board, which is a major component of a comprehensive national employment and training system. It was pointed out in chapter 2 that the Swedish government spends a far higher percentage of Gross Domestic Product on adult training than does any other of the nations considered. Functioning independently of the regular educational infrastructure, the National Employment Training Board operates a nationwide system of 100 skill training centers. Each skill center offers basic education courses as well as several hundred vocational training curricula lasting up to a year or more.

Creation of a government training system like that found in Sweden is not practical in the United States because of our extensive postsecondary school system (see criterion 5). Nevertheless, there are at least three important lessons to be learned from the Swedish experience. First, training should be provided to the extent possible in an environment resembling a workplace rather than a classroom in a school. In connection with the second criterion, it was emphasized earlier in chapter 1 that displaced workers are interested in jobs, not training. In Sweden, a modular system allows training programs to be individualized and self-paced, and instructors relate to trainees less like teachers lecturing students than like supervisors interacting with employees.

A second lesson is that program curricula should be directly responsive to market demand so that program graduates possess job skills that are salable (criterion 4). Sweden has traditionally approached this problem by appointing business and labor members to the national and local boards that supervise the training system. The 1986 reorganization of the system was designed to increase its flexibility and responsiveness by decentralizing decision making within the National Employment Training Board and making it financially self-supporting.

Finally, the Swedish adult training system operates successfully as the most common way for Swedish workers to enhance their vocational skills. This is true whether they are jobless and classified as displaced or economically disadvantaged workers or they are currently employed individuals interested in upgrading their skills to qualify for a promotion or to move between employers. The broad usage of the system has two substantial advantages in comparison to the narrowly targeted approach used in the United States. One advantage is that the Swedish system avoids the stigma often attached by employers to graduates of programs specifically targeted to the low skilled or to welfare recipients. The other is the equity issue involved in allowing some jobless individuals access to a government-funded program, but denying access to others who appear to be equally in need (for example, access to the Trade Adjustment Assistance program in the United States is restricted to trade-displaced workers).

Although adult training in Sweden is generally highly praised, the system has been subjected to several criticisms. One is that it "warehouses" substantial numbers of workers for whom training is unlikely to improve their long-term earnings prospects (see, for example, Bendick 1983, p. 216). More recently, Ramaswamy (1994) argues that Sweden's government training system imparts mainly general skills, whereas modern technology requires a greater emphasis on workplace-specific skills. But employers' willingness to offer in-house training depends, at least in part, on the freedom they have to devise their own internal wage structures and promotion schemes to retain the services of newly trained workers. In Ramaswamy's view, rigidities imposed by centralized bargaining and a national policy of wage equalization remove the flexibility Swedish employers need to offer wage-tenure profiles that are steeply enough sloped to retain the services of trained workers. The consequence is an underinvestment in firm-specific training. This argument may help to explain the absence of evidence noted in chapter 4 of a positive earnings effect of Swedish adult training programs. Finally, Forslund and Krueger (1994) emphasize that Sweden's heavy investment in adult training and active labor market programs in general failed to fend off the extraordinarily large rise in the Swedish unemployment rate beginning in 1991.

Firm-Based Training

From the criterion 4 perspective that training programs must supply marketable skills, the firm-based model is most likely to be successful since workplace training has the benefit of providing demand-related training. Baily, Burtless, and Litan (1993, p. 126) note that while graduates of public training programs often end up with skills they do not use on their next jobs,

> [P]rivate employers, who at least understand their own training needs, enjoy significant advantages in assigning workers to courses of instruction. Chances are good that if an employer is paying for part of the training investment, the training will be used in the worker's next job.

Since the training is strongly linked to jobs (as opposed to simply more schooling), firm-based training also satisfies an important need expressed in criterion 2. Considered in detail in chapter 4 were the firm-based training systems in place in Germany and Japan.

The German dual system of apprenticeship training has recently received considerable attention in this country because of the Clinton administration's advocacy of a nationwide system of youth apprenticeship programs designed after the German model (see Heckman, Roselius, and Smith 1993). As described earlier, apprenticeship training in Germany lasts from two to three and one-half years; and apprentices complement their on-the-job training with one or two days a week of off-the-job training in a state vocational school. The workers produced by this system are generally thought to be highly skilled—as opposed to highly specialized—as called for by the "high-performance workplaces" described in chapter 1 in the context of criterion 6. Although the German dual system is currently of interest to policy makers seeking to smooth the school-to-work transition of American youth, the earlier discussion also pointed out that adult workers in Germany have the opportunity to continue their occupation-specific training in a *Meister* or a Technician program. In the case of the displaced, ad hoc agreements worked out between employers, local government officials, and worker-elected works councils frequently allow redundant workers to receive government-subsidized retraining. The objective of the government subsidy is to allow workers to remain on the employer's payroll or, in the case of a permanent plant closure, to entice new management to take over the closed facility and its workers.

The transferability of the German dual system of apprenticeship training to American workers is considerably enhanced by the commitment within the United States to provide ready access to community college and vocational/technical school training. Indeed, the community college system is currently undergoing a fundamental transformation. Historically a springboard to four-year colleges and a source of vocational training for youth, community colleges are emerging as the nation's largest provider of adult worker retraining. Along with standard classes in basic literacy and math skills, community colleges are increasingly linking up with local employers to develop technical courses tailored to meet their individual demands for skilled workers (see Lynch 1993b, p. 1301; and Osterman and Batt 1993, pp. 460-61).

This trend toward greater utilization of existing education and training institutions to meet firm-specific training needs is very much consistent with criterion 5.

Hashimoto (1994) reports that while the use of formal training by Japanese employers is increasing, informal training in the workplace still characterizes Japan's firm-based training system.[4] The Japanese model is built on a school system that produces students competent in basic skills and possessing the abilities to learn and to function as team members. Once hired, large Japanese firms offer an internal labor market structure within which workers can expect to receive life-long training opportunities through a process of job rotation supplemented by self-study. The combination of high-quality schooling and intensive informal training produces workers widely viewed as capable of meeting the many challenges imposed in high-performance workplaces. That is, Japanese workers covered by lifetime employment guarantees tend to be highly skilled, able to work in teams, flexible in their ability to adjust quickly to changes in product demand, and capable of solving problems on their own.

Although Germany and Japan are still widely regarded as producing world-class skilled workers, some criticisms of their firm-based systems are beginning to surface (see, for example, Heckman, Roselius, and Smith 1993; and *The Economist* 1994b). The German apprenticeship system has been criticized as being inflexible in responding to shifts in the occupational demand for labor. Moreover, questions have recently been raised about whether occupation-specific training is sufficient to allow workers to be competitive in labor markets that appear to be placing increasing value on workers' abilities to perform multiple tasks and to retrain themselves in new skills. Apparently young Germans recognize that apprenticeship training may no longer guarantee a secure job. *The Economist* (1994c) recently reported that the number seeking places in the dual system of apprenticeship training is falling and that, for the first time, more Germans are choosing to enroll in universities than to enter the dual system.

The viability of the Japanese model is also being questioned as, due to the lingering effects of the worldwide recession of the early 1990s, fewer young workers are being extended lifetime employment contracts by their employers. Japanese employers are instead making increasing use of temporary or contract workers for whom continued employment and salaries are renegotiated annually and pay is tied strictly to performance. At the same time, chapter 4 presented anecdotal evidence for Japanese as well as German transplant firms located in the United States, which indicates that the firm-based training systems of both nations are economically feasible with American workers.

In the absence of the high value placed on skilled workforces in Germany and Japan, an approach to increasing firm-based training in the United States is the imposition of a payroll training tax along the lines of the Australian Training Guarantee discussed in chapter 4. Australian employers are required to document that they spend 1.5 percent (as of 1992) of their payroll on formal training; otherwise, they have to make up the difference between what they spend and 1.5 percent of payroll in a tax payment. These tax payments are presumably used to fund government-sponsored training programs. The training tax offers the advantages of increasing the priority employers place on training and of reducing the incentive to poach already-trained workers, since all firms that benefit from training share in the costs. Nevertheless, the earlier discussion of the Australian Training Guarantee centered on two difficulties in implementing a training tax. The first of these was the problem of verifying reported expenditures on programs and trainers since companies have an incentive to overstate their training expenditures. The second was the difficulty of making sure that access to training actually increases for less-skilled workers and for employees of small firms.

In advocating a 2 percent training tax levied on payrolls, Baily, Burtless, and Litan (1993, pp. 128-31) are optimistic that these two problems can be overcome.[5] To ensure that training opportunities are directed to the less skilled, they recommend that employers be required to devote at least a specified percentage of their payrolls to training workers whose formal education ended with high school or who have no more than a year of college. On the problem of verifying employer training expenditures, the authors suggest that for the first several years after the training obligation has been imposed, approved training expenses should be defined loosely to reduce the shock of the new mandate and to minimize potential adverse effects on employment. Gradually, the definition of allowable training would become more strict in the sense that employers would be expected to demonstrate that the training they provide leads to a mastery of occupational skills as certified by nationally recognized credentials.

Lynch (1993a) and Osterman and Batt (1993) take a less optimistic view of the feasibility of the training tax. They argue, based on experience gained in Australia as well as in France, that no matter how the tax is structured, there will always be some firms that manipulate expenditures to beat the system, and that a tax rate high enough to increase the level of training will be a heavy burden on small firms that are already struggling. Bishop's (1993) description of the French experience with a training tax includes the finding that the incidence of training increases with firm size and, within each firm size category, with skill level. In particular, he points out that small firms have a comparative advantage at providing informal training, but that the training tax furnishes a strong incentive to substitute formal for informal training. Because formal training is subject to substantial economies of scale, small firms are at a disadvantage in responding to this incentive unless they can join forces in a cooperative effort to achieve the scale necessary to make formal training economically feasible.

Employer-Led/School-Based Training

Following on the heels of this discussion of apprenticeships and firm-based training, it is interesting to note that, as described in chapter 4, Britain overhauled its training system in 1988, moving away from an apprenticeship system and to a decentralized employer-led/school-based system. As discussed by Dolton (1993, p. 1266), the primary problem with the union-controlled apprenticeship system administered under the Industrial Training Board (ITB) structure was that some unions feared the consequences of new technology and clung to obsolete demarcation lines between skills. Union apprenticeship programs were thus viewed as an anachronism by a Thatcher government seeking policies intended to restrict the power of institutions like the ITBs and to stimulate market competition and entrepreneurship.

The key element of the 1988 reform was the creation of a national network of consortiums called Training and Enterprise Councils (TECs). Each of the 100 TECs is composed of local employers given the mandate to plan and deliver training services and promote small business development in their geographic regions. The national government provides funding, while each TEC contracts out to local training institutions for provision of the actual training programs. Advantages of the TEC approach are twofold. First, decentralization increases the responsiveness of the training system to the needs of local employers. Second, access to training of employees of small firms is enhanced by spreading fixed costs of training programs over the greater number of workers covered by the consortium. As discussed in chapter 4, performance standards are imposed on individual TECs to make sure that their efforts are consistent with national policy goals. The earlier discussion suggested that performance standards can be specified to minimize the problem of creaming in the selection of program participants.

To date, the main difficulty with the TEC system involves inadequate revenue. The old ITB system received government funding, but each ITB was also permitted to impose levies on participating firms within its industry. In contrast, TECs face the obligation to deliver services required by existing programs with limited government funding and little incentive for participating employers to commit themselves financially to training programs. It appears that at present TECs can do little more than provide training allowances to youth and members of the long-term unemployed, respectively, who are eligible for the Youth Training and Employment Training programs.[6]

Employment Services

The discussion in chapter 5 centered on two important categories of government-funded employment services—job matching (or labor exchange) services and job search assistance. Job matching is the core employment service provided by public employment agencies in most industrialized nations, including the United States. In addition to this core service, public employment services typically play the supportive roles of gatekeeper in allocating retraining and transitional employment opportunities and of enforcer of job search requirements imposed in unemployment insurance programs. Job search assistance (JSA) services typically go beyond the traditional labor exchange function of public employment services in terms of reaching out to the unemployed, providing them with counseling, improving their job search skills, and assisting them to locate jobs that are not listed or advertised by employers. JSA services are key components of the packages of services offered in the U.S. displaced worker demonstration projects carried out during the 1980s and early 1990s. Yet these services are not commonly available on a permanent and nationwide basis to displaced American workers.

The limited empirical evidence available on the effectiveness of job matching services provided by the U.S. and Canadian public employment services is not especially encouraging. For American men, in particular, a well-known study by Johnson, Dickinson, and West (1985) finds that an Employment Service (ES) referral had no significant effect on earnings and weeks to first job during the six-month period following application to the ES. In other words, unemployed men who did not receive a referral located jobs on their own as quickly as men who received an ES referral. Moreover, the jobs found by the not-referred paid as much.

It is not difficult to explain these discouraging results. As described in chapter 5, the U.S. Employment Service has been obliged to shift its priorities over time from serving all job seekers to focusing on the placement of disadvantaged workers. At the same time, U.S. employers are under no obligation to list their job vacancies with the ES. The consequence of these two factors is a dynamic process of adverse selection, the outcome of which is that the ES is limited to referring low-skilled workers to low-paying and often temporary jobs listed by local employers.

A recent survey by Jacobson (1994) of largely unpublished papers and government reports offers a less pessimistic evaluation of the Employment Service. Two of his points are particularly worth considering. First, he argues that the ES has an important role to play as a "backstop" aiding job seekers who lack good information about alternative job opportunities or those who have tried, but failed, to find jobs using other job search methods. That is, the ES does a reasonably good job of helping unskilled workers find relatively low-paying jobs. Second, despite reductions in resources and increased responsibilities that detract from its effectiveness in providing labor exchange services, Jacobson concludes that the ES offers enough potential that marginal changes in management procedures and funding could dramatically improve its performance.

Sweden offers an example of a well-funded national employment service that provides labor exchange services to a broad cross section of workers. As described in chapters 2 and 5, the nationwide system of employment exchange offices operated by the National Labor Market Board is the focal point of Swedish labor market policy. An unemployed job seeker who registers with his or her local employment exchange office becomes the responsibility of a case manager who is responsible for the case until the worker becomes reemployed. Clients who are not job-ready may be referred to specialists within the National Labor Market Board for counseling or to an adult training program. Because Swedish law requires employers to list vacant jobs with the public employment service, job-ready clients have access through their local employment exchange office to information on the full range of employment opportunities available across Sweden. This makes it attractive for skilled as well as unskilled job seekers to make use of the public employment service. At the same time, employers can be confident that employment exchange referrals will not be limited to the low end of the skill distribution.

Displaced workers have been characterized throughout this monograph as experienced, frequently well-paid adult workers who have been permanently laid off from their jobs. Because of their often lengthy tenure with their prelayoff employers, the job search skills of the displaced are likely to be rusty and they are unlikely to possess up-to-date information on alternative job opportunities. While an argument can be made that the U.S. Employment Service performs a useful function for individuals least able to help themselves (see Jacobson 1994), it seems clear the ES could become substantially more helpful to many displaced workers if it were redirected to serve a broader cross section of workers, and if it were able to list more of the good job openings available. Following the Swedish model, the latter objective could be accomplished by requiring employers to list all job openings with the ES except for those intended to be filled through internal promotions or job reassignments. If, as seems likely, this kind of government coercion is ruled out, the alternative is to induce voluntary employer cooperation by improving the quality of services that both workers and firms can expect. In Sweden, a fully computerized job placement system in place since the late 1980s provides each employment exchange office with on-line access to information on job seekers and job vacancies across Sweden. An underfunded U.S. Employment Service has been slow to utilize computers in developing a referral system that is national in scope. As noted by Baily, Burtless, and Litan (1993, p. 138),

> [A]lthough developing software for interstate job referrals is a formidable problem, it is solvable given the dramatic reductions in the cost of computation over the past two decades. Moreover, the burdens of writing job referral software are hardly unique. Missile defense, the space program, and air traffic control all required enormous investments in software development. We wonder whether the problems of the U.S. Employment Service have received less attention because policymakers erroneously believe that labor market exchange is a straightforward and relatively unimportant public function.

Employment and Immigration Canada (1989b, chs. 5 and 6) summarizes the results of a survey of Canadian Employment Centre staff in which they were asked to evaluate the effectiveness of a computerized on-line system of processing job orders and worker client data. As described in chapter 5, over three-quarters of responding CEC staff members cited the on-line system as improving the quality of services delivered to both worker clients and employer clients.

Turning to job search assistance, chapter 3 summarized in some detail the evaluation evidence gathered for JSA services from the U.S. displaced worker demonstrations. JSA services offered in the four demonstration projects include various combinations of the following: (1) outreach; (2) orientation; (3) assessment and testing; (4) job search workshops, resource centers, and job clubs; (5) follow-up counseling; and (6) job development. Evidence from the demonstrations indicates quite clearly that JSA speeds up the reemployment of displaced workers. Given their modest cost per worker, moreover, the evidence suggests that JSA services are cost effective.

There is also limited evidence available on the labor market effectiveness of some of the individual JSA services. These include job counseling, job clubs, and job development. Using data from the New Jersey UI Reemployment demonstration, Anderson (1992) examines the reemployment impact of the job counseling provided as part of job search workshops offered all treatment group members. In principle, job counseling might achieve its desired result in either of two ways: (1) helping displaced workers to more correctly assess and revise downward their recall prospects, or (2) teaching more efficient job search methods. The results of her analysis indicate little support for the second possibility, while counseling did appear to accelerate reemployment by putting workers in closer touch with the realities of the job market.

Chapter 5 noted that in Sweden a response to rising unemployment (from a very low level) during and immediately after the recession of the early 1990s was the expansion of existing job search training activities to include job clubs. Trehörning (1993) reports evidence that these job clubs were effective in helping club participants uncover job openings that had not been advertised or listed with the public employment service. Similarly, the job development service provided by the Canadian Industrial Adjustment Service has received highly favorable assessments over its nearly forty years of existence. An evaluation by Employment and Immigration Canada (1993) emphasizes that the positive labor market impacts of the agency hinge on its job development activity. That is, the effectiveness of the Industrial Adjustment Service appears to be seriously diluted when program participants are channeled into related services, including retraining.

Still other studies examine, for recipients of unemployment compensation benefits, the effectiveness of linking enhanced JSA services to stricter enforcement of work search rules determining continuing eligibility for benefits. For the long-term unemployed in Britain, mandatory attendance at a job search workshop—called Restart courses—is reported by the OECD (1992, annex 3.D) to have resulted in a sharp decline in the number of unemployment compensation recipients claiming benefits. Although this reduction in claimants could be reflecting increased reemployment, the OECD suggests that it is more likely to be capturing access to other sources of income, in which case the benefit claim status of recipients was probably fraudulent. For the United States, similar evidence has been obtained for job search experiments carried out in Charleston, South Carolina, New Jersey, and Washington State that combined enhanced JSA services and tightened UI eligibility checks. Evidence yielded by these three experiments indicates that the measured reduction in length of UI receipt was primarily the result of claimants being dropped from UI rolls either by choice or by being formally denied benefits, rather than their leaving UI because of improved reemployment opportunities. At the very least, these results indicate the importance of linking receipt of UI benefits to work search requirements and, for those who need them, enhanced JSA services.

An Agenda for Assisting Displaced Americans

The distinction between passive and active labor market programs has come up repeatedly in this monograph. Among passive programs, the unemployment insurance system in place in the United States is quite limited, particularly in the duration of UI benefits, in comparison with unemployment compensation systems in most of the other nations considered. While U.S. policy makers are currently concerned about what appears to be a rising incidence of long-term unemployment among the unemployed (see U.S. Department of Labor 1993), the problem of long-term unemployment was seen in chapter 2 to be much less severe in this country than in most of the others countries examined. The perspective taken in this final section is therefore one of developing an active labor market policy intended to meet the needs of displaced workers that builds on the foundation of the existing UI system. The one change in the UI system that might be considered is making UI benefits available on a longer-term basis to workers enrolled in an approved training program lasting longer than six months. Displaced workers may apply for the existing Pell Grant and Guaranteed Student Loan programs, but the maximum amount a student can receive through these programs is substantially less than regular UI assistance. Indeed, Smith (1994, p. 12) argues that an indication of the pent-up demand for income support during training is the large number of displaced workers who have recently applied for Pell grants. It might also be noted that extended UI benefits for eligible displaced workers undergoing retraining is a major feature of the proposed Reemployment Act of 1994.

The agenda outlined here envisions three levels of active labor market services directed toward three categories of displaced workers broadly defined according to services required. Since the displaced are by definition experienced workers who have permanently lost their jobs, the first level of services is a nationwide labor exchange system offered by a revitalized and adequately funded Employment Service. It is critical to reverse earlier policies restricting the ES to servicing only targeted groups such as economically disadvantaged workers. Such policies tend to stigmatize workers in the targeted groups. Moreover, displaced workers may not be easily distinguished from other unemployed workers, particularly early during their spells of unemployment. Early contact with the service delivery system is essential to prevent a period of idleness during which apathy, bitterness, self-doubt, and other negative attitudes have a chance to fester and grow, thereby destroying workers' effectiveness in seeking reemployment. A recent study of the Canadian Revitalization strategy indicates that a short (typically about 11 minute) interview with new UI claimants is sufficient to distinguish the job-ready from claimants who require JSA services or retraining before they can be said to be job-ready (Employment and Immigration Canada 1989b). Recent innovations in the active labor market programs offered in Britain and Australia also seek to identify early in the unemployment spell those claimants likely to have difficulty finding reemployment without assistance. Such "profiling" is encouraged by 1993 federal legislation authorizing extended UI benefits to unemployed American workers.

In an initial visit to his or her local Job Service office, a displaced worker should be able to register for UI benefits and begin the job referral process. The objective is to minimize the time an individual spends filling out forms and waiting in line at different offices and to maximize the time he or she has available for engaging in active job search. It is interesting to note that both the Job Training 2000 program proposed by President Bush and the Clinton administration's proposed Reemployment Act of 1994 emphasize the importance of providing services in a single location—currently termed "one-stop shopping."[7] It was noted in chapter 2 that one-stop job centers are an essential feature of Germany's employment and training system.

To keep the individual from getting lost within the system, a desirable approach is the Swedish procedure in which each client is assigned a case manager who is responsible for the case until the worker finds a new job. A primary task of the case manager is to select an individualized set of services for each client. Although these services may be provided within the system by specialists in assessment and testing, training, and job development, the case manager is the continuing point of contact between the client and the system. Britain's scheduling and programming strategy is also designed to develop a good working relationship between the job seeker and a particular claimant advisor. The overall goal of this first level of the service delivery system is to make job matching services of the ES sufficiently attractive that most job seekers—employed as well as unemployed—will make the local Job Service office their first stop as they initiate their job search process.

These Level 1 services involving basic orientation, access to labor market information, and referrals to potential employers through the job matching system should be sufficient for perhaps a minority of displaced workers who are job-ready and who possess basic job search skills. But there is likely to be a sizable additional group of the displaced whose job search skills are more seriously deficient or whose morale is so low that it inhibits active job search. For these workers, a second level of job search assistance services is required. Appropriate JSA services include training provided in a job search workshop followed by access to either a resource center or a job club. It is also useful to supplement the efforts of individual workers in finding their own job leads with job development assistance on the part of Employment Service staff members. Finally, a strong linkage should be established between receipt of UI benefits and active participation in JSA services.

The JSA services available in Level 2 of the service delivery system are relatively cheap and should be freely available to all individuals whose case managers feel they would benefit from them. On the other hand, the third level of services involving access to training programs is substantially more expensive. Careful attention to assessment and testing is required to limit access to only those individuals who require retraining to qualify for jobs in other industries or to meet the higher skill requirements of jobs in their current industries. Clearly to be avoided is the criticism of the Swedish training system that substantial numbers of workers for whom training is unlikely to improve their long-term earnings prospects are warehoused in training programs.

While it is reasonably easy to make the case for including retraining in the menu of services that should be made available to displaced workers, it is more difficult to specify precisely how an adult training system should be put together. One point is clear. The current hodgepodge of categorical programs should be consolidated into a single adult training system. Although it may have made political sense in the past to design a specific program for each identifiable group of workers displaced due to a particular policy action (e.g., workers displaced from their jobs due to Nafta-induced lowering of tariffs), the present maze of programs is inefficient, inequitable, and serves only a minority of workers in need.

A recurring theme in chapter 4 is that other nations engaged in restructuring their adult training systems are paying particular attention to increasing the involvement of private-sector employers in the training process. There appears to be no other satisfactory way to ensure that training program graduates will possess skills that are salable (criterion 4). In Sweden, the 1986 reorganization of the adult training system was intended to increase responsiveness to market demand by decentralizing decision making and requiring the National Employment Training Board to be financially self-supporting. Similarly, Britain took action in 1988 to make training locally based rather than industry-based and to put decision making under the control of local employers. And Canada's Employability Improvement Program enacted in 1991 seeks to decentralize decision making by giving local Canadian Employment Centre counselors additional flexibility to design reemployment plans more closely aligned with the needs of individual worker clients.

Possibly the most direct way to strengthen the interest of employers, particularly the interest of small employers, in providing additional training is to impose a payroll tax which can be avoided only by increasing formal training expenditures. This approach was taken by the Australian government with the passage of a training tax in 1990 called the Training Guarantee. A serious disadvantage of a training tax policy, however, is the potential adverse impact of an additional payroll tax on the hiring of permanent employees. In addition, as emphasized by Bishop (1993b), it is not clear that small employers should be encouraged to substitute formal training for the kinds of informal training they excel at providing.

More viable approaches to delivering marketable training are either to (1) subsidize the direct purchase by individual displaced workers of training services supplied by private-sector employers or institutional training providers, or (2) subsidize firm-centered training offered through agency-based training programs.[8] The first of these approaches has already been implemented at the federal level through the Pell Grant/Guaranteed Student Loan programs subsidizing investments in postsecondary education. Directed specifically to the displaced, another federal program implementing the direct-purchase approach provides training vouchers to trade-displaced workers under the Trade Adjustment Assistance program (see chapter 3). Training vouchers were also an integral part of the 1992 Job Training 2000 proposal of the Bush administration. Trade Adjustment Assistance vouchers are primarily used to purchase training from vocational/technical schools or community colleges, while training vouchers under the Bush proposal could have been exchanged for on-the-job as well as classroom training. In Britain, Cappelli (1993b) reports that by 1996 the current Youth Training program will be replaced by a system of vouchers intended to increase access of youth to entry-level jobs that offer training opportunities. However, he also notes that while the voucher program is still in its pilot stage, it has been difficult to induce employers to offer positions.

As indicated by experience gained from the Trade Adjustment Assistance program, training vouchers have the advantage of increasing the opportunity of displaced workers to enroll in training programs offered by our extensive system of public postsecondary institutions, thus satisfying criterion 5. That experience is buttressed by evidence reported by O'Neill (1977) in a study of the GI Bill. O'Neill's results suggest that the voucher-delivery system of the GI Bill allowed eligible individuals most in need of training—blacks and educationally disadvantaged veterans in this study—to substantially increase their enrollment in training programs following completion of their military service. Indeed, holding prior schooling and a measure of ability constant, black veterans were found to use the GI Bill to a greater extent than nonblack veterans.

Given the interest of the displaced in training that is directly related to jobs, an increase in their effective demand should enhance the incentive of training institutions to establish closer linkages to local employers, a process that for community colleges already appears to be well under way. Good counseling by Employment Service personnel is a necessary condition for displaced workers to make appropriate decisions on training providers and curricula. A national system of occupational credentials would perhaps also be helpful in guiding individuals' choices toward those training institutions that are most effective in providing skills in recognized occupations and away from the least effective providers. However, a potential problem involved in formal occupational testing is that training instruction will be directed toward performing well on standardized tests rather than toward providing job-related skills demanded in the local labor market (see Heckman, Roselius, and Smith 1993).

The alternative approach to delivering marketable training—the employer-centered/agency-based training model— is intended to more directly involve employers in the design and implementation of training programs. At the federal level, this approach is found in the decentralized systems of decision making presently existing in Britain and under JTPA in this country. The basic concept is that federal dollars are channeled through local boards to subsidize the costs of training programs proposed by employers. Local boards may be patterned after either Private Industry Councils created under JTPA or British Training and Enterprise Councils. In either case, substantial employer representation on the boards is the essential feature, although as chapter 4 described not all British employers appear to be enthusiastic supporters of their local TECs. In both the TEC and JTPA systems, the federal government ensures that its policy objectives are satisfied by imposing performance standards on local boards which, in turn, may withhold partial payment to training providers if these standards are not met. Performance standards may be crafted to emphasize training directed to the low skilled.

At the state level, chapter 2 pointed to the California Employment Training Panel as a leading example of an innovative state-funded agency mandated to stimulate the volume of training activity and to assist in state economic development. This model encourages employers to identify training needs and develop training proposals. If a proposal receives Employment Training Panel funding, employers take the lead in designing curriculums and establishing program admission and completion standards. In exchange for the public funding of their programs, employers obligate themselves to hire successful program graduates. Along with its employer-driven approach to training, the

Employment Training Panel is well known for its extensive use of stringent performance standards.

Under the employer-centered/agency-based training approach, it is likely that many firms will propose cooperative programs established jointly with local training institutions. Participation of small and medium-sized employers may be increased by making smaller firms a priority for funding at the national or local level. To the extent that small firms are especially likely to lack in-house training capacity, groups of small employers can be encouraged to enter into consortiums in which they contract with a local institutional provider to furnish training tailored to meet their specific requirements.

A major advantage of the firm-centered/agency-based approach in comparison to public education-based systems is the direct involvement of employers. In addition, agency-based programs may be quicker to respond to changes in technology and shifts in labor demand. They are also able to draw upon a broader range of training providers. On the other hand, Osterman and Batt (1993) argue that agency-based programs tend to be project-oriented, and thus they do not contribute to the development of a strong training system. In their words (1993, p. 464),

> [T]he most compelling reason for system building is that the training problem is too big for a project-based approach to have much impact. There are too many firms relative to any conceivable level of public funding. Instead, scarce funds should be expended to build institutions that outlive a particular project and that continue to address the issue after the project funds are expended.

From this perspective, the ongoing institutional presence of public training institutions is an important advantage. Fortunately, the increasingly entrepreneurial orientation of community college systems in developing programs tailored to meet the training needs of specific employers is causing public education-based training to more closely resemble firm-centered/agency-based programs in terms of direct employer involvement. At the same time, community colleges are permanent fixtures in their communities. Regarding the value of community college education, it is worth noting that a recent major study by Kane and Rouse (1993) finds that community college students enjoy the same rate of return for every year of credits completed as do students at four-year institutions.

The agenda to assist displaced workers developed in this final section is both conservative and doable in the sense that the three levels of services suggested build directly on lessons learned from experiments and demonstration projects carried out in this country and from permanent, nationwide programs implemented in other highly industrialized nations. It is also of interest, however, to briefly consider a more radical proposal that has recently been suggested as an alternative to more traditional employment and training programs.

Termed "earnings insurance" by Baily, Burtless, and Litan (1993, p. 204) and an "earnings subsidy" by Jacobson, LaLonde, and Sullivan (1993b, pp. 160-71), the objective of this proposal is to cushion the heavy financial blow associated with displacement by supplementing earnings after reemployment. At the same time, the proposal would increase the incentive to find a new job quickly. In the more fully developed earnings-subsidy program, Jacobson, LaLonde, and Sullivan suggest that a subsidy be paid to reemployed workers that is based on their predisplacement earnings. In this way, the subsidy is largest for those workers who bear the greatest losses from displacement. Given the level of predisplacement earnings, the incentive to return to work is strengthened by reducing the subsidy only gradually (i.e., avoiding a 100 percent implicit tax rate) as postdisplacement earnings rise to 100 percent of the level of predisplacement earnings. That is, a worker who is able to quickly find a new job but at a much lower wage than he or she previously earned would be eligible for a sizable earnings subsidy. Under the present UI system, the reemployed worker would of course no longer be eligible for benefits.

Despite these attractive features, there are several reasons for questioning the immediate applicability of a wage-subsidy program to displaced workers in the U.S. labor market. First, evidence from the reemployment bonus demonstration projects discussed in chapter 3 indicates that bonuses offer little promise of speeding up the reemployment process above the effects of much cheaper JSA services. Second, as noted earlier, displaced workers may not be easily distinguished from other unemployed workers, especially early in their spells of unemployment. An advantage of job search assistance services is that their cost is sufficiently low that they can be made available to all unemployed workers, whether or not they were displaced from their previous jobs. A wage-subsidy program, on the other hand, is likely to be substantially more expensive and would thus need to be carefully targeted. Third, a recent simulation study carried out by Davidson and Woodbury (1994) indicates that a wage-subsidy program would indeed provide employment gains to displaced workers, but that these gains would come at the expense of other groups of workers. The authors also find that the displacement effect is widely dispersed. This evidence on displacement certainly appears to reduce the attractiveness of the wage-subsidy proposal as a policy option. Nevertheless, the finding that displacement is widely dispersed can be viewed as positive evidence for a wage subsidy from the perspective that the proposal successfully shelters the displaced from the full labor market costs associated with industrial restructuring without dramatically harming any other particular group of workers.

Finally, the cost of a wage-subsidy program is potentially quite high. Jacobson, LaLonde, and Sullivan (1993b, pp. 167-68) offer one cost estimate of $9 billion annually, noting that this estimate is meant only to be illustrative. By way of comparison, the Clinton administration's budget released in February of 1994 for fiscal year 1995 proposed to spend slightly under $1.5 billion for displaced worker assistance. This consolidated program features both job search assistance and retraining, with another $250 million proposed for a one-stop career shopping program. Also worth noting is that the estimated price tag for the administration's proposed Reemployment Act of 1994 is $13 billion spread over five years, or about $2.6 billion per year.

Wage-subsidy proposals appear to merit further development and study. Given the current state of our knowledge and resources, however, the more prudent course of action to assist displaced Americans in the near term is to proceed as described earlier in developing and implementing a more conventional active labor market policy. The three major elements of such a policy should be a nationwide labor exchange system, job search assistance services that are freely available to those whose job search skills are deficient or whose morale is low, and an adult training program utilizing our postsecondary educational institutions that is carefully limited to those individuals who require retraining to qualify for jobs in new industries or to meet rising skill requirements in their current industries.

NOTES

1. The first industrial revolution took place in England from the late eighteenth through the early nineteenth centuries, and the second took place primarily in the United States from the mid- to the late nineteenth century.

2. Other categories of active labor market programs distinguished by the OECD are job creation/employment subsidies, special youth measures, and programs for the disabled. Because of their work experience, special youth measures and programs for the disabled are not typically relevant to the displaced. Programs falling under the job creation/employment subsidies category are not emphasized in this monograph because their usual purpose is either to maintain employment in depressed industries or to provide temporary employment in the public sector. In other words, job creation/employment subsidy programs may have the perverse effect of slowing down the transition of displaced workers to their higher valued uses in growing industries.

3. Since the late 1970s, the OECD has issued a series of policy statements urging the implementation of active labor market policies. For example, the OECD (1990, p. 8) recommends that

> [P]riority should be given to active measures such as training, placement and rehabilitation programmes for the unemployed, the inactive and those on welfare in order to break dependency cycles, reduce inequality in the access to jobs and generally integrate people into the mainstream of productive activity. These priorities should be reflected in the allocation of resources.

The OECD goes on to suggest that, in practice, this priority implies the coupling of measures to promote active job search with income support programs designed to avoid work disincentives.

4. Large Japanese establishments are more likely to conduct formal training programs in-house in company training centers, while smaller firms tend to rely of courses taught at vocational training schools and other outside providers.

5. The 2 percent training tax is part of the authors' three-pronged proposal to increase the level and quality of workplace training. The other two prongs are the establishment of nationally recognized credentials to certify occupational skills and the creation of a national apprenticeship system directed toward non-college-bound youth.

6. It is interesting to note the report in *The Economist* (1994b) that in its most recent budget, the British government unveiled a scheme for reintroducing apprenticeship training.

7. Also worth noting is that the administration's proposal allowed room for privatizing the provision of some reemployment services by permitting private-sector firms to bid for the right to open and operate the one-stop career centers.

8. Still another approach is to subsidize institutional training providers to supply additional classroom training slots to displaced workers. This approach has been taken in programs in both Canada with the Direct Purchase option and Australia. While it has the advantage of increasing utilization of the existing training infrastructure by the displaced, the disadvantage of this approach is that there is no incentive for training institutions to focus their programs on meeting the needs of local employers.

References

Abraham, Katharine G., and Susan N. Houseman. 1993. *Job Security in America: Lessons from Germany.* Washington, DC: Brookings Institution.

Addison, John T., and Pedro Portugal. 1989. "Job Displacement, Relative Wage Changes, and Duration of Unemployment," *Journal of Labor Economics* 7 (July): 281-302.

Anderson, Kathryn H., Richard V. Burkhauser, and Jennie E. Raymond. 1993. "The Effect of Creaming on Placement Rates Under the Job Training Partnership Act," *Industrial and Labor Relations Review* 46 (July): 613-24.

Anderson, Patricia M. 1992. "Time-varying Effects of Recall Expectation, a Reemployment Bonus, and Job Counseling on Unemployment Durations," *Journal of Labor Economics* 10 (January): 99-115.

Anderson, Patricia, Walter Corson, and Paul Decker. 1991. "The New Jersey Unemployment Insurance Reemployment Demonstration Project Follow-Up Report." Unemployment Insurance Occasional Paper 91-1, U.S. Department of Labor.

Atkinson, Anthony B., and John Micklewright. 1991. "Unemployment Compensation and Labor Market Transitions: A Critical Review," *Journal of Economic Literature* 29 (December): 1679-1727.

Baily, Martin N., Gary Burtless, and Robert E. Litan. 1993. *Growth with Equity: Economic Policymaking for the Next Century.* Washington, DC: Brookings Institution.

Barnow, Burt S. 1992. "The Effects of Performance Standards on State and Local Programs." In *Evaluating Welfare and Training Programs*, Charles F. Manski and Irwin Garfinkel, eds. Cambridge, MA: Harvard University Press. Pp. 277-309.

Batt, William L., Jr. 1983. "Canada's Good Example with Displaced Workers," *Harvard Business Review* 61 (July-August): 4-11.

Bednarzik, Robert W. 1993. "An Analysis of U.S. Industries Sensitive to Foreign Trade, 1982-87," *Monthly Labor Review* 116 (February): 15-31.

Bendick, Marc, Jr. 1983. "The Swedish 'Active Labor Market' Approach to Reemploying Workers Dislocated by Economic Change," *Journal of Health and Human Resources Administration* 6 (Fall): 209-24.

Bendick, Marc, Jr., and Mary Lou Egan. 1987. "Transfer Payment Diversion for Small Business Development: British and French Experience," *Industrial and Labor Relations Review* 40 (July): 528-42.

Benjamin, Daniel. 1993. "Giant Under Stress: With Unemployment Climbing in Germany, So Are Social Tensions," *The Wall Street Journal* (November 4): A1, A8.

Benus, Jacob M., Michelle Wood, and Neelima Grover. 1994. "A Comparative Analysis of the Washington and Massachusetts UI Self-Employment Demonstrations." Abt Associates (January).

Bishop, John. 1993a. "Improving Job Matches in the U.S. Labor Market," *Brookings Papers on Economic Activity: Microeconomics* 1: 335-90.

_______. 1993b. "The French Mandate to Spend on Training: A Model for the United States?" Industrial Relations Research Association Series, *Proceedings of the Forty-Fifth Annual Meeting* (January 5-7): 285-95.

_______. 1994. "The Incidence and Payoff to Employer Training: A Review of the Literature." National Center on the Educational Quality of the Workforce, University of Pennsylvania (June).

Bishop, John H., and Mark Montgomery. 1986. "Evidence on Firm Participation in Employment Subsidy Programs," *Industrial Relations* 25 (Winter): 56-64.

Björklund, Anders. 1991. "Evaluation of Labour Market Policy in Sweden." In *Evaluating Labour Market and Social Programmes: The State of a Complex Art*. Paris: OECD. Pp. 73-88.

Blanchflower, David G., and Lisa M. Lynch. 1994. "Training at Work: A Comparison of U.S. and British Youths." In *Training and the Private Sector: International Comparisons*, Lisa M. Lynch, ed. Chicago: University of Chicago Press. Pp. 233-60.

Blank, Rebecca M., and David E. Card. 1991. "Recent Trends in Insured and Uninsured Unemployment: Is There an Explanation?" *Quarterly Journal of Economics* 106 (November): 1157-89.

Bloom, Howard S. 1990. *Back to Work: Testing Reemployment Services for Displaced Workers*. Kalamazoo, MI: W. E. Upjohn Institute for Employment Research.

Bloom, Howard S., Larry L. Orr, George Cave, Stephen H. Bell, and Fred Doolittle. 1992. "The National JTPA Study: Title II-A Impacts on Earnings and Employment at 18 Months." Abt Associates (May).

Bloom, Howard S., Larry L. Orr, George Cave, Stephen H. Bell, Fred Doolittle, and Winston Lin. 1994. "The National JTPA Study. Overview: Impacts, Benefits, and Costs of Title II-A." Abt Associates (January).

Bound, John, and George Johnson. 1992. "Changes in the Structure of Wages in the 1980s: An Evaluation of Alternative Explanations," *American Economic Review* 82 (June): 371-92.

Brown, Clair, Michael Reich, David Stern, and Lloyd Ulman. 1993. "Conflict and Cooperation in Labor-Management Relations in Japan and the United States." Industrial Relations Research Association Series, *Proceedings of the Forty-Fifth Annual Meeting* (January 5-7): 426-36.

Burghardt, John, Anu Rangarajan, Anne Gordon, and Ellen Kisker. 1992. "Evaluation of the Minority Female Single Parent Demonstration: Summary Report." Vol. 1. Rockefeller Foundation.

Burtless, Gary. 1985. "Are Targeted Wage Subsidies Harmful? Evidence from a Wage Voucher Experiment," *Industrial and Labor Relations Review* 39 (October): 105-14.

_______. 1987. "Jobless Pay and High European Unemployment." In *Barriers to European Growth: A Transatlantic View*, Robert Z. Lawrence and Charles L. Schultze, eds. Washington, DC: Brookings Institution. Pp. 105-74.

Cappelli, Peter. 1993a. "Are Skill Requirements Rising? Evidence from Production and Clerical Jobs," *Industrial and Labor Relations Review* 46: 515-30.

_______. 1993b. "British Lessons for School-to-Work Transition Policy in the U.S." National Center on the Educational Quality of the Workforce, EQW Working Paper 19, University of Pennsylvania.

Card, David, and Richard B. Freeman. 1994. "Small Differences That Matter: Canada vs. the United States." In *Working Under Different Rules*, Richard B. Freeman, ed. New York: Russell Sage Foundation. Pp. 189-222.

Carrington, William J. 1993. "Wage Losses for Displaced Workers: Is It Really the Firm that Matters?" *Journal of Human Resources* 28 (Summer): 571-92.

Commission on Workforce Quality and Labor Market Efficiency. 1989. "Investing In People: A Strategy to Address America's Workforce Crisis." U.S. Department of Labor (September).

Corson, Walter, Rebecca Maynard, and Jack Wichita. 1984. "Process and Implementation Issues in the Design and Conduct of Programs to Aid the Reemployment of Dislocated Workers." Mathematica Policy Research (October 30).

Corson, Walter, Sharon Long, and Rebecca Maynard. 1985. "An Impact Evaluation of the Buffalo Dislocated Worker Demonstration Program." Mathematica Policy Research (March 12).

Corson, Walter, David Long, and Walter Nicholson. 1985. "Evaluation of the Charleston Claimant Placement and Work Test Demonstration." Unemployment Insurance Occasional Paper 85-2, U.S. Department of Labor.

Corson, Walter, Shari Dunstan, Paul Decker, and Anne Gordon. 1989. "New Jersey Unemployment Insurance Reemployment Demonstration Project." Unemployment Insurance Occasional Paper 89-3, U.S. Department of Labor.

Corson, Walter, Paul Decker, Shari Dunstan, and Stuart Kerachsky. 1992. "Pennsylvania Reemployment Bonus Demonstration: Final Report."

Unemployment Insurance Occasional Paper 92-1, U.S. Department of Labor.

Corson, Walter, Paul Decker, Phillip Gleason, and Walter Nicholson. 1993. "International Trade and Worker Dislocation: Evaluation of the Trade Adjustment Assistance Program." Mathematica Policy Research (April).

Craig, Michael. 1993. "The Role of Performance Incentives in Government-Provided Job Training: The Case of the Job Training Partnership Act." Presented at the Canadian Employment Research Forum Workshop on Labour Adjustment, Vancouver, B.C., June 25.

Crawford, Clarence C. 1993. "The Job Training Partnership Act: Potential for Program Improvements But National Job Training Strategy Needed." Testimony before the Subcommittee on Employment, Housing, and Aviation, Committee on Government Operations, House of Representatives (April 29).

Crossley, Thomas F., Stephen R. G. Jones, and Peter Kuhn. 1994. "Gender Differences in Displacement Cost: Evidence and Implications," *Journal of Human Resources* 29 (Spring): 461-80.

Davidson, Carl, and Stephen A. Woodbury. 1991. "Effects of a Reemployment Bonus under Differing Benefit Entitlements, or, Why the Illinois Experiment Worked." Unpublished working paper.

_______. 1993. "The Displacement Effect of Reemployment Bonus Programs," *Journal of Labor Economics* 11 (October): 575-605.

_______. 1994. "Wage Subsidies for Dislocated Workers." Presented at the Canadian Employment Research Forum Workshop on Displaced Workers and Public Policy Responses, Montreal, December 2-3.

Department of Employment. 1988. *Employment for the 1990s*. London: Her Majesty's Stationary Office (December).

Dertouzos, Michael L., Richard K. Lester, and Robert M. Solow. 1989. *Made in America: Regaining the Productive Edge*. Cambridge, MA: MIT Press.

Dickinson, Katherine P., Richard W. West, Deborah J. Kogan, David A. Drury, Marlene S. Franks, Laura Schlichtmann, and Mary Vencel. 1988. *Evaluation of the Effects of JTPA Performance Standards on Clients, Services, and Costs*. Washington, DC: National Commission for Employment Policy.

Dolton, Peter J. 1993. "The Economics of Youth Training In Britain." *Economic Journal* 103 (September): 1261-78.

Dolton, Peter J., Gerald H. Makepeace, and John G. Treble. 1994. "Public- and Private-Sector Training of Young People in Britain." In *Training and the Private Sector: International Comparisons*, Lisa M. Lynch, ed. Chicago: University of Chicago Press. Pp. 261-82

Dore, Ronald, Jean Bounine-Cabalé, and Kari Tapiola. 1989. *Japan at Work: Markets, Management and Flexibility.* Paris: OECD.

The Economist. 1994a. "Training: A Lousy Job." January 15, p. 62.

_______. 1994b. "Training for Jobs: O Brave New World." March 12, pp. 19-26.

_______. 1994c. "Education in Germany: The Next Generation." August 20, p. 44.

Economist Intelligence Unit. 1994a. *Country Report: Germany*. First quarter.

_______. 1994b. *Country Report: Sweden*. First quarter.

Employment Department Group. 1991. "Just the Job." England (September).

Employment and Immigration Canada (EIC). 1989a. "Success in the Works: A Policy Paper." April.

_______. 1989b. "Evaluation of the National Employment Service: An Overview Report." Program Evaluation Branch (April).

_______. 1991. "Employment: New Programs and Services 1991-92." July.

_______. 1993. "Industrial Adjustment Services Program Evaluation: Final Report." Job Creation and Employment Services Division, Program Evaluation Branch (November).

Farber, Henry S. 1993. "The Incidence and Costs of Job Loss: 1982-1991," *Brookings Papers on Economic Activity: Microeconomics* 1: 73-119.

Flaim, Paul O., and Ellen Sehgal. 1985. "Displaced Workers of 1979-83: How Well Have They Fared?" *Monthly Labor Review* 108 (June): 3-16.

Forslund, Anders, and Alan B. Krueger. 1994. "An Evaluation of the Swedish Active Labor Market Policy: New and Received Wisdom." NBER Working Paper No. 4802 (July).

Friedlander, Daniel, James Riccio, and Stephen Freedman. 1993. "GAIN: Two-Year Impacts in Six Counties." Manpower Demonstration Research Corporation (May).

Green, David A., and W. Craig Riddell. 1993. "The Economic Effects of Unemployment Insurance in Canada: An Empirical Analysis of UI Disentitlement," *Journal of Labor Economics* 11 (January, Part 2): S96-S147.

Hamermesh, Daniel S. 1987. "The Costs of Worker Displacement," *Quarterly Journal of Economics* 102 (February): 51-75.

_______. 1989. "What Do We Know About Worker Displacement in the U.S.?" *Industrial Relations* 28 (Winter): 51-59.

Hamilton, Stephen F. 1990. *Apprenticeship for Adulthood: Preparing Youth for the Future*. New York: Free Press.

Harhoff, Dietmar, and Thomas Kane. 1993. "Financing Apprenticeship Training: Evidence from Germany." NBER Working Paper No. 4557 (December).

Hashimoto, Masanori. 1993. "Aspects of Labor Market Adjustments in Japan," *Journal of Labor Economics* 11 (January, Part 1): 136-61.

_______. 1994. "Employment-Based Training in Japanese Firms in Japan and in the United States: Experiences of Automobile Manufacturers." In *Training and the Private Sector: International Comparisons*, Lisa M. Lynch, ed. Chicago: University of Chicago Press. Pp. 109-48.

Haveman, Robert H., and Daniel H. Saks. 1985. "Transatlantic Lessons for Employment and Training Policy," *Industrial Relations* 24 (Winter): 20-36.

Heckman, James J. 1978. "Dummy Endogenous Variables in a Simultaneous Equations System," *Econometrica* 46 (July): 931-59.

_______. 1979. "Sample Selection Bias as a Specification Error." *Econometrica* 47 (January): 153-61.

Heckman, James J., V. Joseph Hotz, and Marcelo Dabos. 1987. "Do We Need Experimental Data to Evaluate the Impact of Manpower Training on Earnings?" *Evaluation Review* 11 (August): 395-427.

Heckman, James J., Rebecca L. Roselius, and Jeffrey A. Smith. 1993. "U.S. Education and Training Policy: A Re-evaluation of the Underlying Assumptions Behind the 'New Consensus'." Working Paper #CSPE94-1, Center for Social Program Evaluation, University of Chicago (December).

Her Majesty's Inspectorate, Department of Education and Science. 1991. "Aspects of Vocational Education and Training in the Federal Republic of Germany." London: Her Majesty's Stationary Office.

Horwitz, Tony. 1991. "No Expectations: Working Class Culture Erodes Britain's Rank in a Unified Europe," *The Wall Street Journal* (February 11): A1, A9.

Hotz, V. Joseph. 1992. "Designing an Evaluation of the Job Training Partnership Act," In *Evaluating Welfare and Training Programs*, Charles F. Manski and Irwin Garfinkel, eds. Cambridge, MA: Harvard University Press. Pp. 76-114.

Houseman, Susan N., and Katharine G. Abraham. 1993. "Female Workers as a Buffer in the Japanese Economy," *American Economic Review* 83 (May): 45-51.

Jacobson, Louis. 1994. "The Effectiveness of the U.S. Employment Service." Report prepared for the Advisory Commission on Unemployment Compensation (March 14).

Jacobson, Louis, Robert J. LaLonde, and Daniel G. Sullivan. 1993a. "Earnings Losses of Displaced Workers," *American Economic Review* 83 (September): 685-709.

_______. 1993b. *The Costs of Worker Dislocation*. Kalamazoo, MI: W. E. Upjohn Institute for Employment Research.

Jensen, Michael C. 1994. "A Revolution Only Markets Could Love," *The Wall Street Journal* (January 3): 6.

Johnson, Terry R., Katherine P. Dickinson, and Richard W. West. 1985. "An Evaluation of the Impact of ES Referrals on Applicant Earnings," *Journal of Human Resources* 20 (Winter): 117-37.

Johnson, Terry R., and Daniel H. Klepinger. 1994. "Experimental Evidence on Unemployment Insurance Work-Search Policies," *Journal of Human Resources* 29 (Summer): 695-717.

Kane, Thomas J., and Cecilia E. Rouse. 1993. "Labor Market Returns to Two- and Four-Year Colleges: Is a Credit a Credit and Do Degrees Matter?" NBER Working Paper No. 4268 (January).

Karr, Albert R. 1991. "Glum Holiday: Unlike Past Recessions, This One is Battering White-Collar Workers," *The Wall Street Journal* (December 2): A1, A2.

Kletzer, Lori. G. 1989. "Returns to Seniority After Permanent Job Loss," *American Economic Review* 79 (June): 536-43.

Kulik, Jane, D. Alton Smith, and Ernst W. Stromsdorfer. 1984. "The Downriver Community Conference Economic Readjustment Program: Final Evaluation Report." Abt Associates (May 18).

LaLonde, Robert J. 1986. "Evaluating the Econometric Evaluations of Training Programs with Experimental Data," *American Economic Review* 76 (September): 604-20.

Leigh, Duane E. 1989. *Assisting Displaced Workers: Do the States Have a Better Idea?* Kalamazoo, MI: W. E. Upjohn Institute for Employment Research.

_______. 1990. *Does Training Work for Displaced Workers? A Survey of Existing Evidence*. Kalamazoo, MI: W. E. Upjohn Institute for Employment Research.

Lerman, Robert I., and Hillard Pouncy. 1990. "The Compelling Case for Youth Apprenticeships," *The Public Interest* 101 (Fall): 62-77.

Levitan, Sar A., and Frank Gallo. 1988. *A Second Chance: Training for Jobs*. Kalamazoo, MI: W. E. Upjohn Institute for Employment Research.

Lynch, Lisa, M. 1992. "Private-Sector Training and the Earnings of Young Workers," *American Economic Review* 82 (March): 299-312.

_______. 1993a. *Strategies for Workplace Training: Lessons from Abroad*. Washington, DC: Economic Policy Institute.

_______. 1993b. "The Economics of Youth Training in the United States," *Economic Journal* 103 (September): 1292-1302.

_______. 1994. "Payoffs to Alternative Training Strategies at Work." In *Working Under Different Rules*, Richard B. Freeman, ed. New York: Russell Sage Foundation. Pp. 63-96.

Marshall, Ray, and Marc Tucker. 1992. *Thinking for a Living*. New York: Basic Books.

McCarthy, Michael J. 1993. "Unlikely Sites: Why German Firms Choose the Carolinas to Build U.S. Plants," *The Wall Street Journal* (May 4): A1, A6.

Milner, Henry. 1990. *Sweden: Social Democracy in Practice*. Oxford: Oxford University Press.

Meyer, Bruce D. 1992. "Policy Lessons from the U.S. Unemployment Insurance Experiments." NBER Working Paper No. 4197 (October).

O'Neill, Dave M. 1977. "Voucher Funding of Training Programs: Evidence from the GI Bill," *Journal of Human Resources* 12 (Fall): 425-45.

Ohmae, Kenichi. 1994. "For Japan's Economy, a Call to Arms," *The Wall Street Journal* (January 13): A14.

Ono, Yumiko. 1993. "Unneeded Workers in Japan Are Bored, And Very Well Paid," *The Wall Street Journal* (April 20): A1, A20.

Organization for Economic Cooperation and Development. 1988. *OECD Employment Outlook*. Paris (September).

_______. 1989. *OECD Employment Outlook*. Paris (July).

_______. 1990. *Labour Market Policies for the 1990s*. Paris

_______. 1992. *OECD Employment Outlook*. Paris.

_______. 1993. *OECD Employment Outlook*. Paris (July).

Osberg, Lars. 1993. "Fishing in Different Pools: Job-Search Strategies and Job-finding Success in Canada in the Early 1980s," *Journal of Labor Economics* 11 (April): 348-86.

Osterman, Paul. 1994. "How Common Is Workplace Transformation and Who Adopts It?" *Industrial and Labor Relations Review* 47 (January): 173-88.

Osterman, Paul, and Rosemary Batt. 1993. "Employer-Centered Training for International Competitiveness: Lessons from State Programs," *Journal of Policy Analysis and Management* 12 (Summer): 456-77.

Park, Norman, W. Craig Riddell, and Robert Power. 1993. "An Evaluation of UI-Sponsored Training." Program Evaluation Branch, Employment and Immigration Canada (August).

Prewo, Wilfried. 1993. "The Sorcery of Apprenticeship," *The Wall Street Journal* (February 12): A10.

Ramaswamy, Ramana. 1994. "The Swedish Labor Model in Crisis," *Finance & Development* 31 (June): 36-39.

Rehn, Gösta. 1985. "Swedish Active Labor Market Policy: Retrospect and Prospect," *Industrial Relations* 24 (Winter): 62-87.

Riddell, Craig. 1991. "Evaluation of Manpower and Training Programmes: The North American Experience." In *Evaluating Labour Market and Social Programmes: The State of a Complex Art*. Paris: OECD. Pp. 43-72.

Rogers, Joel, and Wolfgang Streeck. 1994. "Workplace Representation Overseas: The Works Councils Story." In *Working Under Different Rules*, Richard B. Freeman, ed. New York: Russell Sage Foundation. Pp. 97-156.

Rollén, Berit. 1988. “Full-Employment Through Training.” Presentation to the World Bank (September).

Ross, Murray N., and Ralph E. Smith. 1993. “Displaced Workers: Trends in the 1980s and Implications for the Future.” Congressional Budget Office (February).

Ruhm, Christopher J. 1991. “Are Workers Permanently Scarred by Job Displacements?” *American Economic Review* 81 (March): 319-24.

Runner, Diana. 1994. “Changes in Unemployment Insurance Legislation in 1993,” *Monthly Labor Review* 117 (January): 65-71.

Salwen, Kevin G. 1993. “The Cutting Edge: German-Owned Maker of Power Tools Finds Job Training Pays Off,” *The Wall Street Journal* (April 19): A1, A7.

Schellhaass, Horst-Manfred. 1991. “Evaluation Strategies and Methods with Regard to Labour Market Programmes: A German Perspective.” In *Evaluating Labour Market and Social Programmes: The State of a Complex Art*. Paris: OECD. Pp. 89-106.

Schlesinger, Jacob M., and Masayoshi Kanabayashi. 1992. “On the Street: Many Japanese Find their ‘Lifetime’ Jobs Can Be Short-Lived,” *The Wall Street Journal* (October 8): A1, A11.

Secretary’s Commission on Achieving Necessary Skills. 1991. “What Work Requires of Schools: A SCANS Report for America 2000.” U.S. Department of Labor (June).

Smith, Ralph. 1994. “An Analysis of the Administration’s Proposed Program for Displaced Workers.” Congressional Budget Office (December).

Sorrentino, Constance. 1993. “International Comparisons of Unemployment Indicators,” *Monthly Labor Review* 116 (March): 3-24.

Soskice, David. 1994. “Reconciling Markets and Institutions: The German Apprenticeship System.” In *Training and the Private Sector: International Comparisons*, Lisa M. Lynch, ed. Chicago: University of Chicago Press. Pp. 25-60.

Spiegelman, Robert G., Christopher J. O’Leary, and Kenneth J. Kline. 1992. “The Washington Reemployment Bonus Experiment: Final Report.” Unemployment Insurance Occasional Paper 92-6, U.S. Department of Labor.

Steedman, Hilary. 1993. “The Economics of Youth Training In Germany,” *Economic Journal* 103 (September): 1279-91.

Swedish Institute. 1990. “Fact Sheets on Sweden.” January.

_______. 1992. “Fact Sheets on Sweden.” December.

Trebilcock, Michael. 1986. *The Political Economy of Economic Adjustment: The Case of Declining Sectors*. Toronto: University of Toronto Press.

Trehörning, Pär. 1993. *Measures to Combat Unemployment in Sweden: Labor Market Policy in the Mid-1990s*. Stockholm: Swedish Institute.

U.S. Department of Labor 1986. "Economic Adjustment and Worker Dislocation In a Competitive Society." Report of the Secretary of Labor's Task Force on Economic Adjustment and Worker Dislocation. (December).

_______. 1993. "The Changing Labor Market and the Need for a Reemployment Response." (December).

U.S. General Accounting Office. 1987. "Dislocated Workers: Local Programs and Outcomes Under the Job Training Partnership Act." (March).

Vandewalle, G. 1991. "An Institutional Approach to the Phenomenon of Unemployment in the United States, Japan, Great Britain, Belgium and Sweden." In *The Art of Full Employment: Unemployment Policy in Open Economies*, C. de Neubourg, ed. Amsterdam: Elsevier Science Publishers. Pp. 453-68.

The Wall Street Journal. 1993. "Day of Reckoning: After Years of Bliss, Canada Faces Trouble From Excess Spending." (August 27): pp. A1, A8.

Wessel, David, and Daniel Benjamin. 1994. "Looking for Work: In Employment Policy, America and Europe Make a Sharp Contrast," *The Wall Street Journal* (March 14): A1, A6.

Wilensky. Harold L. 1985. "Nothing Fails Like Success: The Evaluation-Research Industry and Labor Market Policy," *Industrial Relations* 24 (Winter): 1-19.

Williams, Michael. 1994. "Japan's Labor System Survives Recession, But Costs of Employment Guarantees Are Huge," *The Wall Street Journal* (November 8): A19.

Woodbury, Stephen A., and Robert G. Spiegelman. 1987. "Bonuses to Workers and Employers to Reduce Unemployment: Randomized Trials in Illinois," *American Economic Review* 77 (September): 513-30.

INDEX

About the Institute

The W.E. Upjohn Institute for Employment Research is a nonprofit research organization devoted to finding and promoting solutions to employment-related problems at the national, state, and local level. It is an activity of the W.E. Upjohn Unemployment Trustee Corporation, which was established in 1932 to administer a fund set aside by the late Dr. W.E. Upjohn, founder of The Upjohn Company, to seek ways to counteract the loss of employment income during economic downturns.

The Institute is funded largely by income from the W.E. Upjohn Unemployment Trust, supplemented by outside grants, contracts, and sales of publications. Activities of the Institute are comprised of the following elements: (1) a research program conducted by a resident staff of professional social scientists; (2) a competitive grant program, which expands and complements the internal research program by providing financial support to researchers outside the Institute; (3) a publications program, which provides the major vehicle for the dissemination of research by staff and grantees, as well as other selected work in the field; and (4) an Employment Management Services division, which manages most of the publicly funded employment and training programs in the local area.

The broad objectives of the Institute's research, grant, and publication programs are to: (1) promote scholarship and experimentation on issues of public and private employment and unemployment policy; and (2) make knowledge and scholarship relevant and useful to policymakers in their pursuit of solutions to employment and unemployment problems.

Current areas of concentration for these programs include: causes, consequences, and measures to alleviate unemployment; social insurance and income maintenance programs; compensation; workforce quality; work arrangements; family labor issues; labor-management relations; and regional economic development and local labor markets.